Judgment & Grace in
DIXIE

Judgment & Grace in

DIX

The
University
of
Georgia
Press
Athens
&
London

Southern
Faiths
from
Faulkner
to
Elvis

Charles Reagan Wilson

This paperback edition published in 2007
by The University of Georgia Press
Athens, Georgia 30602
© 1995 by Charles Reagan Wilson
Preface to the 2007 Edition
© 2007 by Charles Reagan Wilson
"The Death of Bear Bryant: Myth and
Ritual in the Modern South"
© 1987 by Duke University Press
Designed by Richard Hendel
Set in Monotype Garamond
by Tseng Information Systems, Inc.
Printed and bound by IBT Global
The paper in this book meets the
guidelines for permanence and
durability of the Committee on
Production Guidelines for Book
Longevity of the Council on Library
Resources.
Printed in the United States of America
11 10 09 08 07 P 5 4 3 2 1

Library of Congress
Cataloging-in-Publication Data
Wilson, Charles Reagan.
Judgment and Grace in Dixie : southern
faiths from Faulkner to Elvis / Charles Reagan
Wilson. — Pbk. ed.
    p.   cm.
Originally published: Athens, Ga. : University
of Georgia Press, c1995.
Includes bibliographical references and index.
ISBN-13: 978-0-8203-2965-9 (pbk. : alk. paper)
ISBN-10: 0-8203-2965-7 (pbk. : alk. paper)
1. Southern States — Religious life and
customs. 2. Southern States — Civilization.
3. Evangelicalism — Southern States —
History — 20th century. I. Title.
BR535.W55 2007
306.60975 — dc22   2007011374
British Library Cataloging-in-Publication Data
available

TO MARIE

Contents

Preface to the 2007 Edition
Popular Religion in the American South since the 1990s

This book, *Judgment and Grace in Dixie,* argues that supernatural outcroppings have been and continue to be part of
the landscape of the American South, both inside and outside of churches. Observers in Memphis, Tennessee, would
likely say "amen" to such an argument when confronted with the seventy-
two-foot-high Statue of Liberation through Christ unveiled in the summer of 2006 on Winchester Avenue by the World Overcomers Outreach
Ministries Church. *Judgment and Grace* stresses religion's role in public
culture as well, and Lady Liberty is a compelling example of popular religion marking an urban southern space with a clear statement of civil
religion.

The Statue of Liberation is a biblically themed statue replicating New
York City's Statue of Liberty but with preeminent religious symbolism.
"Jehovah" is inscribed on her crown, the Ten Commandments are under
her arm, and she holds high not a torch but a large gold cross. As inter-

preted by local church members, a single tear stains her face as she cries for the nation's growing wickedness. The statue cost $260,000 and was unveiled at a religious-political ceremony on the Fourth of July. On that day, a crowd—many of them church members wearing sea-green foam Lady Liberty crowns—assembled on the church grounds to eat hamburgers, drink grape soda, spin on carnival rides, and smoke meat in a barbecue cook-off. Speeches and prayers preceded the consecration of the statue. "I decree the spirit of conviction on this intersection," said Apostle Alton R. Williams, pastor of the church. "This statue proves that Jesus Christ is Lord over America, he is Lord over Tennessee, he is Lord over Memphis." This was a ritual of the American civil religion, seeing religious meaning in national experience, but Williams's rhetoric localized it to particular state and local contexts of the American South. A Memphis woman who observed the unveiling added an explicit regional context, using a term long associated with evangelical-dominated religion in the South. "I can't see anything wrong with it," she said. "This is the Bible Belt."

This civil-religious ceremony in Memphis witnessed for a new dynamic in the recent South: the campaign to achieve public recognition of the nation as a Christian civilization. Apostle Williams explained that the statue's main purpose is to indicate to passersby that Christianity should be the guiding ethos of the nation. The teardrop, he added, is a response to such ills as legalized abortion, a lack of prayer in schools, and the nation's toleration of "New Age, Wicca, secularism, and humanism." As a black minister to a biracial but predominantly African American congregation, Williams put himself in league with the predominantly white Christian Right and its moral agenda, an agenda that increasingly brings morally conservative evangelicals together across the color line.

The decade or so since publication of *Judgment and Grace in Dixie* has seen many dramatic changes in religion in the American South, which have helped produce stories such as that of the World Overcomers Outreach Ministries Church and its Statue of Liberation. The South remains, to be sure, the most churched region of the nation, one still dominated by an interdenominational evangelical Protestant tradition, with more Baptists than members of any other religious group. The Bible is still *the* book, with unusual authority in the region, and the Spirit is still alive and active for many believers. The terrorist attacks of September 11, 2001, confirmed the dark presence of evil as a tangible force that has long haunted the southern worldview. But "What a Friend We Have in Jesus" is a song that still expresses a core belief in the hope of salvation and ultimate redemption. These attitudes remain the background to the continuity of many expressions of popular religion.

Samuel S. Hill notes, however, that purity is "the new driving force of the southern religious community," not just the traditional concern for purity of moral behavior but also "purity in the form of absolute devotion to the truth." The conservatives who took over the Southern Baptist Convention in the last two decades, the zealous red-state political warriors of the Christian Right who have become ever more prominent in George W. Bush's presidency, and the on-the-street protesters against abortion all see ideological tests as essential in affirming a black-and-white, good-or-evil version of the truth faith. Moral relativism and theological heresy are the enemies, often summed up in the term "liberal." The new ethical agenda focuses on sex and gender issues, such as abortion, homosexuality, and the public role of women. Evangelical Protestants long took for granted that the South was an evangelical Zion, the last bastion of a hegemonic Christian society, but the loss of that sense of dominance in recent decades has energized the southern faithful to a new ideological focus on not only the southern community but national life as well.

How have these changes affected popular religiosity in the South? The civil-religious ethos that injects religion into activities outside of churches has taken even deeper root than it did earlier, as have expressions of popular piety. A concern for ideological purity rests comfortably with evangelically based devotionalism, creating a distinctive context for popular religion. The Ten Commandments, for example, took on new symbolic meaning in the early years of the twenty-first century when Alabama Supreme Court chief justice Roy Moore directed workers to place a 5,280-pound granite monument he had designed, displaying the Ten Commandments along with quotations from the Bible and the Founding Fathers of the American Republic, in the rotunda of the state judicial building in Montgomery. His action was only the most dramatic of those in many southern states that reflected popular fervor for state and local governments to acknowledge Christian symbols. One poll found that 90 percent of Alabamians favored keeping the monument in place, but a federal court ordered the monument removed as a violation of the separation of church and state. Popular religion preserved the focus on the moral meanings and public display of the Ten Commandments, using such grassroots means as cardboard yard signs and personal lapel pins with an image of the Ten Commandments tablets.

Popular religion has recently taken deeper root in specific social spaces within the South. *Judgment and Grace in Dixie* looks at football as an example of the role of sports in the civil religion, as seen in the ritual of Bear Bryant's funeral. More recently, NASCAR has emerged as a spectator sport of enormous popularity and national significance, with rich symbolic meanings for religion's role in popular culture in the South. Formed in 1949, NASCAR started as a southern phenomenon, reflecting the piedmont and mountain culture of moonshine-running fast cars. The live sporting events now attract 6 million fans annually, and the sport is second to the National Football League (NFL) in television viewers, with 105 million people tuning in—another 60 million listen on radio. Although NASCAR has become a national phenomenon, it retains deep southern anchorings. The South has the largest concentration of races and fans, with twenty-two of thirty-nine events taking place in the region. Stock car racing retains clear social class significance as well, an expression of the southern working class, with 56 percent of NASCAR fans earning less than forty thousand dollars a year and 71 percent having less than one year of college.

Distinctive religious rituals and symbolism mark NASCAR events. The NFL long ago did away with an invocation before games, as a way to attract a broader audience, but NASCAR races still begin with such, usually by a local Baptist or other evangelical church minister. Jesus is usually mentioned explicitly, so the generalized American civil religion of the Judeo-Christian tradition is not invoked as much as an intentionally evangelical ethos. The South's religion of the Lost Cause is displayed through the waving of Confederate flags and the sporting of bumper stickers that affirm southern heritage. Crews typically pray together before a race, and thanks are often given to Jesus in postrace interviews. Drivers frequently place a Bible verse on their dashboards where the in-car cameras can flash the verse to viewers. Drivers and crews embody an old evangelical imperative, using their sport to witness for their faith. When Morgan Shepherd put a Jesus decal on the hood of his car, he noted that in doing so he hoped that "somebody's life will be changed." Popular religion in the South touches on many genres, which often overlap. Bobby LaBonte's hood decal in 2004 was a scene of the Crucifixion of Christ, used to promote the Mel Gibson film *The Passion of the Christ*, a film that evoked extraordinary enthusiasm among evangelical churches.

While both sporting events and films have been carriers of southern popular religion, television has extended that reach through televangelist broadcasts. Southern preachers, of course, have long claimed the airwaves, whether through broadcasts of Billy Graham's crusades, Oral Roberts's faith-healing ceremonies, or Jimmy Swaggart's emotional church services. Jerry Falwell and Pat Robertson, likewise, have used television broadcasts to spread their call for ideological religious purity. Recent additions to the televangelist ranks, however, suggest new models of popular religiosity. Joel Osteen pastors one of the nation's largest megachurches, Lakewood Church, in Houston, Texas. The son of pastor Joe Osteen, Joel made his mark in the early 1980s setting up his father's television ministry, with the services eventually airing in 140 countries. When his father died in 1991, he expanded Lakewood's media productions, targeting the nation's top twenty-five television markets and broadcasting the church's services during prime airtime slots. Lakewood's televised services can now be seen in 92 percent of the nation's households. The services are high entertainment, with a twelve-piece band providing lively music and a lighting designer assuring quality production. Wooden pews have given way to padded seats, a stage has replaced the altar, and three large projection screens show song lyrics so that hymnals are no longer required and PowerPoint sermons can highlight Osteen's main points. A giant globe rotates on stage as Osteen speaks, reflecting the worldwide impact of the broadcast. The church is housed in a former sports arena, and the outside façade still retains that look, with no churchly symbolism, reinforcing the idea that religion is just a part of everyday life. Churchly religion – normally confined inside the church doors – now blurs itself with the popular religion outside.

Televangelists increasingly are allied with another expression of popular religion, megachurches. While popular religion is separate from denominational, official religion, megachurches are both churchly congregations and expressions of popular religiosity. They are usually nondenominational and reflect a sensitive understanding of religion's relationship to popular culture. Reflections of suburban sprawl, marketing, consumer demand, an entertainment culture, and a yearning for community life, megachurches provide social services that mainline denominations can seldom afford.

Various World Changers Ministries through the South operate music studios, publishing houses, computer graphic-design suites, and record labels. The Memphis World Changers Ministries has a school, a bowling alley, a roller skating rink, a bookstore, and twelve thousand members. Osteen's Lakewood Church has twenty-five thousand members, and its retail store sells baseball caps with religious slogans (WWJD – What Would Jesus Do?), jewelry, bumper stickers, skateboards, and even fortune cookies with Bible verses. Such material culture takes religious messages outside the congregation into the secular world, spreading popular religiosity along the way. Megachurches often witness as well for the new dynamic of ideological purity, as they serve as organizing sites for Christian Right political activity and grassroots campaigns against abortion and for school prayer. As with NASCAR, megachurches provided a site for the popularization of Mel Gibson's film *The Passion of the Christ*, which he especially previewed for evangelicals in many megachurches across the South. *Judgment and Grace* argues that the lines between official, ecclesiastical religion and popular religion blurred in the late twentieth century, and this trend has surely escalated, as seen by the activities of megachurches.

Judgment and Grace includes several chapters on creative expression of popular religion, and literature and music have found new embodiments in recent years that reflect this religiosity. Bibles, prayer books, religious tracts, and religious newspapers and magazines have long blanketed the South, and self-help books, best-selling Christian-themed novels, compact discs, videos and DVDs, and the Internet offer more-recent examples of media being used to promote religion outside the church doors. Millennialism, and its accompanying apocalyptic imagery, has often been a popular theme in religious literature in the South, as seen in Hal Lindsey's books *Late Great Planet Earth* (1970) and *Satan Is Alive and Well on Planet Earth* (1972). These writings linked good and evil to such then-current events as war in the Middle East and the cold war between the United States and the Soviet Union. They nurtured a sense of evil in the world, the expectation of a time of coming tribulation, and the need for direct access to the supernatural if good is to survive.

The *Left Behind* series of novels, written by Jerry B. Jenkins and Tim LaHaye and published since 1995, have drawn from the same themes, selling over sixty-two million copies in the process. The novels bring a "book of Revelation" sensibility to current events. When the Iraq War began, the nation's most popular novel was Jenkins and LaHaye's *The Remnant*, which portrayed a world tyrannized by a former leader of the United Nations who operated his global force of storm troopers (called "peacekeepers") from Baghdad. Throughout the saga, Baghdad is Satan's headquarters. Market research has shown that 40 percent of the series' readers reside in the South, with the core buyer a married woman between twenty-five and fifty-four years of age who attends weekly worship services at an evangelical church. Odds are she bought the book at Wal-Mart, which markets the books prominently.

Religious music has long been an expression of popular religiosity that took a peculiarly southern shape, with southern and African American gospel music the traditional outlet for believers to express their faith outside the church. Gospel music of various types has long been centered in the South, with the Gospel Music Association, headquartered in Nashville, counting four thousand biracial members. The Southern Gospel Music Association, in Pigeon Forge, Tennessee, has as its main purpose the operation of the Southern Gospel Music Hall of Fame and Museum, located inside the Dollywood theme park. "We believe Southern Gospel Music is the musical arm of our Lord's evangelical church, without regard to denomination," says the association's mission statement. Further, the museum sees its job as using all available means "to praise and spread the name of Jesus Christ." Recently, southern gospel music has seen a new popular hymnody, one associated with Bill and Gloria Gaither. These are songs that hit one particular theme, that of wonder and amazement at God's glory. This outlook avoids denominational theologies and concentrates in good popular religious fashion on an underlying spirituality that grows out of an evangelical sensibility. The Gaither Homecoming Tours, started in 1992, have sold over a million tickets and have been featured in various media productions, including being shown regularly on Public Broadcasting stations.

Since its emergence in the 1970s as a separate industry from gospel, contemporary Christian music–rock and folk consciously modeled on American pop music but with religious lyrics–has shown considerable vitality. The industry has its own radio formats, publishing houses, and music production companies, most of which target young white evangelicals. One of the genre's most successful performers, Amy Grant, has crossed over into secular pop music stardom, raising questions about the commitment of Christian music entertainers to their music's spiritual mission. The contemporary Christian music industry has often faced criticism from churches and pastors because of its zealous commercialism. Popular religiosity always blurs sacred-secular lines, and the social authority of popular music in the nation creates special temptations for religious music to embrace the world in hopes of dispersing its message to a wider audience.

Holy hip-hop, a genre separate from contemporary Christian, reflects even more the attempt to fashion a pop spirituality within a consumer-oriented modern American culture. This genre has largely been underground in big cities, finding its base in inner-city youth groups, but the movement has also had mainstream success, as evidenced by the album sales of the Christian rap group The Cross Movement. Southern cities like Atlanta, Memphis, and Jackson, Mississippi, are now recognized for their distinctive southern rap traditions (the "Dirty South"), and one of its stars, Kanye West, revealed a religious dimension to that southern school of rap with his 2006 song "Jesus Walks." Confessing his earlier failures and weaknesses, he recalls that "My momma used to say only Jesus can save us." He sings that people are at war with "society, racism . . . , terrorism," but he adds that, deeper than those conflicts, we are "at war with ourselves." He comes back to the Jesus of his youth, singing, "Jesus Walk – God show me the way because the devil tryna break me down." A mainstream artist here embraces popular religiosity, showing again the permeability of the lines between sacred and secular.

Finally, I return to the issue of sacred spaces with which I began. Roadside crosses are one of the most intriguing examples of southerners claiming new spaces that represent a faith that thrives outside churches. As with so many other examples we have reviewed, roadside crosses represent a popular religiosity that, while not unique to the American South, have widespread and distinctive expressions there. Mexico and the American Southwest have a long tradition of roadside crosses, reflecting a Roman Catholic popular religiosity. The purpose for placing these crosses was often to acknowledge the sudden deaths of people who were unable to receive last rites from the church. Each cross would likely be part of construction that included not only the crucifix but also candles, images of Catholic saints, rosary beads, or representations of the preeminent symbol of Hispanic popular piety – Our Lady of Guadeloupe. Roadside crosses in the South typically mark the sites of accidental automobile deaths, and the religiosity expressed comes from a generalized evangelical Protestant sensibility, with images of saints unlikely. Instead, magical-religious tokens such as angels, candles, flowers, and American or Confederate flags are not unusual, nor are items such as teddy bears or dolls that belonged to the honored one. The southern Protestant aesthetic often incorporates verbal expression into vernacular art, and such language is alive through such written statements as "Alive in the Lord" found alongside roadside crosses. The organization Mothers Against Drunk Drivers erects crosses for victims of drunk drivers, which have an expressly ideological purpose in reminding the community of the need for laws and prosecution, but most crosses are vernacular creations, welling up from grief and the need to mark sites of loved ones' deaths. When families can do so, they will maintain these sites year round, decorating them for the seasons.

Civil-religious imagery and ritual are often in public space, and highway roadsides are regulated public spaces, resulting in civil authorities having to negotiate public and personal concerns in dealing with these popular expressions of piety in the face of death. State and local governments often see the crosses as a threat to safety, distracting drivers from the road. They can be a nuisance to transportation crews cleaning roadside as well. The cross is an explicitly Christian icon, sometimes raising issues for protestors of separation of church and state when displayed on roadside right of ways. The status of a roadside cross is thus always in flux, with authorities sometimes tolerating it because of its symbolic power to the families involved. Some states now ban the crosses, however, preventing any possibility of permanence.

Since *Judgment and Grace in Dixie*'s original publication, popular religiosity such as that seen in roadside crosses has taken new and distinctive forms in the American South, reflecting an evolving social and cultural context. These southern expressions resonate with popular religion elsewhere. Frances Mayes, the Georgia-born writer who achieved international acclaim in the 1990s for her book *Under the Tuscan Skies*, makes a global tie between the South of her upbringing and the Italian world she adopts in the book. Popular religion is the connection that gives meaning to her view of these two places. "In my South, there were signs on trees that said 'Repent,'" she recalls. "Jesus Is Coming" cried out from another sign she remembers. In her Italy, on the car radio a "lulling voice implores Mary to intercede for us in purgatory." A church near her Tuscan home has a phial of Holy Milk as a relic. She understands the primal culture of her new home partly because "this everyday wildness and wonder came back so naturally from the miracle-hungry South."

Meanwhile, Hispanic immigrants have come to Mayes's Georgia and other parts of the American South in increasing numbers since the mid-1990s, suggesting that the southern cultural context may produce a very different popular religiosity in the future. Images of Our Lady of Guadeloupe now grace processions and churches in such deeply southern places as Mississippi and North Carolina on her feast day in December. She is the premier icon of Mexican civil religion, and her image is a Hispanic contribution that may increasingly enrich the South's public spaces and its private devotionalism in coming decades, producing new configurations in the South's popular religion.

Preface to the Original Edition

The essays in this book were originally prepared for different occasions. Three came from symposia, several from scholarly journals and books, and a few from popular periodicals. One was the foreword to a book of photographs, and another was an Op-Ed feature in the *Atlanta Journal-Constitution*. The essays were thus originally of differing lengths, styles, and approaches.

These essays represent, though, an interconnected view of religion's role in southern culture. The distinctiveness of evangelical Protestantism in the South is explored in chapter 1, but most of the essays take off from that assumption, examining cultural implications of evangelical Protestantism's long hegemony over southern life. This book is less about what happens inside the churches and more about how the dominant strain of southern religion seeped into many features of regional life. Religion is not seen in isolation from other aspects of southern culture but as interacting with them.

Acknowledgments

I am grateful to the original publishers of these essays for permission to reprint them. They appeared originally as the following: "The Southern Religious Culture: Distinctiveness and Social Change," *Amerikastudien: American Studies*, 38 (1993), 357–67. "'God's Project': The Southern Civil Religion, 1920–1980," *Religion and the Life of the Nation*, ed. Rowland A. Sherrill (Urbana: University of Illinois Press, 1990), 64–83. "The Death of Bear Bryant: Myth and Ritual in the Modern South," *South Atlantic Quarterly*, 86 (summer 1987), 282–95. "William Faulkner and the Southern Religious Culture," *Faulkner and Religion* (Jackson: University Press of Mississippi, 1991), 21–43. "Southern Religion and Visionary Art," *Mississippi Folklore Register*, 15 and 16 (1991/92), 1–10. "Digging Up Bones: Death in Country Music," *You Wrote My Life: Lyrical Themes in Country Music*, ed. Melton A. McLaurin and Richard A. Peterson (Philadelphia: Gordon and Breach, 1992), 113–30. "The South's Torturous Search for the Good Books," *Publishing Research Quarterly*, 9 (winter 1993/94), 3–16. "The Iconography of Elvis," *Rejoice*, 1 (summer 1988), 32–33. "Sunday at the First Baptist Church," in *Reckon*, 1/2 (premiere 1995): 148–49. "The

Cult of Beauty," *The Encyclopedia of Southern Culture* (Chapel Hill: University of North Carolina Press, 1989), 600–603. "Unifying the Symbols of Southern Culture," *Atlanta Journal-Constitution,* 2 April 1989, 1B-2B. "Sacred Southern Space," *Sacred Spaces* (Jackson: University Press of Mississippi, 1994), foreword.

I am grateful to many people for their assistance in the long course of writing these essays. The University of Mississippi has provided an extraordinary context for studying the South over the last decade and a half, during which I have taught history and southern studies there. Robert Haws, chairman of the history department and a good friend, has encouraged me in countless ways, but his most helpful assistance has been as intellectual sparring partner. His incisiveness, iconoclasm, and rigor always make me think and rethink any nasty glib generalizations I might make.

The Center for the Study of Southern Culture has provided many institutional supports. Director Bill Ferris has enormous enthusiasm for the work of all attached to the Center, and we have worked well together over a very long time now. Associate Director Ann Abadie deserves special appreciation for her work with Bill in coordinating and managing the Center's activities. She has given me many particular opportunities to prepare lectures and articles that appear in this volume. Whenever I have requested assistance with my research, Ann has always somehow found a way to help.

So many other people at the University of Mississippi are interested in southern culture and have shared ideas and thoughts with me that I fear I cannot mention them all. In particular, I have discussed the ideas in these essays with Ted Ownby, Bob Brinkmeyer, Lisa Howorth, and Jack Bass, and I have appreciated their reactions along the way. The College of Liberal Arts has assisted me financially in the summers, and I am grateful to Dean Dale Abadie and the College's committee for their support. My graduate students, in both history and southern studies, will be familiar with the ideas herein, and I thank them for their thoughts in seminars. For tangible assistance with this project, I should especially thank Susan Glisson and Amy Wood. I am most grateful to Michelle Weaver for making the manuscript presentable and for assisting me in many ways.

My thanks go to Alfred Hornung, Rowland A. Sherrill, Cheryl Thurber, and Tom Rankin for giving me the opportunity to write material that appears in this volume. In some cases, they gently insisted I do it well after I told them I would, and in retrospect I am grateful for their patience. Tom Rankin, a friend at the Center for the Study of Southern Culture, is an uncommonly talented photographer and folklorist. He and I share an interest in popular and folk religion in the South that has helped me especially in conceptualizing this book. I appreciate his help with the illustrations herein. Susan Lee, an insightful southern photographer interested in religion, has contributed several fine illustrations to this book and has helped with its preparations as well.

Samuel S. Hill's influence will be apparent throughout this study, as he has shaped my views on southern religion. He also embodies a humane ideal of the scholar-teacher that I admire. John Shelton Reed and Jim Cobb read the manuscript and made valuable suggestions. My work in general profits from ongoing dialogues with them. I first thought about this book while conducting a National Endowment for the Humanities Summer Seminar in 1992, and I am grateful to the seminar members for their insights. Malcolm Call, former director of the University of Georgia Press, has been a pleasure to work with, as has Karen Orchard. The Press is an "author-friendly" place.

Kees, Jean, Fiona, and Adrienne Gispen have been supportive friends, and Kees, as a European historian, is another colleague who helps me keep the larger intellectual context in mind while looking for regional particularities.

My parents, as always, have my love and respect for their support of my work, and this book on southern religion touches an area of special concern to them. I share so many general interests and beliefs with my brother Martin that he should be singled out as well for helping to shape my own worldview.

This book is dedicated to my wife, Marie Antoon. She has been with me throughout the gestation and writing of each of these chapters. She has listened to my half-formed speculations, sat through my public lectures, and read the drafts of my essays, all of which have been strengthened by her own insights. No one, I suspect, but she and I know how much she has contributed to this book.

Introduction

James McBride Dabbs, the South Carolina farmer, writer, and social reformer, coined the term "God's project" to refer to the South. "I know how all this sounds," he admitted. Critics of the South would conclude that "if the South is evidence of God at work, then the sooner he quits work the better." Dabbs believed that southern history was a mystery, and religion therefore was especially appropriate to understanding it. "Perhaps the mystery," he mused, "lies in the fact that God is working here, and, as men have long realized, he works in mysterious ways."[1] The term "God's project" evokes the ironies and heavy cultural burdens associated with the religion-culture ties explored in this book.

The essays in this volume are unified by two broad themes. The first one is religion's role in the South's public culture. My earlier book, *Baptized in Blood: The Religion of the Lost Cause, 1865–1920* (1980), argued for the significance of a southern civil religion, which used regional religion to sanctify the memory of the Confederate experience and, more broadly, the southern way of life. This book is a contribution toward drawing out further implications of the southern civil religion for the twentieth century. Related and intertwined with this first theme is a second one: religion's role in southern creative expression. The essays discuss literature, music, folk art, and sports. We meet herein such southern cultural icons as William Faulkner, Hank Williams, Martin Luther King Jr., Elvis Presley, Eudora Welty, the southern Agrarians, and Bear Bryant. We also, though, spend time with less well known but also significant figures, including Dabbs, such visionary folk artists as Howard Finster and Gertrude Morgan, and African-American church people in the Mississippi Delta.

Popular religion is used here as a vehicle to examine southern culture in the twentieth century. Peter W. Williams defines popular religion as spiritual phenomena mostly outside formal church institutions, transmitted through nonecclesiastical channels, and concerned especially with specific outcroppings of the supernatural in the secular world.[2] It is the religion of the people, rather than of leaders or institutions. Roman Catholic popular religiosity emphasizes God's active presence in places, images, and material things, such as pilgrimage sites, candles, holy waters, and icons of the saints. Protestant examples would include radio and television evangelists, Billy Graham's newspaper columns, Oral Roberts's faith healings, best-selling devotional books, millennialist popular writings, prophetic interpretations of signs and wonders, and eclectic combinations of unorthodox spiritual phenomena. All of those Protestant forms have flourished in the modern South.

Examples of popular religiosity especially well rooted in the South's predominant evangelical Protestantism and popular culture include funeral home paper fans with religious scenes, interdenominational gospel songs sung at secular music concerts or at social gatherings, prayers before high school football games, and images of Jesus on black velvet. The regional civil religion appears as popular religion on Confederate battleflags with Elvis Presley's image in the middle and on special-issue Coca-Cola bottles with Bear Bryant's image on them. Such popular religiosity draws on symbols that touch deep feelings and express sentiments that reveal, if obliquely, the ultimate concerns that characterize religious behavior.

Popular religion often flourishes during times of cultural crisis, and this describes the twentieth-century South undergoing slow but wrenching economic modernization and dramatic social change in fundamental social arrangements. Traditional religion has been disrupted by modernization. Religious activity frequently becomes abstract and rationalized as a by-product of modernization, and traditional forms of symbolic life are relegated to what Peter W. Williams calls "the interstices of society," thus becoming the nucleus of popular, extraecclesiastical religion.[3]

Organized, official religion in modern societies is often desupernaturalized, with fewer parishioners believing in the direct wonder-working power of the spirit. Supernaturalism may well have survived more clearly in mainstream southern evangelical religion than in the churches elsewhere in modern America. But it surely thrives at the popular level. Southerners have long believed that God works directly through southern history—as reflected in the title of this volume and explored in chapter 2 especially. Many Southerners also expect the second coming of Jesus Christ. Some of them see God guiding the work of visionary painters. A few believe that Elvis Presley lives. A famous painting in Alabama shows Bear Bryant walking on water.

The South's predominant evangelical Protestant heritage, its "official" religion explored in chapter 1, creates peculiar conditions for a southern version of popular religion to flourish. The official religion of the South, embodied in the three largest denominations—Baptist, Methodist, and Presbyterian—has always seen the spirit as alive and well. Certainly, Presbyterian theology and creedalism have been less inclined to this feeling than the Baptists have, but the "power of the blood" is not simply of historic interest to most churchgoing Southerners. With such an official position, popular versions of supernaturalism have had an especially rich ground in which to grow. Indeed, Samuel S. Hill uses the term "popular" to describe mainstream southern denominations because their beliefs are so widespread, inside and outside of the churches.[4]

One example of the complex ties between "official" religion and "popular" religion is civil religion, the close relationship between nation and religion, or, in this case, region and religion. It has been embodied in the official religion of the churches, but it has also been diffused through southern culture, appearing at such rituals as football games, beauty pageants, and rock and country music concerts. The official religion of modern southern churches increasingly becomes routinized and bureaucratized; the passion of evangelical religion then survives best as part of popular, extraecclesiastical religion. Popular religion in a modernizing South may represent, though, a countermodernization, a reassertion of supernaturalism in a region increasingly incorporated into a homogenized, desacralized national culture.[5]

Popular religion is also closely related to southern folk religion. Folk religion is the religious belief and practice of a specific group, one that is, according to folklorist Jeff Todd Titon, outside the power structure of a society. This definition emphasizes "differences in wealth, status, education, and most of all economic and political impact" between those in "official" mainstream churches and "folk" traditional churches. Folk religion is relatively unorganized, and Don Yoder even calls it simply the "religious dimension of folk culture."[6]

Folk religion is characterized by scriptural literalism, consciousness of God's providence in human affairs, evangelism, informality, emotionalism, sectarianism, egalitarianism, isolation of church facilities if organized, and demonstrative performance style. All of those traits can also characterize popular religion, especially in the evangelical cauldron of the South. But other folk religious aspects do not seem to fit as well. Folk religion tends to be based in oral tradition, oriented toward the past, and morally rigorous. In contrast, popular religion is more often based in mass-produced ways of communication, at least in the twentieth century, which is the focus of this book. It seems less oriented toward the past than folk religion because it is less rooted in a discrete folk group with a distinct heritage. It may or may not be morally rigorous, although the consumer society in which American popular religion thrives has sometimes produced figures that use religiosity for indulgence rather than abstinence.[7]

In the "modern" South, which has been neither fully "modern" nor fully "traditional," popular religion has drawn from the beliefs and practices of folk religion and preserved them in new formats, albeit changing them in the process of adapting them to mass society. While one can, moreover, rationally categorize these differing varieties of religion in the South, most Southerners would likely see them as artificial divisions. True believers would see less difference than scholars would see between the inherited folk meanings of religion and modern popular meanings. Southern Protestants who take their faith seriously try not to separate, for example, the secular and the sacred.

Part I, "Civil Religion," focuses most specifically within this volume

An arrow points the way to wanderers seeking a folk church for worship near Carthage, Mississippi. (Photo by Tom Rankin)

on the evangelical Protestant tradition that has dominated not only the churches but the culture of the South, and it details the transformation of the religion of the Lost Cause into a biracial southern civil religion. Chapter 1, "The Southern Religious Culture: Distinctiveness and Social Change," is a synthetic essay based in the collective findings of recent southern religious history. Little in it will surprise specialists in the field, but its intent is to provide in one spot a readable overview of southern religious distinctiveness as background for other chapters. Chapter 2, " 'God's Project': The Southern Civil Religion, 1920–1980," examines the stages in the transformation of the sacralized South from a whites-only vision of the Confederate Lost Cause into a post-1960s ideal of racial integration. Chapter 3, "The Death of Bear Bryant: Myth and Ritual in the Modern South," looks at the funeral of football coach Bear Bryant as an example of civil religious behavior in the modern South.

Modernity often is accompanied by the removal of religion from the public stage to more private areas, and Part II, "Expressive Culture," turns from the issues of southern public culture to more private, especially creative, uses of religion. Chapter 4, "William Faulkner and the Southern Religious Culture," argues that the key to understanding Faulkner's portrayal of religion is not the Calvinism usually stressed by scholars but rather his understanding that the South's evangelical Protestantism and its Confederate heritage had become intertwined by the early twentieth century. If the result of this was pathological to Faulkner, the folk religion of plain white folks and blacks offered a vision of spiritual hope. Chapter 5, "Southern Religion and Visionary Art," relates visionary artists to such factors as their denominational backgrounds, poverty, and social class positions in the South, the importance of "the Word" in the region, and Holiness-Pentecostalism as a specific source nurturing a religion of the spirit that inspired their artistry. These artists are especially intriguing examples of southern traditionalism developing into popular religion at a time of regional modernization.

"The Word," whether sung or read, is the focus of the next two chapters. Chapter 6, "Digging Up Bones: Death in Country Music," reflects the preoccupation of southern popular religion with mortality. It is framed in terms of the distinctiveness of southern death attitudes within the American context. Chapter 7, "The South's Torturous Search for the Good Books," deals with religion as a key aspect influencing the development of a book culture in the South. This chapter is about southern culture in general but sees religious fundamentalism as a major obstacle to a widespread acceptance of a book culture in the region, because it embodied a rigid orthodoxy that worked against the free play of ideas. On the other hand, the Bible was *the book* in the South, the good book, and it played an enormous role in fostering creativity.

Part III, "Icons and Spaces," contains briefer observations about certain images and places embued by Southerners with religious significance. These are more observations than systematic analyses but reflect this volume's goal of seeing how religion penetrates regional life in general. Chapter 8, "The Iconography of Elvis," looks at Elvis Presley as a "saint" of the modern southern popular religion. The essay's character comes from thinking of the singer in visual terms rather than as an embodiment of southern sounds. Chapter 9, "Sunday at the First Baptist Church," describes a visit to Dallas First Baptist Church, home of the Reverend W. A. Criswell. Chapter 10, "The Cult of Beauty," looks for popular religious meanings in the beauty queen, another icon of the southern civil religion. Chapter 11, "Unifying the Symbols of Southern Culture," considers the controversy over the continued display of Lost Cause symbolism in the recent South and new regional symbols that may be developing. It follows suggestions in chapter 2 that the South's biracial folk culture is the source of a new southern civil religion. Chapter 12, "Sacred Southern Space," an afterword of sorts to this book, was originally the foreword to Tom Rankin's photographs of African-American religion in the Mississippi Delta. The essay is focused sharply on the Delta, but the implications are much broader, with contemporary black Delta religion representing a transition from traditional black folk religion to the modern black church.

Richard M. Weaver once noted that "what the Southerner desired above all else in religion was a fine set of images to contemplate."[8] This volume is cultural history, preoccupied with images, icons, symbols, and rituals. We know much about the oral tradition in southern culture and particularly how central it was to evangelical Protestantism. This book argues for more attention to the visual aspect of southern culture, especially for what it can reveal about the worldview of the region's people.

Elvis Presley
1956

ELVIS PRESLEY
GRACELAND
MEMPHIS
1935 — 1977

Civil
Religion

The Southern
Religious Culture:
Distinctiveness
and Social Change

Tennessee governor Frank Clement delivered a rousing key-
note address at the 1956 Democratic National Convention in New York
City, but some of the delegates thought he had confused the convention's podium with a pulpit from back home. Clement prophesied the
approaching exodus of the Republicans from the White House, when
"the opposition party of privilege and pillage passes over the Potomac
in the greatest water crossing since the children of Israel crossed the Red
Sea." In outlining what he saw as the Republicans' many grievous sins, he
used the refrain, "How long, O America, How long, O Lord, shall these
things endure?" When he closed, the convention band played his theme

song, an old gospel tune, "Precious Lord, Take My Hand, and Lead Me On," to rousing cheers from the delegates.[1] Frank Clement, a devout Methodist raised by a pious mother in a small southern town, had been criticized throughout his political career for "Bible-toting" – displaying often his knowledge of the Good Book and appealing to it in judging his opponents – but the critics had no impact on his success in Tennessee. The words and images of evangelical Protestantism came naturally to him and to his constituents. But Clement's address at the convention was a different matter: he was no longer speaking within the religious culture of his region, and the result was controversy. Billy Graham, to be sure, liked the speech, but not everyone else did so. The frank use of religious themes and language so familiar in Tennessee failed to please some listeners outside the region. From Brooklyn came a letter saying, "I was shocked to hear our Lord's Gospel being used for political ends." The delegates themselves certainly applauded the old-time, stem-winding rhetoric, but the speech killed Clement's chances of national election because of his open use of evangelical Protestantism in a national cultural context. What worked in Tennessee did not necessarily convert those elsewhere.[2]

Frank Clement was a product of the religious culture that has dominated the American South since the early nineteenth century, a culture that blurred the distinctions between the secular and the sacred. Southern churches have been, as historian John Lee Eighmy notes, in "cultural captivity," affirming the values of secular southern culture; yet, they have also shaped that culture, making the American South's way of life distinctive within the American context. This essay will highlight the historical contours in the relationship between religion and southern culture, examine the distinctive aspects of that religious culture, and briefly examine continuities and changes in the southern religious culture today.[3]

The history of the southern religious culture, the story of how the ties between religion and culture become so close, can be seen in terms of historical moments. In the colonial era, a traveler asking to visit the "Bible Belt" would likely have been taken to New England. Colonists founded Massachusetts Bay and Plymouth for specifically religious reasons, as societies seeking holy righteousness. The South by contrast attracted individuals seeking self-betterment and approaching their goals in individualistic terms rather than in the communalism of New England. Anglicanism became the established church of the southern colonies, but its decline after the American Revolution led to a new voluntary system of religious affiliation.[4]

The turning point in southern religious history was the Cane Ridge Revival, which began in Kentucky in August 1801 and quickly spread revivalism throughout the rural and frontier South, establishing a central evangelical belief system. On the frontier, the Methodists, Baptists, and Presbyterians soon emerged as dominant denominations among people whose religious needs had been earlier unmet. This powerful emotional faith suited the spiritual needs of the rural South, and institutional arrangements such as the camp meeting, circuit rider, and lay preacher, offered organizational methods that extended organized religion's influence in new, effective ways.[5]

Southern Evangelicalism in the early nineteenth century was part of a broad national transformation and democratization of religion, which led to the rise of the same denominations – Methodists, Baptists, and Presbyterians – in the North as in the South. But a turning point for regional religion came in the 1840s with the separation of southern Methodists and Baptists from their northern brethren. When the Methodist General Assembly prohibited slaveowners from holding the office of bishop, Southerners left the denomination and formed the Methodist Episcopal Church, South. When the Baptists forbade a slaveowner from serving as a missionary, Southerners withdrew and set up the Southern Baptist Convention. Later, when the Civil War began, southern Presbyterians similarly established what later became the Presbyterian Church in the United States as a distinctly regional denomination. Southern religious people thus seceded before political secession led to the Civil War. The Protestant churches defended slavery and blessed Confederate soldiers going off to war, signs of the close ties that had developed between regional culture and religion.[6]

The religious separation was more enduring than the political separation. After the Civil War ended, none of the three religious families reunited, so that the southern churches became the repositories of the southern identity, the prime institutional embodiment of southern regionalism, and the treasuries of the region's religious folklife. After the war, ministers became the priests and prophets of a religion of the Lost Cause, which saw spiritual significance in the Confederacy as the focus of a new civil religion.[7]

The Reconstruction era after the war, from 1865 to 1877, represented another landmark in the development of a southern religious culture. These years witnessed the profound racial separation of southern blacks and whites. Under slavery, a biracial church tradition had taken root, with blacks and whites worshiping together in the same church buildings, albeit in segregated seating. Evangelical congregations offered African Americans a larger share of acceptance and of equality with whites, based in spiritual equality, than was found in any other area of southern culture. But with Emancipation, freedmen and freedwomen demanded true equality, including the right to hold church offices and serve as ministers. White Christians refused this essential demand, leading to the organization of separate black denominations. A racial color line was now established in religion, a precursor to the political and legal color line achieved in the 1890s through Jim Crow laws and disfranchisement.[8]

During the 1880s, southern ideology shifted from the dominant prewar agrarianism to a New South of economic diversification and a larger business-oriented middle class. Urban churches and the denominational press became closely allied with New South advocates, so that Methodist bishops were icons of the new materialism as well as advocates for spiritual values. They blessed the region's new millionaires while asking them to donate to good causes. Nashville emerged as a combination Mecca and Vatican of the South, the center of Baptist and Methodist denominational life and a great religious publishing center.[9] But this outcropping of materialism, this age of gilded Evangelicalism, left much spiritual uneasiness. The mainstream churches themselves launched crusades against gambling, Sunday recreation, theaters, novels, and above all, the sale and consumption of alcoholic beverages. Blue laws prohibiting the sale of merchandise on Sundays began as a New England invention, but after the Civil War Southerners came to see them as a part of their way of life. The spiritual uneasiness of the late nineteenth century was also apparent in the appearance of energetic sectarian groups with pronounced class dimensions. The holiness churches, Pentecostalism, the Churches of Christ – all of these denominational traditions expressed a repugnance to the materialism and seemingly formal spiritual life of the mainstream evangelical Baptist, Methodist, and Presbyterian churches. Sharecroppers and textile-mill workers were plain white folks who created the churches that became their own unique expressions of the region's dominant religious orientation.[10]

The 1920s witnessed conflict of another sort for southern churches. They were key years in the confrontation between modernism and orthodoxy. Despite their racial and social class divisions, southern churches had traditionally united in defending theological orthodoxy. The South produced dynamic revivalists but few eminent theologians, a revealing sign of the overall orientation of the tradition. Darwinian science, higher criticism of the Bible, a liberal theology that offered easy salvation – all of these challenges to American religion were overcome by the orthodoxies of southern religious traditionalism. The churches maintained in the 1920s, though, a moderate position in this ongoing controversy. The mainstream Southern Baptist Convention, Methodist Episcopal Church, South, and Presbyterian Church in the United States all faced efforts by Fundamentalists to take over their organizations, yet the Fundamentalists were unsuccessful. Still, their defeat was no victory for theological liberalism.[11]

By the 1920s, southern religious distinctiveness was clear, measured by the predominant patterns of southern religious life and their contrast with those in other parts of the United States. The distinctiveness of southern religion did not come from any one trait but from a peculiar combination of characteristics and their long dominance of a regional group. Above all was Protestant dominance. This dominance did not mean other religious traditions did not exist in the South. Roman Catholics were among the earliest settlers of the South, especially in Maryland, the colony founded as a refuge for them, and Catholics were found throughout southern history, even dominating in such border areas as south Louisiana, south Texas, and south Florida. Jews also were early southern colonists, establishing historic synagogues in Charleston and Savannah, and the Jewish merchant became a figure from regional folklore. But Southerners who have joined religious groups have overwhelmingly joined Protestant ones. Significant differences existed between the Presbyterian Church in the United States and the Assemblies of God, the southern Baptists and the Methodists, black Methodists and white Methodists, and all of the above have differed from the Fire Baptized Holiness Church members. But beneath these differences is a broad, interdenominational tradition of shared

Protestantism within an American culture that is much more religiously diverse than the South.[12]

The second characteristic of the distinctive southern religious culture is its evangelical nature. American Protestantism has many branches: a liturgical dimension epitomized by the Episcopalians and Lutherans; a theological tradition best seen in the Congregationalists and Presbyterians; a social gospel embodied by the social activist agencies within modern, mainstream Protestant groups and by the activities of the interdenominational National Council of Churches. None of these traditions has ever dominated the South. Evangelicalism is that branch of Protestantism that has dominated the South, embodied institutionally in Baptists, Methodists, Pentecostals, and affecting even groups not normally a part of the tradition.[13]

Evangelicalism says that the most important aspect of Christianity is experiential. As historian Samuel S. Hill notes, the central theme of southern religious history is the search for conversion, for redemption from innate human depravity. With a Calvinist-inspired dim view of human nature, it is a religion of sin and salvation. Evangelicalism does offer assurance, however; unlike the Calvinist's insecurity, the evangelical, through direct access to God, can be born again, touched by the Holy Spirit and cleansed – "washed white as snow," as the old hymn says, by the "Precious Blood of the Lamb." That experience then becomes the foundation for a new, transformed life. The dynamic of Evangelicalism is conversion, and proselytizing becomes not one aspect of religion but the central concern of individuals and the church as a community. Evangelical groups exist in other parts of the United States and indeed Great Britain and elsewhere. The distinctiveness of southern religion is that this tradition has been the dominant tradition for so long, since the early nineteenth century, and its orthodoxy has remained that of the region.[14]

The third characteristic of southern religion that collectively has made it distinctive is Fundamentalism. Observers often use "Fundamentalism" as the main descriptor of southern religious groups and do not clarify its analytical distinction from Evangelicalism. Evangelicalism and Fundamentalism are two quite distinct categories, although believers frequently hold both concepts. Evangelicalism is about "getting right with God," about that saving moment of religious revelation from which the convert can date the real beginnings of the Christian life, no matter when baptism or confirmation may have occurred. Fundamentalism, on the other hand, suggests adherence to certain doctrines, demanding affirmation of an identifiable creed, statement of belief, or agenda. Evangelicals and Fundamentalists in the South share the belief that right behavior is essential to "being religious." [15]

Fundamentalism became an organized socioreligious movement in the early twentieth century. A series of twelve pamphlets called *The Fundamentals* (1910–15) outlined the basics of conservative theology, especially defending the inerrancy of the Bible and the belief in salvation by Christ's atoning death. This classic version of Fundamentalism was apologetic, making the case for its beliefs, aiming at a comprehensive explanation of the faith, striving to make it believable by high intellectual standards. Southern Fundamentalism has been, however, less intellectual than this and, until recently, less concerned with defending a faith under attack. That is because within the southern religious culture Fundamentalism has remained a key aspect of the regional worldview. Fundamentalism in the South has meant a literal-mindedness about Scripture, and that has indeed characterized the southern social as well as religious outlook. Southern Fundamentalism affirms key beliefs, ideas, and stories based on the Bible and combines them into a system used as supporting evidence for the Great Commission – Christ's admonition to go into the world and convert lost souls. [16]

The fourth characteristic of the interdenominational Protestantism that has dominated the South is moralism. Ethics has been a central concern of southern churches, but it has been understood in a particular sense. Morality is individualistic. One learns the "finger sins" in Sunday school: do not lie, do not cheat, do not covet your neighbor's possessions, do not lust even in your heart, do not drink alcoholic beverages. Count off on your fingers the sins you do not commit and you have a claim on righteousness. A broader understanding that morality may be judged by whether a society's overall institutional structures are just is alien to the predominant views of southern religion. The social gospel tradition has been weak. This is not to suggest that courageous and even prominent individuals within the Southern Baptist Convention and other denominations have not witnessed for social justice. They have, but their views have indeed been those of the courageous fighting the majority will. [17]

The fifth identifying characteristic of the southern religious tradition

1. Protestantism
2. evangelicalism
3. Fundamentalism
4. moralism
5. expressiveness/emotionality

In Southern Evangelicalism, "The Word" is spread any way possible—even on the side of a truck in Colquitt, Georgia. (Photo by Tom Rankin)

is its expressiveness. Emotion has frequently been present and is encouraged, a sign of the intensity and seriousness with which spiritual matters are treated. The logic of Evangelicalism suggests the importance of spreading the word, so the faithful talk openly about faith. The South's culture has been an oral one, producing great lawyers, politicians, singers, storytellers, and preachers – anyone handy with the spoken word. Testimonials are a vital part of the faith: showing how wicked you were only makes your conversion more convincing evidence for the power of the Gospel. Churches create the context to encourage expressiveness, with informality and hospitality emphasized. A sign in front of a Southern Baptist Convention congregation in El Paso, Texas – on the western margins of the southern cultural region – typically invites worshipers to "A Friendly Southern Baptist Church." This folksy style, generated in the South's earlier rural, face-to-face society and expressed in the regional vernacular, is still cultivated in the modern South and remains an important distinguishing trait of style compared to churches in other parts of the nation.[18]

If these characteristics have been the key ones in suggesting the nature of the southern religious culture, then its racial caste and social class aspects are revealing of the conflicts within that culture and yet of religion's role in unifying society in spite of its divisions. Sunday morning at eleven o'clock – church time, as Martin Luther King Jr. used to note – still is the most segregated time in the South. Blacks attend separate churches from whites – the National Baptist Convention, not the Southern Baptist Convention; the African Methodist Episcopal Church, not the United Methodist Church; the Church of God in Christ, not the Church of God. Black churches are historic, deeply rooted in a separate black religious tradition. Churches served as crucial institutional centers of black life. Under Jim Crow segregation, they were the centers of African-American social life – the shelter from the storm and the training ground for leaders. Churches had a prophetic dimension, judging society's failures to deal justly with racial issues. Finally, pronounced differences in worship can be seen between the churches of whites and blacks in the South. Worship in African-American churches is not simply a part of the broad goal of evangelism but an end in itself, a joyous expression of faith. Folklorists studying black religious rites have shown that black worship is characterized by pronounced spontaneity, bodily movements in dancing and movement, and a call-and-response pattern of preacher-congregation interaction. Scholars have traced some of these behavioral aspects back to African antecedents.[19]

Seen from a slightly different perspective, though, the southern religious culture has been a biracial tradition. The traits outlined as characteristics of a predominant style of religion in the South are as true for black Southerners as for white. Blacks join evangelical Baptist and Methodist churches in even greater percentages than whites. Differences exist between rural and urban congregations, middle class and working class, and uptown Baptist and edge-of-town Pentecostal. But southern black worship services tend overall to be expressive, their preachers inculcate individualistic moral virtues, and the Bible serves as the literal word of God, wholly sufficient for understanding religious truth. Historians have shown that slaves who attended early camp meetings with their masters influenced the style and substance of the revivalism that would dominate the region. Black churches have thus socialized generations of people into the southern religious culture, reinforcing its predominant patterns because they helped to shape those patterns. When the civil rights movement challenged the racially segregated aspects of that culture, it naturally spoke in religious language understood by the region's blacks and whites, bringing social change in the process. African Southerners are thus the quintessential religious representatives of the region.[20]

The equally complex relationship between religion and social class in the South was seen in the agrarian rebellion embodied in the Farmers' Alliance of the late nineteenth century. The Alliance organized agrarian discontent, a forerunner of the Populist Party of the 1890s. Spokesmen for the major southern denominations and editors of the religious press were predominantly town- and urban-centered by this time, and most of them gave at least tacit approval to the New South's economic diversification and thus were unsympathetic to the calls from the countryside for public policies to benefit farm society. But the membership of most southern Protestant groups was still rural, and these rural church members did not blindly affirm the New South myths. The agrarian revolt precipitated serious cleavages within the major denominations, the same town-rural division that one saw in other areas of regional life.[21]

The official spokesmen for the denominations were not alone, then, in expressing their religious views in politics. Reformers divided the world between those who were with them and those who were against them. As one Allianceman said, "Many who are trying to follow Christ will be found on the Lord's side and some who are vainly trying to serve God and gold will sooner or later be found on the other side. The Lord's side is the side of the oppressed; the other side is the side of the oppressor." The issue was fought out at the local level, involving countless congregations and their Baptist and Methodist pastors who took stands, or failed to do so, for the agrarian reformers.[22]

These reformers were well integrated into their regional religious culture. They used the rhetoric of evangelical Protestantism to lay out clear-cut, right-and-wrong moralistic responses to issues. They used local churches as gathering spots for their Alliance meetings, which resembled revival meetings. They were claiming the culturally approved evangelical symbols rooted in a distinctive religious culture to buttress their appeal for reform. Two decades later, rural Socialists active in east Texas and the "Little Dixie" area of southeastern Oklahoma befuddled northern Socialists by similarly using evangelical language and images to explain Socialist doctrine in terms that disenchanted southern farmers would respond to. Karl Marx and Jesus Christ were united in a distinctive rural South reform tradition.[23]   *Acts 2:44*

What of this southern religious culture today? "We have moved through the last forty-odd years as if through a millennium," noted Wilmer C. Fields, an official with the Southern Baptist Convention in a 1983 assessment of southern religion. He used a striking term with clear religious overtones to describe the dramatic transformation of the South's political, economic, racial, and social institutions in the period since World War II. Fields argued that "sectionalism is growing less distinct in religious faith as in social class and family style." Much evidence supports this viewpoint, but other facts suggest that in religious matters Southerners show more continuity with their past than in any other area of contemporary life.[24]

Nine out of ten Southerners, for example, still identify themselves as Protestants, compared to only six out of ten non-Southerners. Nearly half of southern Protestants are Baptist, confirming the views of cultural geographers who categorize the South as one of the nation's most clearly defined religious regions. Southerners' responses to questions about religion on public opinion polls show a continued orthodoxy: they believe overwhelmingly in a personal, anthropomorphic God, in Jesus Christ as the Son of God, in Christ's second coming, and in life after death. One survey showed that 86 percent of Southerners believed in the devil, whereas only 52 percent of non-Southerners so believed. Southern Protestants show greater hostility to ecumenical involvement with Roman Catholics than do nonsouthern Protestants.[25]

As Southerners have moved to cities, and the majority of them have moved from rural working-class status into the middle class since the 1960s, they have continued to affiliate mostly with the same Baptist and Methodist churches as their ancestors, giving the church tremendous power socially, economically, and even politically. The greater prosperity of the recent South compared to the past has enabled churches to expand, keeping pace with growth in population. A recent Southern Life poll conducted by the *Atlanta Journal-Constitution* showed that Southerners were more likely than other Americans to take their children to church and to teach them to say grace before meals. Religion likely has been the key force providing stability in the region as its people have gone through the "millennial" changes of the last decades that saw concentrated, rapid modernization.[26]

But this rapid modernization has led to much anxiety because of the accompanying secularism. Urbanization and suburban living have meant increased anonymity as well as tolerance, but both have decreased the sense of security associated with the predominantly rural, small-town living of the southern past. The security of southern religious traditionalism came with a good deal of authoritarianism, and modern life has undermined that force. People are subject to many cultural forces now, through higher levels of education, greater travel, media exposure to other worlds, and increased population diversity in the growing cities of the region. Even though Southerners continue to join evangelical churches, the entire context of their lives has so changed that the meaning of those churches may well be different now.[27]

Certainly, churches themselves reflect the materialistic values. Southern cities are famous for their super sanctuaries – giant "family life centers" that provide multitudinous functions for their members. The First Baptist Church of Dallas, Texas, for example, has 27,000 members. It provides fitness training through twin gymnasiums, a skating rink, bowling alleys, racquetball courts, and a sauna. The church has twenty or

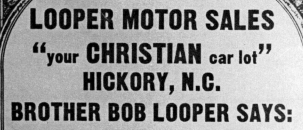

LOOPER MOTOR SALES
"your CHRISTIAN car lot"
HICKORY, N.C.
BROTHER BOB LOOPER SAYS:

NOAH CONDEMNED THE THEN KNOWN WORLD WHEN HE BUILT THE ARK. BROTHER BOB LOOPER CONDEMNS THE WORLD COUNCIL OF CHURCHES and EVERY OTHER CHURCH THAT DOESN'T TAKE THE TRUE NAME AND DOCTRINE.

Please **STUDY**- don't just read -**ACTS 20:28**
ALSO **STUDY**- not read -**1ST TIMOTHY 2:4**
NOW **STUDY**-**1st CORINTHIANS 1:27**

IT DOES SOUND FOOLISH FOR A USED CAR DEALER TO TEAR UP FALSE RELIGION, BEING AS CROOKED AS THEY ARE SUPPOSED TO BE, also the WEAKER THINGS OF THE WORLD TO CONFOUND THE THINGS THAT ARE MIGHTY, BEING AS I HAVE BEEN A PATIENT IN SIX MENTAL INSTITUTIONS.

WE ARE NOT AGAINST THE PEOPLE — ONLY AGAINST FALSE RELIGION. HAVE HOPE. It says in the evening time there shall be light. It's pretty dark right now all over the world.

**"Reminding you that God loves you
and we do, too."**

*A North Carolina used-car dealer displays his faith through his leaflet.
(Photo by Tom Rankin)*

so choirs for those people who like to sing, a school for children from kindergarten through the twelfth grade, an FM radio station. It also sponsored a Fellowship of Christian Truckers who evangelized and ministered to those they met on the road.[28]

The anxieties of southern evangelicals in a new secular age have led, then, not to a withering away of southern religious orthodoxy but to an assertiveness of it. This was clear in the two most notable religious developments of the 1980s. One was the rise of the Electronic Church and accompanying New Right political activities of the televangelists. This was not exclusively a southern phenomenon. But many of the leading televangelists easily emerged from the southern religious culture – Pat Robertson and Jerry Falwell in Virginia, Jimmy Lee Swaggart in Louisiana, Oral Roberts in Oklahoma, James Robertson in Texas. Even non-Southerners like Jim and Tammy Faye Bakker had to come south, to North Carolina, to make their evangelical empire of the air. The Electronic Church projected a modern, high-tech Gospel to its television congregations. Its format was modern, but its message was an old-fashioned one of sin and salvation, of redemption and security. The audience was national, representing an Americanization of the southern religious culture.[29]

Similarly, the assertiveness of southern traditional religion was seen in the battle for control of the Southern Baptist Convention (SBC). Beginning in 1979, Fundamentalists within the SBC launched a long-range plan to take control of the church through electing conservative presidents who would then appoint their true believers to the agency boards that run the denomination. The plan worked, and moderates who had long controlled the SBC found themselves shut out of power, as Fundamentalists began to demand ideological purity of all leaders. This development grew out of Fundamentalist fears that they had lost control of their world. Indeed, they were right: the southern culture that was once dominated by conservative orthodoxy had been challenged by modernization. Fundamentalist demands for ideological purity represented the triumph of their creedal orientation over the traditionally dominant evangelical experientialism in the South. If the battle within the SBC represented the assertiveness of orthodoxy, the uncompromising militancy of Fundamentalists weakened the SBC by pushing moderates into a newly emerging organization, the Southern Baptist Alliance.[30]

Flannery O'Connor once wrote that the South produced great literature during the Southern Literary Renaissance because of its historical experience of Civil War defeat and a predominant religion that told its believers about the sinful nature of humanity. "We have gone into the modern world," she wrote of Southerners, "with an inburnt knowledge of human limitations and with a sense of mystery which could not have developed in our first state of innocence – as it has not sufficiently developed in the rest of our country." O'Connor wrote those words in the 1950s. Four decades later, when the South seems to be more in a postmodern world than concerned for modernization, does the region still have a religious culture that teaches such lessons? No one can answer that question yet, but it is instructive to consider the opinion of a wise visitor. V. S. Naipaul visited the South in the mid-1980s and reported on "the great discovery of my travels": "In no other part of the world had I found people so driven by the idea of good behavior and the good religious life. And that was true for black and white." The southern religious culture continues to teach its lessons.[31]

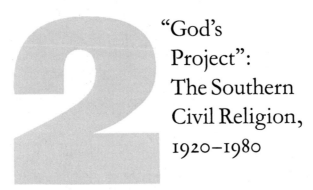

"God's Project": The Southern Civil Religion, 1920–1980

In *The Broken Covenant: American Civil Religion in Time of Trial* (1975), Robert N. Bellah suggested that scholars look beyond the American civil religion to alternative visions of American destiny. Among other possibilities, he offered the experience of the South, although he noted that the region's sentimentalization of the past and its militarism tempered its realism and its willingness to look critically at national life. The South's history, however, has been notably different from the national experience, and in considering the possibility of American recovery of meaning one should look carefully at the lessons of the southern past. The period from 1920 to 1980 is revealing, in particular, because it witnessed the profound transformation of a southern civil religion. Noting that "civil religions have come into being in America and passed away again," John F. Wilson has asked in *Public Religion in American Culture* (1979) whether "a public religion once substantially depleted in a democratic society can be revitalized." Examination of the southern civil religion in the twentieth century offers the opportunity to observe the adaptation of one such public religion to new social and cultural conditions.[1]

In the years from 1920 to 1980 the southern civil religion evolved from a public faith celebrating the virtues of a religiously sanctioned regional culture to preoccupation with what the region's new destiny was on the national and indeed universal human scale. The term "civil religion" can be used to describe the post-1920 effort of Southerners to place their historical experience in cosmic perspective. The new visions that Southerners offered of their destiny may now provide visions for America's renewal. The transformation of an earlier civil religion also provides the hope that America's mythic structure can be refocused on humane concerns that will still reflect the best of the nation's heritage.

Historians have never been able to agree on when a southern identity, a regional consciousness, emerged, but the Civil War experience and Confederate defeat surely gave a new meaning to that identity as a separate southern people within the American nation. It now had mythic dimensions. Historian George Tindall has described myths as mental pictures summing up a people's experience, and he argues that the South is especially given to myths because they appeal to the Southerner's love of concrete images and dramatic stories. Out of the experience of defeat came the myth of the Lost Cause, which centered on the efforts of Southerners to come to terms with defeat, embodying the idea that the South had been destined to lose because of the sheer force and power of the North. Much of this effort involved trying to justify the actions of the South and of Southerners. Long after the war ended, political leaders like Jefferson Davis wrote books still insisting that secession was legally defensible. Military leaders wrote books explaining that their military maneuvers during the war had been correct and the real blame lay elsewhere.[2]

Religious interpretations of the war and defeat also appeared. Ministers and churches during the war had insisted that the Confederacy was a crusade against the evil empire of the Yankee. It was a holy war, but how does one come to terms with losing a holy war? In *Baptized in Blood:*

The Religion of the Lost Cause (1980), I discussed the way the Confederate experience led Southerners to see their historical past in transcendent, cosmic terms. Southerners came to believe that God had not abandoned them but instead had chastised them, in preparation for a greater destiny in the future. The South has given rise, of course, to many myths – the Old South, the New South, Reconstruction, the savage South of violence, the decadent South of Tennessee Williams, and now the Sunbelt. The unique aspect of the myth of the Lost Cause in the late nineteenth century was the structure that existed around it. It became the basis for what anthropologists would see as a functioning religion. It was not a formal religion; no First Church of the Lost Cause ever existed. But it was the focus for a complex of religious phenomena.

The Lost Cause had icons, including pervasive images of Robert E. Lee, Jefferson Davis, and Stonewall Jackson – the Lost Cause Trinity. Southerners portrayed the Confederate heroes as saints, prophets, and martyrs. Their images were found in schools and on the stained glass windows in selected churches. Southerners had their sacred artifacts, such as the Confederate battle flag, the song "Dixie," and the ubiquitous Confederate monuments. The people of the region celebrated distinctively southern rituals, such as Confederate Memorial Day, the dedication of Confederate monuments, the funerals of Confederate veterans, and the reunions of living veterans. These rituals were the focus for prayers, sermons, and speeches recalling the Cause and the failed Confederacy. Institutions gave the Lost Cause an organizational structure. Southerners could join the United Confederate Veterans, the United Daughters of the Confederacy, the Sons of Confederate Veterans, and the Children of Confederate Veterans. The Protestant churches were crucial in keeping alive a religious interpretation of the Lost Cause. The Baptists, Methodists, and Presbyterians remained regionally organized after the Civil War, and their ministers played an active role in nurturing the idea that the South's past had continuing spiritual significance. The Episcopalians were even more prominently involved as leaders of southern society.

These were not unrelated parts but aspects of a well-organized spiritual movement, a cultural revitalization movement emerging out of the fear that the South would not survive as a distinct entity after its military and political defeat in the Civil War. Two key theological concepts were at the heart of the religious interpretation of the Confederate experience

– Southerners were a Chosen People, but they were also a Tragic People. They had been destined to crusade with honor for a cause they saw as right, but they had been destined to lose and suffer.

The Lost Cause became a popular movement, and through its various activities, Southerners in the late nineteenth and early twentieth centuries were regularly taught to retain a sense of southern identity. Southerners were told that they were different and that difference had spiritual significance. Historian C. Vann Woodward has written that Southerners came to have a tragic view of life because of their historical experience. The southern people of the late nineteenth century did indeed know this because their culture embodied it for them in a culture religion, or, more accurately, a civil religion, which saw religious significance in the Confederate nationalist experience in particular and in regional culture in general.[3]

The Lost Cause as an organized movement had a long history; indeed, it still exists. Yet the vitality of the movement had begun to ebb by World War I. That war represented a landmark in the reincorporation of the South back into the Union, and the Lost Cause increasingly seemed out of date. What happened to the "religion of the Lost Cause," to the belief that the Confederate nation, in retrospect, had spiritual meaning? Consideration of the topic offers a way to examine the decline and transformation of one variety of civil religion in America. The decline of the Lost Cause as an explanation of southern mission set the stage for the emergence of new dreams of southern destiny.[4]

In sociological terms, the religion of the Lost Cause failed to make the transition from cult status to denominational status. It gradually declined in cultural significance as a popular movement, as those associated with the Confederacy died. The veterans themselves had been a constant reminder to Southerners not to forget their past, but as the ranks of the veterans thinned out, Southerners as a people had less reinforcement for remembering the war. As time went on, the Lost Cause ceremonies and activities were less likely to evoke spiritual feelings. The pattern of life had changed in the South, and it seemed that the issues that the Lost Cause addressed were no longer of central concern to Southerners. Lost Cause activities became less and less full community events. To be sure, the forms were still followed, but without the same spirit and community importance. Confederate Memorial Day still exists and the faithful still honor it, but it is no longer a community event: the Fourth of July is more likely to be a social and community happening. Lee's birthday is still a holiday, but newspapers rarely publish editorials about it anymore. Confederate monuments still dot the landscape, but the young have little sense of what they mean. Young Southerners are much like youthful Americans across the country. They know more about Madonna than about Robert E. Lee, thanks to the media and to modern cultural ideals.[5]

Although the ritualized, institutionalized spiritual aspects of the Lost Cause religious movement have been eclipsed since 1920, the Lost Cause, the memory of Confederate defeat, has played a role in regional and national life. It has been used in many ways by different kinds of Southerners. The first phase of the modern southern civil religion was the literary Lost Cause. The years from 1920 to 1950 witnessed the Southern Literary Renaissance, a flowering of culture such as the South had never seen. The perfect Confederate novel did not come out of this, although many Civil War novels and biographies of Confederate leaders did appear. Writings of the period certainly praised the virtues of the Confederates. W. J. Cash in his classic work, *The Mind of the South* (1941), lauded their "honor, courage, generosity, amiability, courtesy." Southern writers also, however, explored the tragic meaning of the southern experience. One feels a sense of brooding about the past in much of this writing. The Lost Cause all along had been to Southerners more than just the story of romantically going off to war. The words themselves give the clue. The Lost Cause was the memory of defeat itself, of struggling with every ounce of heroic effort, and then failing and having to live with the results of the past. In this era it was no longer just a regional story. As poet Allen Tate said, these modern southern writers converted the memory of the regional past "into a universal myth of the human condition."[6]

Southern writers such as William Faulkner and Robert Penn Warren had profound things to say about the South, about its grandeur and its tragedy. Some scholars argue that southern literature and history have been used "as sacramental acts," intended by writers to counter the instability and chaos they perceive in the modern world. "By such an interpretation," C. Hugh Holman writes, "literature ultimately becomes a religious act, and the distinctiveness of southern writing rests not on its view of social structures or the facts of history but upon the religious orientation of the region."[7] The writers of the Southern Literary Renaissance, then, in one sense extended the religion of the Lost Cause. They converted the southern experience into high art, into parables of the human condition, conveying the southern experience to the rest of the world.

Claiming the Confederate legacy, the belief that the southern past still offered meaning for the region and the nation, was not easy, perhaps no easier for southern intellectuals of the 1920s and 1930s than it had been for the post–Civil War generation. Their efforts should be seen in the context of the 1920s. This was a decade when the region appeared to the world as the "Benighted South," to use George Tindall's phrase, the savage South of the Ku Klux Klan, chain gangs, lynchings, the Scopes trial, and hookworm and pellagra. On the other hand, the internal leadership of the South was in the hands of the boosters, the forces of modernization. Southern intellectuals and artists, including writers, generally faced an identity crisis, caught between the older South and a newly emerging ✓ one, neither of which they fully approved. Southerners of the post–Civil War era had turned to the southern past, to the Lost Cause, to help cope with their identity crisis as a defeated people, and now, in the 1920s and 1930s, southern intellectual leaders again turned to the past.[8]

Allen Tate perhaps best embodied the southern identity crisis and the belief that the South of the Lost Cause still had meaning. Born in Winchester, Kentucky, Tate attended Vanderbilt University and came away a self-conscious intellectual, firmly aware of and committed to the latest modernist literary outlook and assumptions. He gravitated to New York City and its sophisticated Greenwich Village scene. But eventually he came to reassess his southern heritage. In the fall of 1926 he began work on "Ode to the Confederate Dead." This poem expresses the frustration of a modern young Southerner standing at the gate of a Confederate cemetery. He thinks of the "inscrutable infantry rising" and of the battles fought. He envies the Confederates their convictions, their knowledge of why they fought and what they believed. The modern Southerner knows too much, in effect, for simple convictions. He doubts and questions, making it impossible to regain the faith and wholeness of the past.[9]

Tate immersed himself in the Lost Cause in the hope of somehow regaining the traditional southern faith. He wrote biographies of Stonewall Jackson and Jefferson Davis. He read southern history, studied genealogy, and toured battlefields. He bought an antebellum home with columns and porches, and he kept a loaded rifle and a Confederate flag over his mantelpiece. All the while, he clung to the image of the Old South as a unified, religiously oriented society, like the Middle Ages. In his essay "Remarks on the Southern Religion" (1930), Tate asks, "How may the Southerner take hold of his Tradition?" His answer is "by violence." By this he meant by an act of the will, and he tried to do this in his own life.[10]

In this period he was obsessed with the southern past and the Lost Cause, but it was not the South of Confederate defeat, it was not the tragic South that had played such a pronounced role in the rhetoric and rituals of the Lost Cause movement of the late nineteenth century. Back then, Southerners lived with the tangible results of the tragedy of war and could not deny it. Tate was interested in the Lost Cause for other reasons – because it offered a vision of southern crusaders, the Chosen People, battling for a way of life they believed in.

In spite of Tate's passionate interest in it, the Lost Cause was no longer a popular movement. He and his literary colleagues were largely without influence with the masses of the southern people themselves. The tragic view of life that many of these writers expressed had once been embodied in the activities of the Lost Cause movement, but in the modern South it seemed that most Southerners preferred to forget the tragic lessons of the Civil War and to think in more upbeat ways. Tate attended a Confederate memorial service in Clarksville, Tennessee, and was told by a local Baptist minister that Confederate defeat was simply God's ordained way to bring about industrial development in a New South. Factories in Clarksville – that was what the war had been about. This was, in fact, a standard interpretation for many Southerners in the 1920s, but it was frustrating to someone like Tate, who saw deeper meanings to the southern experience in war.

Tate's alienation from this common interpretation of the war reflected the alienation of southern writers from their community and people. They had grown up at a time in the early twentieth century when they could see the truly distinctive South before later changes; they had also lived outside the region and were involved in modernist intellectual currents. They were transitional figures. They saw spiritual meaning in the southern experience, a deeper meaning than Southerners themselves wanted to hear.[11]

Regional writers kept alive, though, the idea of the South as a potentially redemptive community. Critic Lewis P. Simpson has argued that "the Southern writer has tended to be a kind of priest and prophet of a metaphysical nation," who has endeavored to "represent it as a quest for a revelation of man's moral community in history." Writers increasingly placed the South's experience in the broadest possible perspective, making their profoundest achievements when, as Simpson says, "they became sufficiently aware that the South is a part of the apocalypse of modern civilization." As among the most sensitive chroniclers of the South's spiritual destiny, the literary community would play a crucial role in refocusing the southern civil religion on concerns beyond the Lost Cause.[12]

In the 1950s and 1960s, Confederate symbolism reemerged in the segregationist Lost Cause, a popular movement in response to the civil rights movement. Spokesmen for the Lost Cause organizations, and especially ministers in them, had rarely discussed racial issues in the post–Civil War era. Perhaps they simply did not have to do so because the southern white consensus on racial supremacy was so great. In any event, to earlier generations of Southerners the Lost Cause symbols had taught complex lessons, including spiritual lessons of human limitation, suffering, the heroic sacrifices of the Confederates, and finally their tragic defeat. But in the 1950s, the Confederate symbols took on a harsher racial meaning. Segregationists used the symbols of the Lost Cause, and they became explicitly, almost exclusively, tied in with white supremacy in a new way. Whether at Central High School in Little Rock in 1957, at Ole Miss in 1962, or at Selma in 1965, segregationists displayed the Confederate battle flag and played "Dixie." After Central High School was integrated at bayonet point, a local official in Forest, Mississippi, told the high school band there to play "Dixie" before football games instead of the "Star-Spangled Banner." During the riot in Oxford in 1962, students pulled down the Stars and Stripes from the flagpole and raised the Confederate flag. This was powerful symbolism a hundred years after the Civil War. The Ku Klux Klan had made that Confederate flag a central symbol in the early twentieth century, the White Citizens' Councils used it in the 1950s, and in the minds of many Americans that is now its prime association. Writer Walker Percy explained the historic shift in meaning of Confederate symbolism, pointing out in 1961 that "racism is no sectional monopoly. Nor was the Confederate flag a racist symbol. But it is apt to be now. The symbol is the same, but the referent has changed. Now when the Stars and Bars flies over a convertible or a speedboat or a citizen's meeting, what it signifies is not a theory of government but a certain attitude toward the Negro."[13]

This phase of the Lost Cause ebbed in the 1970s, with adjustment to the end of legal segregation and less explicit expression of racism. As a result of the linkage in the 1950s with racial confrontation, the South has seen a decline of Lost Cause symbolism. Most southern universities dropped the playing of "Dixie" during sporting events, a practice that was once common throughout the South. The University of Mississippi, however, retains "Dixie" as a school song, and some public schools and private academies still use the flag.[14]

The third phase of the modern Confederate memory was the Civil War centennial in the early 1960s. The centennial was a national fad, a modern American event that advertisers love – "If General Lee could have had an automobile, he would have wanted a Chevy." To be sure, it also occasioned the display of more Lost Cause symbolism and brought much interest in battle reenactments. Newspaper editorials appeared, and Southerners bought national books and magazines and even wrote many themselves. Shelby Foote's magnificent multivolume narrative history of the Civil War began appearing, and interest in military history – always strong in the South – reached a high point. It was all tied to the southern passion for genealogy and social activities. Faulkner had anticipated this. In *Requiem for a Nun* (1951), he wrote that "the old deathless Lost Cause had become a faded (though still select) social club or caste," and that was indeed what had happened. But the striking fact is that Southerners as a group in this era showed little interest in being reminded of defeat. Southerners were interested in the Confederacy of 1861, in the fighting itself, not in the South of 1865. Nor did the war occasion many southern reflections upon the idea of the region's destiny. Those twin concepts of the older Lost Cause – the Chosen People, the Tragic People – were, then, rarely mentioned during the centennial. Again, it seemed that the spiritual meaning, the religious significance, of defeat, which Southerners had once dwelled upon, had been forgotten.[15]

Two perceptive literary Southerners, Robert Penn Warren and Walker Percy, did see deeper meaning in the Civil War centennial. To them, the Civil War was an ongoing process in their own age. The Civil War had produced great leaders and noble deeds, but the South of their own age produced neither. "Even now," Warren wrote in *The Legacy of the Civil War: Meditations on the Centennial* (1961), "any common lyncher becomes a defender of the southern tradition, and any rabble-rouser the gallant leader of a thin gray line of heroes." Warren argued that the modern Southerner's protests against racial changes were "nothing more than an obscene parody of the meaning of his history." The Confederates offered the lesson that human dignity and grandeur are possible, even amid human weakness and vice, but the actions of contemporary southern leaders were a debasement of the Southerner's history, "with all that was noble, courageous, and justifying bleached out, drained away." He found it inconceivable to picture General Lee, a symbol of integrity, shaking hands with Orval Faubus.[16]

Walker Percy made the same point about the modern South. "When Lee and the Army of Northern Virginia laid down the Confederate flag in 1865, no flag had ever been defended by better men. But when the same flag is picked up by men like Ross Barnett and Jimmy Davis, nothing remains but to make panties and pillowcases with it." That is a prophecy that has come true. The Lost Cause souvenir industry, which seems to operate out of Taiwan, turns out Confederate flag beach towels, cigarette lighters, oversized T-shirts, and, perhaps the best, the southern yuppie version of the Lost Cause – Confederate flag jogging shorts.[17]

Percy's novel *The Last Gentleman* (1966) can be read as an ironic commentary on the centennial. The protagonist, Will Barrett, is a modern Southerner suffering cultural amnesia. He can remember bits and pieces from the past, but they have no coherent meaning. The novel is filled with Civil War references – battles, forts, and generals. Barrett admires the Confederates, but he can find no leader in his own age worth following. Even Barrett cannot bear to face the realities of the Lost Cause in the modern age. Barrett reads Douglas Southall Freeman's biography of General Lee, but eventually he gives it up. "He was tired of Lee's sad fruitless victories and would as soon see the whole thing finished off for good." Barrett was another centennial-era Southerner who could not accept the deepest meaning of the Lost Cause.[18]

Most recently, the Confederacy has served as the basis for a popular culture Lost Cause – the Lost Cause as entertainment. This has sometimes involved nonsouthern attempts to market the South. *Dukes of Hazzard* on television, for example, included a souped-up automobile called the General Lee, with a Confederate flag on its roof. But Southerners themselves made Lost Cause symbolism part of a cultural revitalization movement in the late 1970s and 1980s. One sees it in sports, for example, and especially in college football. The god of southern football is a tribal god, a god of the Chosen People. When Alabama played Notre Dame in the 1970s, Southerners from many states waved the flag and rooted for their legions against the Yankees. The evangelical fervor of the South met squarely the Catholic crusaders. In his last years, and especially after his death in 1983, Bear Bryant was as close to a southern saint as the modern South has produced, with frequent comparisons to General Lee. One also sees a renewed southern spirit in country music, another form of indigenous southern culture: Charlie Daniels consciously evokes the image of a Rebel and uses Confederate symbols as he sings "The South's Gonna Do It Again"; Hank Williams Jr. sings "If Heaven Ain't a Lot like Dixie, Then I Don't Want to Go"; the group Alabama displays the Confederate flag on virtually every record album, and one of their latest songs was "If It Ain't Dixie, It Won't Do." Bob McDill's song "Good Ole Boys," recorded by Don Williams, evokes a whole series of southern images, recalling his youth when a picture of Stonewall Jackson hung above his bed at night.[19]

The popular culture use of the Confederate symbolism is good-natured. If young Southerners do have an image of the Lost Cause, it is probably this one. The Confederate symbolism does not seem as racially charged as it did in the 1960s, but neither is it historically as meaningful. After analyzing a 1971 North Carolina public opinion survey, sociologist John Shelton Reed concluded that, although the flag and "Dixie" still bring to mind the Confederacy, these symbols have become simply "badges of regional identification and objects of conventional piety for many white Southerners, regardless of whether the beholder has any particular interest in the history that they represent." When faced with the Confederate symbolism, most blacks thought not of the Confederacy but of the more recent white resistance to racial equality. In both cases, the meaning of the Civil War historical experience itself, and especially any spiritual significance in it, seems to be of little interest or importance to modern Southerners. Lost Cause symbolism has not disappeared, but it certainly lacks the tragic dimension it once had for Southerners.[20]

Although the Confederate past no longer seems to evoke profound sentiments on the part of modern Southerners, serious efforts have been made to show the continuing relevance of the southern past. The two concepts of the Chosen People and the Tragic People have survived, although not always in association with the Confederate memory itself.

The religious dimension of the Lost Cause all along had addressed the issues of who the southern people were, what their distinctive identity was, and whether they had a destiny under God. The evangelical churches have at times suggested that the South's destiny is to be a great evangelical empire, eventually conquering the nation and the world. Southerners represented, in this interpretation, the last stronghold of pure religion. Segregationists of the 1950s argued that the South's destiny was as one of the last defenders of racial purity in the Western world.[21]

Two dreams of the South's destiny seem to be enduring because they are rooted in the region's distinctive history and represent a continuing critique of dominant American patterns. The southern Agrarians of *I'll Take My Stand* (1930) embodied one variety of the southern civil religion – the antimaterialist South. The Agrarians believed that southern identity had religious significance. As Richard M. Weaver wrote, "Being a Southerner is definitely a spiritual condition, like being a Catholic or a Jew." But the Agrarians lived during the time of a regional spiritual crisis, which was an identity crisis. Louis D. Rubin Jr. has suggested that the Agrarian manifesto "was an assertion of identity, an assertion made necessary precisely because the identity was, in part at least, no longer present." All Southerners had to face this, but by the 1920s, more clearly than ever before, the traditionalists were on the defensive. In the New South, business-industrial advocates were ascendant. The booster outlook seemed triumphant and, unlike the New South advocates of the late nineteenth century, these boosters had little use for the past.[22]

The Agrarians were thus embattled. They saw industrial advocates within the region as their enemy, but they continued the tradition of regional defensiveness by focusing their fears upon the abiding external enemy, the North. Frank Lawrence Owsley wrote of the northern "war of intellectual and spiritual conquest" against the South, and John Shelton Reed argues that *I'll Take My Stand* was "the opening salvo of a counterattack in this spiritual and intellectual war." He sees the Agrarians as cultural nationalists trying "to rejuvenate a culture." The civil religion issue was central to their efforts because religion, along with rural living, was the key to their defense of the region. Their advocacy of the religiously based agrarian way of life had a dignity to it that reinforced lagging southern self-esteem at the end of the 1920s. The religion of the Lost Cause in the post–Civil War era had provided a mythic reassurance of

southern worth, in spite of the reality of defeat, and the Agrarian manifesto had a similar psychological origin and function. "It even suggested
that the South might be a beacon, an example for the rest of the world
to emulate," writes Reed. Instead of the New England city on a hill, the
Agrarians, in effect, pictured a farm on a hill to be admired and copied.[23]

The rejuvenation of southern culture was important not only to Southerners but to the world. The Agrarians saw the South's destiny in terms
of the decline of western civilization. The South was thus potentially the
savior for a disturbed world, because it was the last western embodiment of a society that had escaped the dehumanization and instability of
modern industrial life. This vision of the destiny of the southern chosen
people was one grand dream of the southern civil religion, a conservative
humanist vision. It hoped the South would profit from its tragic history.
Forced by the war into generations of deprivation, the South had gained a
spiritual superiority to the North, a superiority that it had to use wisely.[24]

Another twentieth-century vision of the South's destiny rooted in the
past was that of the biracial South. It was a southern liberal dream, stated
succinctly in 1961 by Leslie W. Dunbar, director of the Southern Regional
Council: "I believe that the South will, out of its travail and sadness
and requited passion, give the world its first grand example of two races
of men living together in equality and with mutual respect. The South's
heroic age is with us now." Southern white liberals had, in fact, expressed
this idea often during the years of segregation. They insisted that southern blacks and whites understood one another better than their counter-
parts in the North.[25]

The southern liberal dream of the South's destiny was rooted in regional evangelical religion. Advocates of the biracial South were generally from evangelical backgrounds, and they came to believe that racial
segregation was a violation of basic Christian ideas. They used religious
language and spoke of "the regeneration of the South." They saw segregation as a moral problem and used the simple ethical teachings of the
Sermon on the Mount as their guide, rather than sophisticated theology.
Like the good Southerners they were, they had grievances against northern liberals, whom they saw as morally complacent about northern society
and "holier than thou" toward the South. The hope was that out of the
South's history of suffering and tribulation would come the realization
that the suffering had been a shared suffering, black and white, and that

the South's destiny was as one society, not two. The end of segregation would free the white Southerner and the black for new achievements.[26]

The ideas of Reinhold Niebuhr helped to shape the vision of the biracial South. On a personal level Niebuhr contributed time and energy to such southern liberal religious efforts as the founding of the Highlander School in 1932 and the Fellowship of Southern Churchmen in 1934. Niebuhr was the preeminent theologian of Neo-orthodoxy, which called into question human institutions, and many Southerners found this religiously based questioning an effective approach to criticizing racial segregation. C. Vann Woodward explicitly applied Niebuhr's outlook to the South in essays such as "The Irony of Southern History" and "The Search for Southern Identity."[27]

The vision of a biracial South was also put forward by southern blacks, especially during the civil rights movement. Martin Luther King Jr. spoke of the movement's national and international significance for black liberation, but he also spoke often of the specifically southern context. Achieving racial justice would contribute, he said, to individual moral health, national political life, the nation's prestige in the world, and "our cultural health as a region." He spoke of "our beloved Southland" and lamented its "tragic attempt to live in monologue rather than dialogue." In a 1961 interview he characterized the South as a land "that has some beauty, that has been made ugly by segregation." "There is an intimacy of life that can be beautiful if it is transformed in race relations from a sort of lord-servant relationship to a person-to-person relationship," he said. He predicted that the nature of life in the South "will make it one of the finest sections of our country once we solve this problem of segregation." Like southern white liberals, King saw regional manners and informal relationships as the source of hope for achieving the biracial South. Noting that southern blacks and whites had the kind of personal contacts that Northerners lacked, King predicted in 1963 that once segregation ended, "I think you'll have a beautiful relationship in terms of brotherhood." He added that "when you find a white southerner who has been emancipated on the issue, the Negro can't find a better friend."[28]

King used the language of the late nineteenth-century Lost Cause, speaking of suffering, tragedy, honor, the need for virtuous behavior, the need of a defeated people to achieve dignity, and the search for group identity and destiny. He compared traditional southern white values and those of black freedom protesters in 1963, noting that "the virtues so long regarded as the exclusive property of the white South – gallantry, loyalty, and pride – had passed to the Negro demonstrators in the heat of the summer's battles." King suggested that the compensation for black physical deprivations was a spiritual maturity – exactly the argument white Southerners had made about their defeated region in the late nineteenth century. King hoped to release "spiritual power" and "soul force" that would transform the South and, from there, the nation and the world. King's "I Have a Dream" speech in 1963 portrayed a redemptive South that would be the scene for national salvation. Reflecting a traditional southern concern for place, he argued that the nation's transformation would not be in some disembodied location but in a specific locale, the South. The region had been the center of black suffering and of flawed humanity, but ultimately the virtue of blacks and decent whites would lead to reconciliation. One day "on the red hills of Georgia," blacks and whites would "sit down together at the table of brotherhood." In the coming day of redemption, even the state of Mississippi, "a state sweltering with the heat of injustice, sweltering with the heat of oppression, will be transformed into an oasis of freedom and justice." [29]

King and other civil rights leaders dreamed, then, southern dreams as well as American dreams. Much has happened since to encourage this vision and much to discourage believers in it. In terms of the South's intellectual life, this remains today perhaps the South's predominant idea of its distinctive regional destiny. Jimmy Carter articulated it in his presidential campaign of 1976, and the national media even suggested the dream was being achieved – a pronouncement that was a bit premature, to say the least. The South has generated yet another mythic view of itself – the myth of the biracial South. [30]

The individual who most fully explored the relationship between the two visions at the heart of the modern southern civil religion was James McBride Dabbs. Born in South Carolina to a family that had been in the state since the colonial era, educated in the South at the University of South Carolina and out of the region at Clark University and Columbia University, a soldier in France during World War I, Dabbs was, at various times, a college teacher, a leader in the southern Presbyterian church, president of the reformist Southern Regional Council, and, for most of his life, a practicing farmer at the family plantation, Rip Raps. In a series of books and in articles in the *Christian Century* and denominational journals, Dabbs brooded upon the southern past. He regarded much of it as shameful, and he examined southern guilt over it, yet he remained very much a Southerner proud of his family ancestry, identifying with his people, and unwilling to repudiate the past. He was prophetic, castigating "the racial sins the white South has committed," which made understandable "the justice of its being defeated and thwarted" in the Civil War. God himself had willed "that defeat and the great lessons it spread before us." He became an active supporter of the civil rights movement, yet retained his influence among his fellow white Southerners. His attempt to take in all of the southern past was reflected symbolically in his own home. Dabbs kept on his living room wall a plaque of recognition from the Detroit NAACP; hanging below it were two crossed Confederate rifles.[31]

Dabbs urged Southerners, black and white, not to accept "the straight American religion" and forget the past. "It seems to me sheer waste to throw away so much only to gain – more shares in General Motors!" The southern experience has been a tragic one, but he believed it had meaning, not only for Southerners but for others as well. He argued that the South had been "a pilot project learning – at terrible expense it is true, but learning doesn't come easy – how to do within a limited area what now has to be done if civilization is to survive." The land itself had been "God's gift to the South," but it became "the Southerner's chief temptation." Southerners exploited the land and tainted it with the sin of slavery. Dabbs understood that, nonetheless, the modern South had lessons to teach on the necessity of preserving the land and of ecological sanity. The southern experience at its best had nurtured an awareness of nature. Southern whites and blacks had been farmers, attuned to nature's ways. Dabbs's first writings were on farming and later in life he frequently quoted the nature poet, Wordsworth, and came under the influence of Thoreau. For Dabbs, farming had religious significance because it nurtured an awareness of the mysteries of life. "The basic religious fact about farming," he wrote, "is the farmer's sense of dependency." Reflecting the Agrarian vision, Dabbs believed that southern farmers, black and white, despite deprivation, had led a deeply integrated life, where spiritual and material values were intertwined, where the meaning of family and work were tied intimately together. Industrialism and its attendant problems threatened the South and the nation. The South needed "men who know that machines are for human use" and that human beings "are here to live, and that life is now, infusing both the means and the ends." Dabbs projected into the future the wisdom of the southern farmer, who had continually learned nature's lessons and respected its rhythms, in a call for redemption of the land through respect for the environment. "This is my religion," he announced in a 1934 article. "The universe throbbing with life gives of this life, carelessly indeed but lavishly, to those who know and are fortunate."[32]

The South's attempt to build a biracial society had taught related lessons. Dabbs pointed out that the "Entity called the South was hammered out by black man and white man working together." The land was the setting for building a biracial community, which was at the heart of the southern way of life. The traits that distinguish those in the South as Southerners, he observed, "are chiefly the result of this basic productive pattern: Whites and Negroes farming, in some sense, together." "Through the processes of history and the grace of God we have been made one people," he wrote, and now "there is no telling what great age might develop in the South." The South was destined to show the way to the rest of the world.[33]

Dabbs repeatedly reiterated "the religious significance of the Southerner's experience." If indeed the South had experience and perhaps even wisdom that might be of use to the nation, "this has happened because of the grace of God. The South has been God's project." The world itself, in a broader sense, is "God's project," he admitted, "only God's hand is more evident in the South than in most other regions." The southern church had a special responsibility to embody this understanding. The church must "make use of the cultural similarity between the races in its attempt to unveil the vision of the religious significance of race relations: to interpret the biracial South as God's Project." Writing in 1964, he charged the church with recognizing "the tragedy of Southerners," which had led, through God's grace and mercy, to the creation of "a common bond between Southern Whites and Negroes."[34]

Southerners have not, to be sure, always understood the experiences that Dabbs explored. The Agrarians, for example, as historian F. Garvin Davenport has pointed out, lacked a sense of irony, lacked enough detachment from the southern experience to see its true significance. Convinced of the essential virtue of the southern past, they were unable to explore fully its deeper meanings. The southern experience has been tragic, but, as Dabbs says, "there is a world of difference between failure interpreted as the experience solely of oneself or one's group and therefore implying injustice, and a failure interpreted as the human lot." The South has been aware of failure in the first sense, and that led to what Robert Penn Warren calls the Great Alibi, by which Southerners have used their history as an excuse for failure to face their problems and deal with them, for nurturing arrogance and resentment.[35] The myth of a biracial South finally recognizes that the southern tragedy is symbolic of the human condition. Southern white narcissism – and American pride – must be repudiated, says this myth, in favor of the awareness of its common lot with the rest of humanity.

Southern white narcissism must be repudiated

As a people, Americans are notoriously ahistorical – looking toward the future, progressive, optimistic. But Southerners have had a deep historical sense, which remains a national resource. Robert Penn Warren has observed that a people with no sense of history "can have no sense of destiny. And what kind of society is it that has no sense of destiny and no sense of self?" The visions of the Agrarian South and the biracial South are not directly related to the myth of the Lost Cause, which once had been the source for the southern civil religion. In the course of the twentieth century the memory of Confederate defeat has been eclipsed by new dreams, which represent potential southern contributions to the nation. Southerners who lived through the social upheaval of the civil rights movement in the 1950s and 1960s had to struggle to seize meaning from a complicated past. To a large degree, there has been an often-unrecognized reinterpretation of the spiritual meaning of southern history. Southerners who have reflected on the meaning of the South's experience when placed in transcendent perspective increasingly hope the southern past can be a resource toward not only racial reconciliation but also national ecological health. Howard Zinn long ago argued that the distinctiveness of the South was in embodying in extreme form certain national tendencies, mostly negative.[36] It may be that the South, the scene of the most dramatic changes in race relations and a radical transformation, with the move from farming to urban industrialization, in the relationship to the land, can distill its concentrated experiences into a national resource.

Robert N. Bellah's original article on the American civil religion pointed toward an emerging world order. Since then he has argued that a new vision of mankind, a new sense of human connection and possibility in an international context, would emerge in the late twentieth century. The modern southern civil religion suggests that the American recovery of meaning must not overlook regional and local resources as well. The American environmental and social justice crises of the late twentieth century are part of a broader international crisis of meaning. The South's struggle to build a biracial society, in particular, will be of special meaning as Americans approach the Third World. Martin Luther King Jr., while founding his vision on the experience of Montgomery and Selma, nonetheless understood the relationship between the civil rights movement in the South and the liberation movements in the developing nations. Such blendings of localism and universalism have continuing relevance in American life. As southern blacks and whites have created elements of a common culture in the South despite the residue of segregation, the story of that attempt to forge a biracial society, out of fear and suffering, despite greed and exploitation, and with sacrifice and inevitable struggle, may help American society recover a sense of meaning as it faces the future and faces the world.

The Death of Bear Bryant: Myth and Ritual in the Modern South

Legend has it that Paul "Bear" Bryant knew he would die if he quit coaching. No folklore has suggested that he predicted the immense scope of his own funeral, though. It lacked the historic sweep and grandeur of the Martin Luther King Jr. funeral and the dramatic, emotional hysteria of the Elvis Presley funeral, but the Bryant funeral, in terms of sheer numbers, was probably unsurpassed in southern history. Atlanta newspaper columnist Ed Hinton, after viewing the funeral procession, referred to it as "the most awesome and overpowering funeral route in the history of Dixie."[1] Political leaders and governmental bodies honored the coach with official gestures of mourning, including statements of the

The Paul W. Bryant Museum at the University of Alabama preserves the artifacts of a sportsman who became a modern icon of the southern civil religion. (Photo by Tom Rankin)

highest praise. Bryant was a hero of the modern South, a historic figure, and the ceremonial reaction to his death and burial suggests much about contemporary southern life. Southerners made him into a modern saint of the civil religion.

Bear Bryant died on Wednesday, January 26, 1983, in a hospital in Tuscaloosa, Alabama. A memorial service was held for Bryant the night before the funeral, and at it one saw the clearest religious overtones to Bryant's life. The service was held at Memorial Coliseum, where a mostly young, university-related crowd of five thousand people attended. Both Christianity and the University of Alabama figured prominently in the service, which opened with the reading of a telegram from Billy Graham, the high priest of interdenominational evangelical religiosity. The vice chancellor for academic affairs, Roger Sayers, praised Bryant for his contribution to the university as a whole, and the service eventually ended with the singing of the Alabama alma mater. Steadman Shealy, one of Bryant's former players and a devoted protégé, gave the eulogy. He told of Bryant kneeling after his last football victory to lead his team in prayer, thanking God for allowing such a long coaching career. The religious sentiment at this service was a generalized spirituality that blended national and regional patriotism with specific references to evangelical Protestantism. It represented the religiosity of the southern middle class, embodying the style of the dominant religion in the South. It showed the interrelatedness of education, sports, and religion.[2]

The funeral was held Friday morning, January 28, at the First United Methodist Church in Tuscaloosa. The church only seated four hundred people, though, and two nearby churches were required to accommodate the crowd. The general public was seated on a first-come, first-served basis at the First Presbyterian Church, while the spillover of family, university officials, coaches, and media representatives went to the First Baptist Church. Despite the theological squabbles of some denominations, the South's shared evangelical Protestantism has long made such interdenominational funeral activities common for public figures. Estimates were that fifteen hundred people attended the service, with ten thousand mourners in downtown Tuscaloosa, most lining the streets to watch the postfuneral procession to the cemetery.[3]

Bryant wanted a simple funeral ritual and that is what he received. There was organ music, but no hymns or eulogies were heard. Normally in the South, a funeral has been the occasion for florid rhetoric. The funeral sermon has typically been evangelistic; just as in the Sunday sermon, the goal is the conversion of the wicked, of which there have always been plenty. The survivors are urged to think of their own wickedness, of their own mortality and readiness for death and judgment. Bryant's funeral sermon was a departure from this – short, unemotional, and rather bland by southern standards. The Reverend Joe Elmore, pastor of the First United Methodist Church, began with the reading of the One Hundredth Psalm, which speaks simply of the fatherhood of God. Elmore called Bryant "a very special man," and he thanked God for Bryant's "long years of influence on young people, challenging them to excellence, discipline, confidence, and hard work." He noted Bryant's "ability to teach and motivate people – to teach them important lessons of life." It was a comforting, low-key sermon, but one that took the terror and mystery out of life and death. Southerners have been used to hearing often of that mystery, but Elmore's sermon was not traditionally southern.[4]

The crowd of mourners outside the churches included students, women, and the elderly who had followed Bryant for years. Class and caste elements were especially noteworthy in observing the mourners. Bear was a working-class hero for a people whose roots were in the countryside. In truck stops across the South, Bryant's death was a major topic for discussion. Football fans in southern states other than Alabama may have looked upon the Bear and his teams as the enemy during football season, and many of them surely hated him and envied his successes because they were not their own, but in death he transcended that status. These people exchanged stories about the hero. They liked his earthiness; his folksy style fit their manner. And they turned out in large numbers to pay tribute.[5]

The involvement of blacks in the ceremonial mourning for Bryant was particularly intriguing. This was the first funeral of a southern celebrity to include prominently blacks and whites. Elvis Presley drew heavily from black culture for his music and his personal style, yet his death turned into a ceremony for southern working-class whites. Blacks were actively involved, though, in Bryant's funeral. The pallbearers in the funeral included black players from the 1982 team, and former black players were among the honored guests. Eddie Robinson, the legendary Grambling coach who ranked behind Bryant in most college football victories, praised Bryant's humility, his lasting influence for good, and his role in breaking racial barriers in the South. "I think the people felt as long as Coach Bryant was doing it, that was fine," Robinson said. Northerners have frequently noted that Bryant was not a bold leader in desegregation, even in the world of football, but the southern myth, spoken by many blacks as well as whites, enshrines Bryant as a harbinger of a biracial South, purged of its sins and united in opposition to, say, Notre Dame.[6]

Bryant's funeral itself was low-key, but the public reaction was colorful. The outpouring of people and their display of imagery on the streets provided distinctive touches to this ceremony. The symbolism was modern with popular culture artifacts reflecting the changing landscape of the South. The University of Alabama campus displayed, to be sure, the traditional black of mourning. Fraternity members and school custodians draped black banners across the Old South columns of fraternity houses and campus buildings. Black paper streamed from car radio antennae. One also saw, though, mourning signs in front of hotels and on motel marquees. "Thank You, Bear, for the Memories," said one sign in Birmingham, in foot-high letters; "Bear Bryant, 1913–1983. We Love You," said a motel sign in Tuscaloosa. Along the procession route, fans displayed banners and signs, many of them homemade: "We Love You, Coach, We Miss You"; "Farewell, Bear"; and perhaps most appropriate, "God Needs an Offensive Coordinator."[7]

Material culture, icons, and relics associated with the University of Alabama were pervasive. The red *A,* like a scarlet letter, adorned jackets, caps, sweaters, and vests. Fans, while waiting for the funeral to end, stocked up on souvenirs to display. It was all highly commercialized. Records and tapes relating to the Bear were sold, and the radio in Tuscaloosa broadcast a song called "The Bear of Alabama." One could buy a T-shirt with a special message – "It Took a Giant to Replace a Bear" – referring to the New York Giants coach Ray Perkins, Bryant's successor as Alabama's coach. A woman who wore one of these shirts had just purchased it for $10.99. "I think Bear would have wanted us to dress like this," she said. Men wore houndstooth hats, in imitation of the hero. Some people had on funeral finery, their Sunday clothes, but the proper etiquette seemed to be to wear Alabama jackets and caps, crimson sweaters, or vests. All of this represented the merchandising of myth. To be sure, it was not as ghoulish and tasteless as outside Graceland during the Presley funeral, which at times resembled a carnival crowd rather than a mourning group.[8]

The floral arrangements also contained unique symbolism and imagery. Floral arrangements at a hero's funeral can mirror the character and life of the deceased. At Jefferson Davis's funeral, combinations of flowers were shaped to form swords, guns, and flags; at Elvis Presley's funeral, one saw flowers in the form of guitars, broken hearts, teddy bears, and hound dogs. For Bryant, one saw likenesses of houndstooth hats in yellow and green chrysanthemums. "We Love You, Bear," said a five-foot, A-shaped arrangement of roses. The most unusual one was a plastic telephone whose receiver was off the hook. Against a background of yellow chrysanthemums, it read, "Jesus Called." Many mourners carried traditional single roses. After the burial, mourners tried to take flowers from the grave and from the floral displays at the gates of the cemetery.[9]

Bear Bryant's funeral procession was one of the most memorable and certainly the most distinctive in southern history. Almost a century before, Jefferson Davis's procession in 1889 from the New Orleans city hall to the Metairie Cemetery was a massive honoring of Davis the man and the Confederate cause he embodied. It was a four-mile procession, which covered two and one-half miles of ground to the cemetery. Trains carried mourners to the burial spot, where ten thousand people had gathered. Essentially, it was a military procession with pomp and ceremony. Martin Luther King Jr.'s procession, or "pilgrimage" as Ralph Abernathy called it, was full of historic overtones. Blacks and whites marched together in the sweltering Atlanta heat, as in a civil rights march. Services were held along the route at Ebenezer Baptist Church, Morehouse College, and South View Cemetery. It covered four and one-third miles from the church to the college, with King leading the way, lying in a mule-drawn farm wagon. Elvis Presley's procession also ranked as one of the South's greatest. As one might expect, it was a flashy motor cortege. All the official automobiles were white, including eighteen gleaming white Cadillacs. Thousands of mourners viewed the cortege, with a half-dozen helicopters hovering above, on its three-mile route.[10]

Bryant's procession was equally impressive; it represented a spontaneous outpouring of simple grief. The motorcade moved through Tuscaloosa after the funeral, past Bryant-Denny Stadium and Memorial Coliseum, shrines in Bryant's athletic domain. Most businesses and offices in the area were closed for the funeral, and school was dismissed, giving mourners the freedom to participate. People stood on the sidewalks, three and four deep at most places, ten deep at a few spots, as the motorcade of three hundred cars moved out Interstate 59 for the fifty-three-mile journey to the cemetery in Birmingham. The procession included nineteen motorcycle policemen, six police sedans, three team buses, various limousines, and assorted private cars. It stretched out for five miles and took two hours to pass. The route was packed with miles of mourners, jamming overpasses, exit ramps, side streets, and bridges and standing on hills and atop automobiles. Estimates of the crowd turnout for the day were between five hundred thousand and seven hundred thousand people, with some observers suggesting as many as a million people. Hundreds of automobiles, in good regional tradition, pulled off on the shoulders of the interstate highway to pay respects, and eventually cars in the opposite lanes of the procession simply stopped in the road.[11]

Police and reporters estimated that ten thousand people participated in the graveside burial at Elmwood Cemetery in Birmingham. A modern lawn-park cemetery established in 1900, Elmwood was chosen for family reasons. Mary Harmon Bryant had bought the space years before as a family plot because members of her family were already buried there. Thus, little thought was given to burial back in Bryant's home state of Arkansas, or on the University of Alabama campus, or on the fifty-yard line of Legion Field in Birmingham, the scene of so many worldly triumphs.

The crowd had started to arrive at the fog-shrouded cemetery by five in the morning. People were casual in appearance and behavior. One reporter described it as "a cold, somber, tailgate party with no cheers or libation to warm the crowd." After the funeral party arrived at the cemetery, the graveside service took only ten minutes, including the reading of the Twenty-third Psalm and the Lord's Prayer. Mourners came in large numbers to the grave for days afterward, and they still come on pilgrimage.[12]

The official and unofficial ceremonies of Bear Bryant's death reflected the legendary qualities of the Bear. The ritual enacted a myth of the modern South. Historian George Tindall, in his article "Mythology: A New Frontier in Southern History," has defined social myths as "mental pictures" portraying the self-image of a people or the view of them by outsiders. He has suggested that because the southern mind is "receptive to the concrete and dramatic image, it may be unusually susceptible to mythology." Studies of southern mythology have proliferated in recent years, but few of them deal with the modern period and none with the importance of sports to the regional psyche.[13]

The Bryant myth begins in the rural South of the Depression. Bryant was born in the backcountry of Arkansas, on what was the southwestern frontier of the nineteenth-century humorists. Like W. J. Cash's classic "man at the center," Bryant seems a simple, rustic fellow, a product of the soil. But his class was sharecropper white, not independent yeoman farmer. The youngest of eleven children, his father was a semi-invalid. His mother supported the family by selling homegrown produce, and young Paul helped her. He always called himself a "Mama's boy." The family was poor, and when he was old enough, Bryant had to do the farmwork that he grew to hate. "For years, the one thing that motivated me," he said, "was the fear of going back to plowing and driving those mules in Arkansas and chopping cotton for 50 cents an hour." So much for agrarianism. The Bear developed an inferiority complex because of the rural poverty he knew. From this source came his enormous drive and ambition to succeed. The demons that made him outwork other coaches and even brutalize his own players in order to succeed came from his own youth, too. Like Davy Crockett, young Paul Bryant wrestled a bear – it was a carnival bear, though – when he was twelve years old, thus earning his nickname. He went on to play football for the Fordyce High School Red Bugs in Arkansas, and then played end at the University of Alabama. Legend has it that his mother took his only pair of shoes to a cobbler and had them cleated; thereafter he wore them everywhere – from the football field to the Sunday school room.[14]

The young Bryant appears as a Faulknerian figure, resembling Labove in *The Hamlet*. Labove was a farm boy who wanted to be a schoolteacher, and the University of Mississippi coach let him attend school with food and shelter in exchange for his playing football and doing chores around the campus. Despite his amazement that anyone would offer him such a deal, Labove accepted the proposal and found in football something for his spirit. When he played football on Saturdays, "despite his contempt, his ingrained conviction, his hard and spartan heritage, he lived fiercely free." One can imagine the young, rawboned Bryant, fresh from the farm, experiencing all this. Faulkner even captures the importance of shoes, as in the myth. Labove's family had few shoes, so he sent them the cleated football shoes he had access to, so that his mother and brothers and sisters walked around in cleats. He was scrupulous and only took a pair of shoes when the team won and he felt he had earned them. This, then, was Labove and the young Bryant of myth – upright, tough, and country naive.[15]

The Bear Bryant myth is a success story, a rags-to-riches American tale, told in the southern vernacular. Like the people of his region, during his lifetime he rose from miserable poverty to increasing material success. He fought his way through football to success; unlike many earlier southern heroes, including the fabled Confederates, he won his wars. He became the most winning college football coach in history, with 323 wins before his retirement at the end of the 1982 season.

Like a good mythic figure, the Bear became the subject of folklore. Above all, there were the descriptions by sportswriters, fans, players, and coaches of Bryant in bigger-than-life terms. "He was a monumental figure in intercollegiate athletics, a man who set standards not easily attainable by men," said Penn State coach Joe Paterno. "He was a giant and we will miss him." "Generations from now they will speak in hushed tones about the backwoodsy man from Fordyce whom the city slickers couldn't beat," wrote Al Dunning of the *Memphis Commercial Appeal*. A column in the *New Yorker* magazine referred to him as an "actual genius." Observers compared him with Douglas MacArthur, John Wayne, and, most frequently, George Patton. Even though Bryant was an old man, his fanatic followers seemed to think this giant would not die. "I thought the man was Immortal and that's why it's still such a shock to me to know that he's gone," said an assistant athletic director at the university. This sentiment should not be surprising, considering that a popular artifact in Tuscaloosa was a portrait of Bryant walking on water.[16]

If indeed he had to die, other folklore stories suggested that the hero had prescience. One legend, as mentioned earlier, was that he coached himself to death. "He grieved himself to death over football, that's what," said a customer in an Aliceville, Alabama, truck stop after Bryant's death. "It wasn't anything else." The popular belief was that he knew the end was coming. Even *New York Times* reporter George Vecsey, not exactly a backwoodsman, suggested as much, intimating that Bryant showed he was "aware of his own mortality by resigning." Perhaps Nina Goolsby, editor of the Oxford, Mississippi, *Eagle,* put it best: "He received that two-minute warning that he was nearing the end of the game." [17]

The rhetoric of the Bryant myth expressed during the death ceremonies suggested that he was most admired in the South because he was a winning leader. For a people whose heroes sometimes symbolized lost causes, Bryant was a change. The consensus of the people of Alabama, at least after his death, was that his abilities could have led to political success. The folklore said that he could easily have been elected governor, if he had wanted to lower himself to that level. His abilities, in other words, transcended sports, a field which some Southerners believed was now producing society's greatest leaders. As one of his ex-players said, "Coach Bryant was the greatest leader this country ever had. And not just the leader of Alabama's football players, but of the whole nation." Bryant's symbolic importance to the nation, as an American figure, was thus noted. President Ronald Reagan described Bryant as a "hard but loved taskmaster." "Patriotic to the core, devoted to his players and inspired by a winning spirit that would not quit, 'Bear' Bryant gave his country the gift of a life unsurpassed," Reagan said. Bryant's coaching colleague Bobby Dodd noted that the "country missed a good bet when it didn't put Paul in charge of negotiations with the Russians." Hyperbole is not unknown to myth, although the image of a one-on-one Bryant-Brezhnev match would have pleased many a sports fan. [18]

The myth was not just one of power and victory, though; it had its sentimental side. "He was a gentle man who cared," said a Memphis reporter. Stories recounted his compassion for injured athletes. The Bear, it was said, stayed up all night with sick friends or called acquaintances going through traumatic experiences. He would read in the newspapers of tragedy and then go out of his way to comfort the afflicted. The stories undoubtedly had a basis in truth, but the mythic process at work led to endless repetition and elaboration in what remains a storytelling, oral culture. The end product reminds one of the Robert E. Lee of legend, the saintly man with a halo. Southerners admired not only Bryant's success but the way he achieved it. Observers stressed his character and class, his concern for making his athletes decent people. The old stories of recruiting scandals thus were forgotten; this hero had to be pure. The Lost

Cause generation of Southerners after the Civil War was told it could be proud for maintaining virtue, despite the tragedy of a failed Confederacy. Bryant's followers attributed to him many of the same virtues as the Confederate heroes, with the added advantage that he achieved success. Southerners for generations after the Civil War were taught not to abandon the virtues of discipline, character, and morality that the Confederates had represented in the southern mind. Bryant confirmed that virtue was not just its own reward, as with the Confederates, but could lead to earthly success as well. The southern commitment to Lost Cause spiritual victories was a profound, yet tenuous, commitment. Given human nature, Southerners could finally relish a hero of victory as well as virtue. Of course, victory was the key to Bryant's appeal. As a *Los Angeles Times* reporter noted, "For Bryant, winning was the ultimate morality."[19]

Bryant's myth occasionally acknowledged human weakness. He had smoked too much, drunk too much, and liked to party. He still would have done so late in life, but his deteriorating health cut back on his pleasures. He was earthy, something that did not bother his rural and working-class followers but did bother his middle-class fans. He cursed and yelled and was generally gruff. He was ornery, even a bully, when younger. He showed downright brutality toward his 1954 Texas A&M football team, which he took by bus to the wilderness of Junction, Texas, and physically tormented in good macho tradition. By the time of his death, this side of his character had mellowed. "He was meaner than hell when he was young and kind-hearted as they come as an old man," said sports writer Rick Cleveland of the *Jackson Clarion-Ledger*. This fit southern expectations perfectly. A people raised on a hard religion based on sin and guilt know that everyone falls short of the glory of God. Bryant's very vices evoked images of the southern past. For a people mired through much of their history in miserable poverty, the only way out indeed seemed to be to fight and claw and scrape to escape it. The southern Protestant religion leaves room for the possibility of redemption, and the worse the sin the better the feelings of salvation. Bear must have had an experience of grace. Unlike another Paul, it was not a blinding revelation on, say, the road to Tuscaloosa, but somewhere along the line, in the 1970s, he mellowed and became an upright figure. Moving home to Alabama, in the myth, was the key factor in his mellowing.[20]

Any hero needs mythmakers, and sportswriters performed that role for Bryant. They shaped the Bryant myth that took such a deep hold on the southern people. Journalists created his image as a folk hero. Bryant made for interesting copy across the nation, but southern reporters were especially fond of ruminating about the coach. When he died, one could observe differences in the reporting between southern and nonsouthern media. The network evening news shows, to be sure, devoted lengthy pieces to the story, as did the national magazines. Northern and western newspapers covered the story as a major event. Front-page photographs appeared in many cases, along with wire service accounts of the death and the funeral. Will Grimsley did a reminiscence for Associated Press that appeared widely. But this represented only the top layer of coverage given to national news at a distance. It was packaged news, uniform across the nation. The *Boston Globe* carried only news service accounts of the death and funeral. The paper devoted no sports columns nor editorials to it. On Friday, the *Cleveland Plain-Dealer* buried the story on the back page of the sports section. The *Los Angeles Times* similarly had no columns or editorials and no stories after the account of the funeral. In contrast, the southern papers carried multiple stories about the death and local reactions to it. Columnists on the feature pages, as well as in the sports sections, for days wrote of the Bear in stories spiced with remembered anecdotes. It was one big "sitting up" ceremony, shared by writers and fans. Weighty editorials even offered Bear as a model for reflection. Special Sunday editions were prepared, filled with fresh accounts of the Bear's life and career and the meaning of his death.[21] Perhaps the point is best made by noting that a *Boston Globe* sportswriter, after listing Bryant's coaching achievements, observed that still, he never had beat Notre Dame; few, if any, southern reporters made a point of that.

Despite his national reputation, Bryant, in fact, had special meaning for Southerners. In the 1960s and early 1970s the South's image was quite negative overall, but Bryant's success gradually became a matter of regional pride. Southerners related to him and his qualities as their own. Although Bryant was an enemy when playing southeastern teams, Southerners rallied behind Bryant when he played teams outside the region. They brought out the old Confederate battle flag, especially when Alabama played a team such as Notre Dame. "When 'Bama went north and east and west, it wasn't going to play just a football game," said Mississippi sportswriter Paul Borden. "It was going on a crusade, and Bear was

48 CIVIL RELIGION

our Richard the Lion-Hearted. Bear was our best, and our best could and did beat the best of anywhere else and that was important to all of us below the Mason-Dixon line." Bryant was compared to Robert E. Lee by Birmingham sportswriter Bill Crowe. Noting that Lee spent more time as a college administrator at West Point and Washington College than as a general, Crowe made the obvious comparison with Bryant the educator. Both were intuitive tacticians and insightful judges of personnel, able to match "personnel to positions." Neither was politically active, but each nonetheless showed "the important qualities: the leadership, the presence, the call to greatness. And the heroism." Like Lee, Bryant could be a unifying figure for Southerners of all sorts.[22]

Even Northerners treated Bryant as a model Southerner. Phil Pepe of the *New York Daily News* wrote after Bryant's death of not understanding the coach until meeting Bryant and observing how people reacted to him. Pepe came to believe that it had "something to do with the South and heroes." George Vecsey, writing in the *New York Times,* noted that "Southerners recognized him as one of their own. He was a huge celebrity in Holiday Inn lobbies, but in truth he was little different from the most successful car dealer in town, or the Southern Baptist preacher or the lawyer who could put his shoes up on his desk and gab with a visitor." Vecsey had seen Bryant impress the families of recruits as a "good old boy with a veneer of college," and his folksy, down-to-earth manner charmed black parents as well as white. Raad Cawthon, a Mississippi reporter who grew up in Alabama as, of all things, a liberal, long-haired student in the 1960s, noted that Bryant was the unifying middle ground for him and his conservative rural southern family. They could share a "common pride" in Bryant's success; the coach had thereby "staked a claim to a piece of my mental landscape."[23]

Bryant was a state hero, but this should not obscure his regionwide significance. Even the popular country-rock singing group Alabama, despite deliberate association with its home state, prominently displays the Confederate flag and other regional symbols. Scholars have long noted the importance of localism and the sense of place as southern regional traits, and Bryant embodied these. His career blossomed when he came "home" to Alabama in 1958. "It was like when you were out in the field, and you heard your mama calling you to dinner," he said of the offer from Alabama. C. Vann Woodward, in his seminal essay "The Search for a

Southern Identity," argued that the South's historical experience had nurtured traits different from those of the North – a sense of guilt over racial problems, defeat in the Civil War, poverty, and a sense of place. The Bear Bryant myth showed that the modern South, or at least its self-conscious mythic image and its national reputation, had changed and overcome the guilt (blacks were now incorporated in a biracial sports South), defeat (Bryant won at football), and poverty (Bryant as rags-to-riches success). In his obvious attachment to Alabama, Bryant showed a continuing southern sense of place, but less a folk version of that than a new middle-class version.[24] Although born in a rural area like most Southerners of his generation, he put down new roots in comfortable suburban life, in this case in Tuscaloosa and Birmingham. Middle-class Southerners were not fanatic over this sense of place business; they could keep it in perspective enough to see "place" in air-conditioned suburbs as well as in decaying farmhouses.

Bryant's mythic imagery as the folksy agrarian could be misleading. In his origins he surely symbolized the poor, rural, Depression-era sharecropper South. But he, and the South with him, evolved into middle-class respectability. He symbolized that change as much as anything else. His association with education was important, as the South's development has been linked to that force. Bryant's South was the new middle-class South of suburbs, white-collar and professional jobs, colleges for sons and daughters, golf courses for dads, and football games for everyone on Saturday. His funeral service itself was a low-key, tasteful, understated affair, which suited this class he represented. It was the kind of funeral *Southern Living* magazine could have done, if it did funerals. It was not a traditional southern funeral – there was no open casket, no "sitting up" ceremony for friends and family to gather at, little hysteria, little explicit old-time evangelical rhetoric. Religion, to be sure, was vital to understanding the funeral, but it was a generalized, modern evangelical ceremony – not the religion of Flannery O'Connor's itinerants burning with the evangelical passion, but the Protestantism of Billy Graham, slick, organized, and successful.

Sociologist John Shelton Reed has noted the need for a new imagery of the middle class in the South. Most regional images have been upper-class and aristocratic in style, or else lower-class, redneck images.[25] Sports, and especially football, are providing images for a new pantheon of southern heroes. Sports figures, perhaps even more than musicians, are becoming prime icons of the modern South, the way the Confederate veterans were heroes in the late nineteenth century. Just as Southerners paid homage to these men to show their commitment to the past, while at the same time pursuing New South business activities, so modern Southerners living in suburbs respond to a folksy, agrarian coach, embodying traditional regional imagery.

The Bryant sports myth embodied aspects of earlier regional mythology – the New South hope of education transforming the region; the fighting South, with football as Celtic sublimation; and the Jeffersonian agrarian dream, although, of course, Bryant came from rural poverty, not agrarian Eden. But the Sports South is a distinct myth and Bryant its greatest symbol. An underlying function of mythology is unification, the development of a sense of community and of common ideals. Myths embody a culture's beliefs about its past and its expectations for the future. The racial dimension of this in the modern South is crucial. Most earlier "southern" myths were, in fact, those mainly of southern whites. No thorough studies of black reaction to southern myths exist, but, clearly, segregated blacks had little impact in formulating the region's predominant mental pictures. In the modern South, though, such cultural phenomena as music and sports offer fresh images of blacks and whites sharing and shaping a common culture.[26] To be sure, mythology cannot deal with the complexity of real life and always simplifies. The danger of mythology is believing myths uncritically. Just because the Bryant sports myth has appealing images of racial harmony on the football field, one should not conclude that the South has achieved a perfect society. But at the mythic level, sports symbolism, and especially football, offers a new model for southern youth, a shared vision, unlike much earlier regional symbolism. It represents the reality of a South moving a bit closer to realization that its once segregated people, black and white, have, after all, shared interests.

Expressive Culture

4

William Faulkner and the Southern Religious Culture

H. L. Mencken would probably snicker at the idea of "southern religious culture." Mencken, of course, was the premier critic of the South in the early twentieth century, and few have had more fun with that position than he. He took a special glee in lampooning southern religion. The root of the problem with the South, as Mencken had it, was the tyranny of the "Baptist and Methodist barbarism" below the Mason-Dixon line. He described the South as a "cesspool of Baptists, a miasma of Methodists, snake charmers, phony real estate operators, and syphilitic evangelists." "No bolder attempt to set up a theocracy was ever made in this world," he said of the South, with his typical restraint and understatement, "and none ever had behind it a more implacable fanaticism." There were no arts except "the lower reaches of the gospel hymn." Sacred Harp singing, he said, combined the sound of a Ukrainian peasant melody with that of a steam calliope.[1]

Mencken was amusing with his diatribes, and he did bring a certain insight to his writing on the South. He coined the term "Bible Belt" to refer to areas of the South and Midwest dominated by conservative Christian concerns. William Faulkner was born in, grew up in, and wrote about the area called the Bible Belt, at a time when popular religion was emerging out of folk and denominational patterns. What was the relationship between the South's religious culture and Faulkner's work?

Faulkner scholars in the past have been slow in exploring this subject. Influential early critics, such as Malcolm Cowley and Irving Howe, rarely even mentioned religion in Faulkner's work. Cowley's famous essay on the Faulkner legend did not include a place for religion, nor did George Marion O'Donnell's article on "Faulkner's Mythology." Later scholars focused on Christian themes. We have read much about the religious symbolism in *A Fable,* for example, or the Christ imagery associated with Joe Christmas in *Light in August.*[2] But this represents "generic" religion – broad themes disassociated from time and place. We know that Faulkner explored place, the particularities of a specific community, as a way to understand the human experience. When scholars examine Faulkner's portrayal of black characters, they do so against the background of the South's tortured history of race relations. When trying to understand Faulkner's world, you must take into account the importance he assigns history, not just abstract "history" but the history of a specific people who experienced slavery, defeat in the Civil War, and poverty afterwards. Scholars in the field of southern religious studies have, over the past generation, moved the study of religion in the region beyond stereotypes of the Bible Belt to a serious exploration of the religious groups and forces in the South that produced Faulkner. The southern religious tradition has been distinctive within the United States in its religious picture. Did this not play a role in Faulkner's fiction?

One aspect of the South's religious tradition has been explored in some depth by scholars. Calvinism was indeed a burden to Faulkner's characters. Faulkner was a critic of Calvinism and saw it limiting human potential. Calvinism teaches the absolute sovereignty of God and the depravity of human beings. They are unable to fathom God's purposes, nor can they dictate their own destinies. Accompanying Calvinism historically has been a pronounced belief in the doctrine of the elect, a conviction that Calvinists are God's chosen. Faulkner surely targeted this Calvinism as a source of southern evil. The absolutism, fatalism, and self-righteousness that exist in the world of his characters and mightily afflict them stem as much from this source as from any other.[3]

Although Calvinism has been a formative influence on southern religion, Faulkner scholarship too often gives the impression that a rigid Calvinism has been the main characteristic of the region's religion and certainly the only trait of it that Faulkner explored in depth. Neither of these propositions is true. The southern religious tradition, to be sure, grew out of Calvinism. Faulkner, like others in his era, often used "Calvinist," "Puritan," and "puritanical" as synonyms, but they have different historical meanings. In the 1920s and 1930s American writers used "Puritan" to stand for, among other things, sexual repression, narrowmindedness, intolerance, and especially anti-intellectualism. This was the meaning Edith Hamilton wanted when she later described Faulkner himself as "a violently twisted Puritan."[4] Historians have shown that the image of dour, sexually repressed colonial-era Puritans is a partial truth, at best; most American hang-ups stem from nineteenth-century Victorianism, not earlier. Perry Miller's studies of the New England colonial mind suggest convincingly that the Puritans were highly intellectual and that later New England rationalism grew out of their work.

The Calvinism that gradually seeped into the southern soul was, in any event, only a distant cousin to its New England relative. Southern Calvinism can be traced as far back as the Presbyterians who were active in the late colonial South. Scotch-Irish settlers in the South had once been Presbyterian Calvinists, although they had lost their churchgoing habits before immigrating to North America, and they preserved Calvinism simply as a half-remembered cultural legacy. Faulkner devotes considerable attention to the Presbyterians, but southern Calvinism did not come primarily from them. Settlers in Mississippi, early or late, did not choose that denomination to join en masse, nor did Southerners elsewhere. Any discussion of Faulkner and the southern religious tradition must confront the denominational issue. The South has been distinguished from other parts of the United States as the region dominated by Baptists and

Methodists. Geographers divide the nation into seven religious regions, each dominated by one religious group or combination of groups. The South has been and still is that region dominated by Baptists, with widespread secondary influence from the Methodists. The Great Revival at the turn of the nineteenth century led to the appearance of camp meetings and revivals, which became the engines that drove these two churches to dominance on the frontier, in the rural areas, and even in the small towns and cities of the South. The Methodists were the largest southern church up to the Civil War, with the Southern Baptist Convention surpassing them after the war, when membership figures in southern churches skyrocketed. In Faulkner's time, Mississippi had one of the highest percentages of enrolled church members in the nation. In 1957 four-fifths of the population belonged to churches, and over half of Mississippians joining congregations were Baptist.[5]

The South, and especially Mississippi, has been Baptist land to both blacks and whites. There it is: the *B* word. A word that Faulkner often used but one that literary critics seem to want to avoid. "Ours was a town founded by Aryan Baptists and Methodists, for Aryan Baptists and Methodists," says Faulkner's narrator, Charles "Chick" Mallison. In recounting the history of mythical Jefferson, Mallison notes that the Episcopal and Presbyterian churches were the oldest in the area, but "the Baptists and Methodists had heired from them, usurped and dispossessed" the others. Faulkner had special fun in sketching the Baptist influence among the Snopeses as they seek success. Ratliff speculates about Flem, for example, that since becoming an "up-and-coming feller in the Baptist church" he seemed to be depending more "on Providence" to get what he wanted, with getting what he wanted still his aim. The Baptist role in the South, in particular, has been extraordinary. The Baptists, writes Samuel S. Hill, began as "a collection of despised and disdained outgroups," who came to dominate the South. Charles Mallison describes them as "incorrigible nonconformists, nonconformists not just to everybody else but to each other in mutual accord." They had not come to the wilderness that was the Deep South for religious freedom but to establish a tyranny "in which to be incorrigible and unreconstructible Baptists and Methodists." This long dominance of a culture remains unique in the history of the Baptists and other evangelical groups. Baptists historically were dissenters in Europe and in most of North America, but in the South they have been a culturally established religion, not just dominating numerically but infiltrating every seam of the region's cultural fabric.[6]

The Baptists certainly inherited Calvinist theology, with its concern for God's omnipotence, human sinfulness, predestination, and other theological features. The Baptists, and the Methodists too, began as frontier religions in the South, and on the frontier this Calvinist legacy was combined with a central stress on free will. This is essential in understanding southern religion. Humans had the ability to decide the all-important question, Where will I spend eternity? "The preachers' appeal was to men's emotions on the route to their will," writes Samuel S. Hill, "precisely because this was the arena wherein, as they reckoned, destinies were determined." As a result, notes Hill, "the Calvinist dimension of the classical Baptist heritage receded under the stress of the frontier preachments."[7]

The religious tradition that has dominated southern culture is Evangelicalism. Both the Baptists and the Methodists are a part of this branch of Protestantism, the distinguishing feature of which is a concern for religious experience. The central theme of southern religion is the need for conversion in a specific experience that will lead to baptism, to a purified new person. The need is to be born again, to "get right with God." Outsiders often see southern religion's central feature as a Fundamentalism stressing orthodox theology, and this outlook has been important in the region's churches. Highly valued is the discipline of a strict adherence to biblical teachings, rigorous morality, and community enforcement of selective religious teachings. But these are secondary; they simply reinforce the essential focus on individualism. The individual must seek the experience of God's grace, and without that, nothing else matters. The spirit is alive in southern religion; the Holy Ghost is a continuing vital presence. This belief is taken to extremes by holiness and Pentecostal groups, but even mainstream Baptists and Methodists believe in it.[8]

The characteristic concerns of Evangelicalism shaped day-to-day life in the South. The region's religious culture was based on the belief in the need to express your religion, to testify to the faith. The South is an oral culture, and religion has reflected that. You stand up in church and recount your sinfulness and the Lord's work in saving you. The minister is judged by how he preaches and how many wayfaring strangers he saves – to the accompanying punctuation of amen from the congregation. Biblical stories and characters are well known. Sermons teach the faith through these stories. The spirituals often recall biblical characters, and gospel songs later did the same thing. Sister Wynona Carr sings "The Ballgame," wherein Satan tosses curveballs to the hitter, Solomon is the umpire, and Job suffers throughout before hitting a home run. Politicians used a biblical shorthand when speaking on the stump, relating the Old Testament's tales of human nature to current governmental struggles. Reformers wanted to throw the moneychangers out of the temple, the temple being the Legislature down in Jackson. The landscape reflected the religious culture with visual messages. "Prepare to Meet Thy God," "Get Right with God," or simply "Jesus Saves" reduced the southern faith to its appropriate essence. Folk artists still produce dramatic visionary paintings and sculpture that translate the religion of the spirit into art.

Faulkner grew up in and knew the southern religious culture. Critics have disagreed on the importance of religion to Faulkner. Some have seen him as essentially an agnostic or atheist, but his explicit statements suggest he claimed a broad Christianity. He attended St. Peter's Episcopal Church in Oxford after his marriage, read the Book of Common Prayer, and was buried with the rites of the church. If you visit his grave, you will find "Beloved, Go with God" there. His Episcopal connection was not an unusual one for southern intellectuals. Others who grew up in evangelical churches have sought refuge in the greater latitude of the Episcopal tradition. Faulkner enjoyed having fun with the connection, too. "Funny going's on in that house," says a character in *Soldiers' Pay*. "And a preacher of the gospel, too. Even if he is Episcopal."[9]

In the context of Faulkner's relationship to the southern religious culture, the crucial issue is not whether he was a Christian or not. Faulkner learned early the religious culture of his time and place. He reflected the usual connection between family and church in the South. His father's family was Methodist, and that denomination was his formative one. It is not a predominantly Calvinist tradition. John Wesley's stress on free will and on the need to cultivate spirituality set it off in the South from the Baptists and Presbyterians, who retained larger elements of Calvinist theology. Faulkner attended Methodist Sunday school when a boy and was baptized at the New Albany Methodist Church. He may have been like Samuel Clemens, who said he grew up learning to fear God and hate the Sunday school. Faulkner's mother took him to country revivals at the Methodist campgrounds near Oxford, where he surely absorbed the atmosphere of rural southern revivalism. One relative taught the religious culture with special effectiveness. When young William Faulkner was at his great-grandfather's house in Ripley, he had to recite a Bible verse before the meal would be served to him. That is a powerful incentive to absorb the features of a culture, willingly or not. Faulkner, in fact, has offered one of the best descriptions of the religious culture of his upbringing. "My life was passed, my childhood, in a very small Mississippi town, and that was a part of my background. I grew up with that. I assimilated that, took that in without even knowing it. It's just there. It has nothing to do with how much of it I might believe or disbelieve – it's just there." [10] That is what culture – and in this case the southern religious culture – is: "It's just there," all around. Faulkner recognized that a specific form of religion was a part of his cultural legacy with which to work.

Faulkner drew from a tradition of literary portrayal of the southern religious culture that goes back at least as far as the southwestern humorists and their accounts of camp meetings. Mark Twain sketched a vivid account of a revival in *Huckleberry Finn*. Faulkner grew to maturity at a time of dramatic events and trends in southern religious history. The Scopes trial, the organized Fundamentalist movement, the growth of the holiness and Pentecostal sects – all of these made for dramatic news and delighted the pen of Mencken and other satirists. Faulkner does not deal at length with many dramatic aspects of the modern religious South. Baptism, for example, is a central ritual in this faith, but he sketched no memorable scene of a baptizing. Few itinerant preachers wander in or out of Yoknapatawpha County. There are no visions nor any dancing in the aisles by those consumed by the spirit. There is no faith healing, speaking in tongues, nor snake handling.

The Georgians seemed somehow closer to that world. Faulkner's contemporary, Erskine Caldwell, dealt often with sectarian religion, but usually for comic purposes, portraying the South's religious forms and impulses as simply a colorful part of the degenerate world of the sharecropper and mill town South. Sister Bessie in *Tobacco Road,* for example, comes from the tradition where having the call to preach makes you a preacher, but Caldwell gives her little credit for any authentic spiritual purpose. Flannery O'Connor uses humor, of course, but she sees in her rural, religiously obsessed characters the raw materials of a religious message. Although a Roman Catholic with serious theological concerns, she made art from the specifics of the Evangelical faith.[11]

Both Faulkner and O'Connor deal often with the spiritually deformed. Old Doc Hines in *Light in August* and Old Tarwater in *The Violent Bear It Away* are kindred spirits of sorts. They are outsiders on the societal fringe, yet they are outsiders only because they have taken to life-and-death extremes key messages of their society. Tarwater is an old prophet obsessed with the need to baptize the young idiot child, Bishop. Hines is twisted by race and religion, preaching a hellfire-and-brimstone version of white supremacy. Both are crazed prophets of spiritual power unrestrained by institutions, and the results of their efforts in both cases are violence. Violence is often a part of O'Connor's world, but in her art violence leads to moments of epiphany, of revelation for the reader, if not for her characters. Faulkner's world, especially in the novels considered his greatest, is sometimes darker: Do the grisly deaths of Joe Christmas and Joanna Burden in *Light in August* have a religious meaning in the same sense that violence in O'Connor leads to spiritual insight? They are related to the stories of spiritual hope embodied by Lena Grove, Byron Bunch, and Gail Hightower, but the deaths in the novel are best characterized not as moments of divine revelation but simply as counterpoints to the other stories. Faulkner's and O'Connor's religious sympathies are with those embodying a simple folk religion, more than with those in the comfortable mainstream town churches. Both writers see mainstream southern Protestant churches as embodying the complacency and self-centeredness of the modern world, but those complacent churches do not exhaust the meaning of religion in the South for either Faulkner or O'Connor.

The religious world that Faulkner sketched in his work was a rich one. The community church occupied a central place in it, and his little postage stamp of native soil had many congregations. Faulkner was not as interested in the wild emotional spirit of the newer sectarian groups that appealed to Flannery O'Connor as he was in the traditions, rituals, and behaviors of what he called "the spirit Protestant eternal" as it had existed since the early days of his county. Young Quentin Compson describes the religion of another Faulkner character as "a granite heritage," while still another character is said to inherit "old strong Campbellite blood," referring to such Restorationist, New Testament churches as the Churches of

Christ.[12] Religion in Faulkner's world, at its best and worst, has contributed through tenacity and strength to the survival of these people.

Institutional religion was in Yoknapatawpha County from the beginning of settlement. Three churches were already there when only thirty homes could be found. The first white settler in Yoknapatawpha County arrived brawling "simply because of his over-revved glands." The earliest ministers came "roaring with Protestant scripture and boiled whiskey, Bible and jug in one hand" and "a native tomahawk in the other." Faulkner leaves little doubt that the taking of land from the Native Americans was a specifically Protestant act making way for capitalist civilization. Religion in Yoknapatawpha County remained a frontier religion for many years indeed. It was a place where, with many churches nearby, men insisted on taking an hour to go five miles to attend a particular denomination, and where Gail Hightower's father rode sixteen miles each Sunday morning to preach. It was a place of revivals. Old Bayard Sartoris of Carolina once pursued his foxes on the hunt through the middle of a Methodist tabernacle, revival in progress, returning later to take part in "the ensuing indignation meeting."[13] Hightower's grandfather, a bluff, hardy Episcopalian who seldom darkened the church doors, liked to attend revivals, luring the congregation away for horse races outside. Those comic scenes are more than counterbalanced by the fearful picture of Joe Christmas disrupting a black revival, killing Pappy Thompson and young Roz as well. The congregation thought he was the devil.

The Bible possessed a near mystical attraction to these folks. Even in dissent, it was the source of all authority, or perhaps dissent was easy because it was the source of authority. The respectable Methodist deacon Coldfield in *Absalom, Absalom!* waited in his room for Confederate troops to march outside, reading from the Bible "the passages of the old violent vindictive mysticism." Evangelical religion and its Scriptures went off to the war and became a part of the New South afterwards. When Flem Snopes takes on the trappings of success, he becomes a Baptist deacon, a natural alliance. A young Baptist minister in *Soldiers' Pay* is described repeatedly as "a fiery-eyed dervish." This New South world is sometimes a less fearful one than before. A character described as "a Rotarian" in *Mosquitoes* proposes that his congregation can achieve 100 percent attendance "by keeping them afraid they'd miss something good by staying away." Circuit-riding fire-and-brimstone preachers were turning over in their graves at the thought of reducing the Gospel to such pragmatism in the Bible Belt.[14]

Preachers were a necessity in this world. Faulkner wrote about at least twelve ministers, but most cannot be described as fitting role models of virtue. As one scholar has classified them, there were "three heavy drinkers, three fanatics, and three slave traders, two adulterers, and two murderers." The Lord works in mysterious ways. Many of Faulkner's ministers are guilty of licentiousness and moral laxity. But this human failing was not the worst offense. A despicable tendency is symbolized by Coldfield, who takes refuge in "the impregnable citadel of his passive rectitude" and raises his daughters "in a grim mausoleum air of Puritan righteousness."[15]

In the end, Faulkner most disliked the austerity and authoritarianism associated with organized religion. Hightower sees churches filled "not with ecstasy or passion but in adjuration, threat, and doom." The professionals who now run the churches had "removed the bells from the steeples" and stood "against truth and against that peace in which to sin and be forgiven which is the life of man." Churches were human institutions and should have more respect for human nature that strives, inevitably fails, but must go on. The sin of the church in the religious legend of Faulkner's Yoknapatawpha world is its failure to come to terms with human nature, to think it is better than the people it serves. Faulkner turns to a cultural experience to convey his ultimate judgment upon the church. As Gail Hightower listens to church organ music one summer night, he fantasizes about the shapes of the music "assuming the shapes and attitudes of crucifixions, ecstatic, solemn, and profound in gathering volume." The music is "stern and implacable," a Protestant music that demands not life and love but "in sonorous tones death as though death were the boon." Hightower moves beyond this judgment on Protestantism to note a grim regional dimension. "Listening, he seems to hear within it the apotheosis of his own history, his own land, his own environed blood: that people from which he sprang and among whom he lives who can never take either pleasure or catastrophe or escape from either, without brawling over it. Pleasure, ecstasy, they cannot seem to bear: their escape from it is in violence, in drinking and fighting and praying; catastrophe too, the violence identical and apparently inescapable. *And so why should not their religion drive them to crucifixion of themselves and one another?* he thinks." This emotional religion driving people to cruci-fixion is the same one that haunts Flannery O'Connor's characters, that confirms W. J. Cash's belief in a tribal southern white God, and that lies on the underside of southern Evangelicalism's call for an ethic of love. Faulkner once described being southern Baptist as "an emotional condi-tion" that came "from times of hardship" when people found "little or no food for the human spirit" and religion "was the only escape they had."[16] At its worst, then, the southern church at the heart of his religious legend of Yoknapatawpha County actually promoted a wild blending of violence and spiritual striving.

Faulkner explored two other aspects of the South's evangelical reli-gious culture. One was the region's civil religion. Sociologist Robert N. Bellah argued in the late 1960s that an American civil religion existed, a body of institutions, myths, values, and rituals that combined religion and nationalism, that saw spiritual significance in the national experi-ence. Since then, other scholars have shown that a variety of civil, or public, religions have existed in the United States. The South has had, as Samuel S. Hill argues, two cultures – a culture of Christian religion and one of southernness. The tension between these two worldviews has helped to shape southern life. In many ways, the churches of the region have been in cultural captivity to regional values.[17] A southern civil reli-gion saw religious significance in the Confederate experience. After the Civil War, Southerners made Robert E. Lee into a saint, Stonewall Jack-son into a prophet, and the Confederacy itself into a sacred memory. This cult of ancestor worship was a central cultural experience to a generation of Southerners. The annual Confederate reunions drew tens of thousands of people, and Confederate memorial day in the typical small town was a key holiday on the ritual calendar. That the South developed a sense of history and an obsession with the past was, then, no accident. This south-ern civil religion flourished especially in the years from 1890 to 1920, the years when Faulkner was growing to manhood, and his writings reflect its pervasiveness in southern culture.[18]

Light in August explores the pathology of the southern civil religion well after its high point. The past lives on in tangible ways in Faulkner's work. Sometimes it is harmless, as Pappy McCallum who has six middle-aged sons, all named for Confederate generals in Lee's army. Sometimes it is the romantic story of soldiers going off to war. But mostly the legacy is a stultifying one. Joanna Burden, for example, represents the sacred past. Her grandfather and brother, Yankee carpetbaggers come south to help the freedmen, were killed in Jefferson during Reconstruction, but, a generation later, "something dark and outlandish and threatening" still attaches to her and to her home. Despite the passage of time, "it is there: the descendants of both in their relationship to one another's ghosts, with between them the phantom of the old spilled blood and the old horror and anger and fear." Fear is an emotion often associated by Faulkner with religion in Yoknapatawpha County, and it was a prominent feature of the sacralized regional culture. Gail Hightower is the embodiment of the civil religion and its evils as Faulkner saw them. He is obsessed with the combination of religion and the Confederacy – with the civil religion. He is oriented toward the past and death itself. He sits "in the August heat, oblivious of the odor in which he lives – that smell of people who no longer live in life: that odor of overplump desiccation and stale linen as though a precursor of the tomb." When he remembers his childhood, he recalls, as phantoms, his father, his mother, and the old black woman who raised him. The formative influence on him was his grandfather, a bigger-than-life character, a Confederate cavalryman who "had killed men 'by the hundreds,'" or so the story went. Brooding on the war led Hightower to "experience a kind of hushed and triumphant terror which left him a little sick," and which also left him with a confused identity. Faulkner has Hightower say his "only salvation" – note the use of that central term in southern Evangelicalism – was "to return to the place to die where my life had already ceased before it began."[19] In a twisted logic, Hightower anticipated salvation not through the blood of the Lamb, but through the blood of the Confederate cavalry.

Hightower comes to Jefferson's Presbyterian church from seminary, refusing any other assignment, to pastor in the town where his grandfather was killed during the war. The congregation cannot make sense of his preaching. Although a seminarian, he appears to his congregation as almost a sectarian preacher, using the emotionalism of a street preacher; the irony is that he is the only member of his sect. People he meets on the street cannot sort out his blending of the Confederate legend and the Christian story. He is "wild too in the pulpit, using religion as though it were a dream." He is a cyclone of energy, and Faulkner mentions "his wild hands and his wild rapt eager voice" in which "God and salvation and the galloping horses and his dead grandfather thundered." He "went faster than the words in the Book," a telling judgment to a people steeped in the Bible. Hightower realizes he is blending Christian dogma with "galloping cavalry and defeat and glory." His obsession with the past leads to personal tragedy, as his wife becomes disenchanted and eventually kills herself in Memphis. The community, needless to say, does not approve of all this, believing "that what he preached in God's own house on God's own day verged on actual sacrilege." In the face of his wild preaching, the elders and the congregation are "puzzled and outraged," and his wife's death leads to his dismissal from the church and ostracism from the community. Byron Bunch's evaluation of all this is that living people cannot do the damage that the dead can do. "It's the dead ones that lay quiet in one place and dont try to hold him, that he cant escape from."[20]

Old Doc Hines is also a product of the South's civil religion, the attempt to make a religion out of its culture. Whereas Hightower's obsession is the Confederate past, Hines's obsession is race. He has the certainty of one who knows God's will. "The Lord told old Doc Hines what to do and old Doc Hines done it." Hines indeed uses Calvinist language in telling Joe Christmas that God "is the Lord God of wrathful hosts, His will be done . . . because you and me are both a part of His purpose and His vengeance." He stands up in prayer meeting, goes to the pulpit and preaches, "yelling against niggers, for the white folks to turn out and kill them all." He becomes an itinerant revivalist of a peculiar sort, wandering into the churches of black folk, seizing the pulpit, and preaching "with violent obscenity" their "humility before all skins lighter than theirs."[21] Hines is not typical of southern religion, but he is an extreme example of tendencies within the faith. He is not in a church, yet he proclaims God's words and teachings with ravings combining God language and racial epithets.

Both Hightower and Hines combine a determinism from Calvinist tradition with the emotional style of an evangelical religion of the spirit. They are outside the community, but Faulkner shows that their beliefs are, in fact, central to the southern culture he inherited. They are only extreme in the violence and the crazed enthusiasm with which they pursue them.

A final overlooked aspect of the religious culture of Faulkner's world is that of folk religion. Historian David Potter once suggested that the South's folk culture was its most distinguishing feature, and religion may well have been the central dimension of it. Southern religious studies has not done an adequate job of exploring this aspect of southern religion. It has much to learn from Faulkner in this regard. This religion is beyond theology. It concerns the beliefs and practices with religious meanings beyond the teachings of organized religion. In Faulkner, folk religion is that among the plain folk, the poor whites and blacks.[22]

The church is a symbol of rural community in Faulkner's religious world. "Shingles for the Lord" is a marvelous evocation of the landscape and spirit of southern rural folk religion. This story is of three men who meet to remove the old shingles from their country church. The church itself is a country church, "an old church, long dried out." The men recognize their obligation to contribute time and labor, although this represents a sacrifice from their own farmwork. But, as one says, they "belonged to that church and used it to be born and marry and die from." The minister, Whitfield, whose name evokes the memory of George Whitfield, the English preacher who effectively introduced the revival to the South in the colonial era, has been pastor for over fifty years. He is a somber-looking man "in his boiled shirt and his black hat and pants and necktie, holding his watch in his hand." He is a stern figure who represents the spiritual life of the few families who live nearby. In the course of the story, the church burns, but Whitfield's response is immediate, calling the men together the next morning to build a new building. As Grier says, "Of course we got to have a church." The young narrator, Grier's son, leaves the reader with the spirit of the church. "I had hated it at times and feared it at others," but "there was something that even that fire hadn't touched." Its "indestructibility" and "endurability" were Faulkner's words to describe it. The preacher knew that the men could only give their labor toward a new church, but they "would be there at sunup tomorrow, and the day after that, and the day after that." So, in a sense, this folk institution "hadn't gone a-tall."[23] Without describing any worship service, Faulkner conveys the spiritual significance of this small institution to its people.

Folk religion in Faulkner involves more than churches. In *As I Lay Dying* it represents the reservoir of biblical teachings, doctrines, sayings, and general folk wisdom that can be summoned. It provides, in some sense, an all-encompassing worldview. References to God are pervasive. This religion is shared among the Bundrens and others nearby. Folklorist

Alan Dundes once suggested studying folk ideas as units of the world-view of a society, and *As I Lay Dying* offers an excellent example. Anse Bundren, husband of the late, lamented Addie, whose corpse holds the story together as it moves to Jefferson for burial, is fond of saying, "If God wills it" and "The Lord giveth." When Tull hears the latter he admits, "It's true. Never a truer breath was ever breathed." The Tulls and the Bundrens are in different social classes, which the Tulls see in moral terms, but the idea that "the Lord giveth" unites the people of this society. The Bundrens themselves do not give evidence of being churchgoers, but they are not outside the religious culture. They have absorbed sayings from the Bible and reflect the emotionalism and the religion of the heart typical of southern Evangelicalism. As Cora Tull says, "Riches is nothing in the face of the Lord for He can see into the heart."[24]

Two characters stand out in analyzing the folk religion of the novel, and neither seems at first glance particularly admirable. Cora Tull appears as a self-righteous, complacent churchwoman, minding other people's business, while Anse is greedy and rapacious. Cora is a more sympathetic character than critics have suggested who paint her as one-dimensional. She can be infuriating, and Faulkner lays it on thick sometimes. Her husband notes that it takes trust in the Lord to get through life, "though sometimes I think that Cora's a mite over-cautious, like she was trying to crowd the other folks away and get in closer than anybody else." Faulkner rarely created one-dimensional characters, and Cora is no exception. She is a specimen from the southern religious culture that spans the institutional and folk religious worlds. She acknowledges that it may be God's will "that some folks have different ideas of honesty from other folks," and she even grants that "it is not my place to question His decree," painful though it is for her not to meddle.[25]

She has her doubts and dark moments, losing faith in human nature, but "always the Lord restores my faith and reveals to me His bounteous love for his creatures." When she sees young Darl watching his dying mother, she is moved by "the bounteous love of the Lord again and His mercy." She can even be compassionate. When Addie dies, Cora's advice to Anse is that it "comes to all of us" and "let the Lord comfort you." She has on her mind the central question of southern Protestantism: Are you right with God? Cora asks it as she watches Addie on her deathbed: "The eternal and the everlasting salvation and grace is not upon her."

Cora has the blessed assurance of the converted, and she is ready to meet her maker.[26]

If Cora is aggressively assured of the state of her soul, Anse explicitly says, "I am not religious, I reckon." But he is judging himself by churchly standards of good behavior. His religion is not that of the respectable society perhaps, but he is within the bounds of folk religion. In his shiftless way, he relies on others, including the religious community of his neighborhood. When Addie passes on, his first response is, "There is Christians enough to help you." "They will help us in our sorrow." They do indeed rally to participate in the death ceremonies and assist the family in various ways through their journey. Folk religion is by definition a shared community experience, and death was perhaps the chief occasion for the display of its rituals. Anse achieves the proper ritual dignity that folk religion demands in the face of death. He is properly, respectably dressed for his journey to bury Addie. Faulkner notes "he is wearing his Sunday pants and a white shirt with the neckband buttoned." He is "dignified, his face tragic and composed." Anse talks of God as Old Marster and refers to "the Lord's earth." His social status and aggrieved position are wrapped up with religion. He notes that "nowhere in this sinful world can a honest, hardworking man profit," but he confesses to expecting "a reward for us above." For him, heaven is the place where the well-off "cant take their autos and such. Every man will be equal there and it will be taken from them that have and give to them that have not by the Lord." He adds, "It's a long wait, seems like." After terrible experiences during part of the journey, he expresses a frustrated sense of Christian destiny as it has worked its way down from the theologians to daily life: "I am the chosen of the Lord, for who He loveth, so doeth He chastiseth. But I be durn if He dont take some curious ways to show it, seems like."[27]

Faulkner portrayed the appreciation in folk religion for ritual and the collective wisdom, but he had special sympathy for simple piety. This becomes especially clear in his portrayal of black religion. Black Southerners stand especially removed from the Calvinist legacy that many critics have seen encompassing all of Faulkner's religious world. Black Protestant churches rejected the harsh Calvinist features of Protestantism in favor of celebratory worship centered on the loving Jesus. They rejected also the South's civil religion of the Confederate past and white supremacy. Slavery was the central event in their religious mythology,

[handwritten margin note: Black Protestants rejected Calvinism & the South's "civil religion"]

and one of Faulkner's most moving scenes is of the promise of freedom to newly freed slaves in *The Unvanquished*. They move collectively down a dusty road, singing of crossing the river Jordan. Black folk religion has always had a pronounced communal aspect; the characteristic evangelical concern for individual salvation has been tempered by the need for collective expression of spirituality.[28]

Perhaps the most famous scene from Faulkner's religious culture of Yoknapatawpha County is Dilsey's attendance at Easter Sunday morning service. The Compson family, for whom she works, serves as a counterpoint to her spirituality. They show no involvement in either organized religion or the folk religion all around them. Reverend Shegog is the visiting preacher from St. Louis, and Dilsey goes to hear him, hoping for a sermon that "kin put de fear of God" into the younger generation. Dilsey takes the idiot Benjy to the weathered old church, ignoring complaints from blacks and whites about this violation of segregation. The processional to the church is important, and Faulkner sketches the sights and sounds of people moving to worship. But the social dimensions of worship do not seem as crucial this day to Dilsey as the search for a renewed sense of salvation. Dilsey is not feeling well, but someone notes that Shegog will "give her de comfort ed de unburdenin."[29]

Shegog is unprepossessing and is portrayed with racist imagery, but he is one of Faulkner's most memorable preachers. He preaches of the Egyptian bondage and the children of God. He preaches of the Crucifixion of Jesus and the Resurrection. He ends with an apocalyptic scene from the Book of Revelation and tells of "de arisen dead whut got de blood en de ricklickshun of de Lamb!" As he preaches, he becomes more emotional, and soon the congregation "just sat swaying a little in their seats as the voice took them into itself." A voice keeps repeating, "Yes, Jesus!" Benjy sits "rapt in his sweet blue gaze." Dilsey "sat bolt upright beside, crying rigidly and quietly in the annealment and the blood of the remembered Lamb." Dilsey is crying when she comes out, having undergone a renewal of her faith. "I've seed de first en de last." "I seed de beginnin, en now I sees de endin." Cleanth Brooks notes that of the characters in *The Sound and the Fury,* she is the survivor because she has gained a sense of eternity.[30] Brooks and others have not noted often enough that this knowledge of her heritage came from southern black religious culture.

The description in the "Appendix" for Dilsey is "They endured." Evangelical religion helped her and other Faulkner characters endure. The religion of black Southerners in Yoknapatawpha County was centered on a personal faith in Jesus, a loving counselor and friend. Flannery O' Connor once noted, of course, that the South was Christ haunted. Faulkner's black characters surely are, but not his white characters. This seems to be the source of some of their problems. The stern Jehovah God is their obsession rather than the loving, forgiving Christ. The name "Jesus" hardly appears in his accounts of white religionists. Faulkner once noted that the faith of southern Evangelicalism as embodied in the southern Baptists represented "the human spirit aspiring toward something," although "it got warped and twisted in the process."[31] That religion was very much a part of Faulkner's mythical Mississippi county. He converted the actual religion of the land into an apocryphal story in which Evangelicalism stood for a twisted striving toward salvation.

Judgmental though Faulkner the moralist was on this religion, he was not at all contemptuous of the search for salvation. A story about the great country music singer Hank Williams sums up the way the southern religious culture appears in Faulkner's world. Williams seems like a character from a Faulkner story. He was from Alabama, the kind of plain southern white boy that could have been the father of Lena Grove's baby in *Light in August*. He was not exactly a typical churchgoing pillar of the community, yet he was a product of the southern religious culture. As well as writing songs about honky tonks, he wrote religious songs, including a classic called "I Saw the Light," which perfectly captures the essence of the born-again religious experience. After wandering aimlessly in a life of sin, he lets his "dear Saviour in." Conversion, redemption, salvation came suddenly, "like a stranger in the night." Praise the Lord, he says, I saw the light. Once, during a country show in El Paso, Texas, shortly before his death at age twenty-nine, another self-destructive, burned-out southern poor boy, Williams was drunk in his car outside the concert, trying to sober up. Another performer, Minnie Pearl, remembers that he started to sing "I Saw the Light." He stopped suddenly. "That's the trouble," he said. "It's all dark. There ain't no light."[32] Faulkner's characters seek the light, seek grace, using the materials their culture gave them. They seem to say to us: "I saw the light, in August. Or did I?"

 Southern
Religion
and
Visionary
Art

Popular religion, to recapitulate the argument herein, has had a particularly southern dimension. Evangelical Protestantism has been at the heart of the religious culture that has dominated the American South, influencing cultural and social activities well beyond the church doors and eventually nurturing an extraecclesiastical popular spirituality. Before the age of media-oriented, blow-dried politicians, a Southerner campaigning for office often spoke in a biblical language, entertaining political rallies with stories from the Old Testament that helped the audience understand how corrupt the incumbent was and why he should be tossed out of office by a righteous people. Hymns and gospel singing were pervasive aspects of daily private life and ceremonial public life. Such secular entertainers as Elvis Presley and James Brown often gained their first musical training in church singings and sometimes continued to perform the old religious songs in their own concerts. Such writers as Flannery O'Connor and William Faulkner drew on religious symbolism and characters from the Bible and from the local religious scene in conveying their deeper truths of the human condition. Visionary art in the South should be seen in terms of its relationship to this regional religious culture. It stands at a particular moment of southern time, when folk and popular religion intersected.[1]

Until the 1960s, scholarly interest in religion in the South did not match the significance of the topic itself, but since then so much work has been achieved that we may speak of a field of southern religious studies. Much of the work has been by historians, including institutional studies of particular denominations, thematic studies of religion's relationship to historical events and forces, and increasingly sophisticated work on evangelical Protestantism's impact on the secular culture in the past. Historian John B. Boles has written of "The Discovery of Southern Religious History," but the study of southern religion has gone beyond any one discipline. Studies relevant to understanding southern religion have appeared from sociologists, literary critics, political scientists, anthropologists, theologians, and scholars in speech communications. Folklorists have added to the understanding of southern religion through their careful fieldwork studies of particular groups and places in the South.[2]

The southern religious tradition that scholars have studied has been an interdenominational one, growing out of the shared cultural assumptions, rituals, beliefs, and customs of the region's predominant Protestants. Those scholars working in southern religious studies have overlooked the rich possibilities of placing the religiously inspired folk art of the region into the specific context of this religious tradition. This is especially true of historians. Historical journals in the South rarely review books about folk art. Samuel S. Hill's mammoth *Encyclopedia of Religion in the South* (1984) is a magnificent achievement, but it has no article on folk art. A brief piece on roadside signs is intriguing, but in general the subject is hardly touched. Hill's *Encyclopedia* is a fascinating source and the best document we have as to the state of southern religious studies. It reflects the broader fact that folk religion in all its manifestations has been overlooked as a resource by many of those who study southern religion. Historians have seen it as a minor theme, best left to other disciplines. Other disciplines, including folklore, often do not explicitly relate field studies to a specifically southern regional context, preferring to understand them in terms of local cultures or traditional folkloristic concern for genres and motifs.

Folklorists and art historians who have studied southern visionary art most carefully have illuminated the African religious sources for the symbolism and themes of these works. Their studies are subtle and imaginative, making valuable connections. Commentators have also noted the regional cultural background to visionary art, but they often portray a stereotypical view of southern religion. The author of an article on a 1986 exhibit of southern visionary art claimed, for example, that in "southern fundamentalist Christian churches, speaking in tongues, seeing God, being called or having visions are accepted realities." Most southern Protestants, in fact, do not speak in tongues nor see visions, and they may more accurately be classified as evangelicals rather than fundamentalists. Establishing the relationship of a particular variety of southern religion to the region's dominant religious forms can be helpful here. While mainstream southern evangelicals in establishment Baptist, Methodist, and Presbyterian churches would flee from ecstatic forms of charismatic religion, those forms grow naturally out of Evangelicalism and can illuminate the sources of visionary art. Understanding southern religious history will enrich the study of these visionary artists, and if historians, for their part, will look more carefully at this art they should be able to see through it new dimensions of Evangelicalism's role in the South.[3]

Religion in the South has been more homogeneously evangelical Protestant and less pluralistic than religion in other parts of the United States. Nowhere else in the world have evangelical groups become so dominant and tied in with a culture as in the South. Even today, despite the dramatic changes in race relations, economic activities, politics, and social life, the dominant religious patterns in the region are similar to those a century ago. Southerners, black and white, continue to worship mostly in Baptist, Methodist, Presbyterian, and Pentecostal congregations. Ironically, black and white Southerners worship in segregated churches and that fact should not be overlooked, nor should it be denied that the differences between a poor rural congregation and a wealthy urban one are profound. But the creativity of southern visionary artists flourished because they lived in places whose people collectively, despite all their pronounced divisions, took seriously the symbols, images, and worldviews of a particular kind of religion; mostly they came out of that tradition, and even those who rejected it often used aspects of it in their work.

Observers have long noted the verbal orientation of southern Protestantism. "It is clear," writes Samuel S. Hill, "that southern churchmen take literally the metaphor, the Word of God, believing that the divine self-revelation proceeds through the agency of the spoken (and heard) word." This tendency toward the word in popular southern Protestantism is, of course, an extreme version of Protestantism in general. Because of the belief that Protestants are oriented toward the word, historians of American religion in general have downplayed the significance of visual representations of religion.[4]

Southern Protestants, though, have developed their own iconography. Within church buildings, the image of Jesus Christ, for example, is frequently displayed in framed pictures of the bearded, long-haired Christ. Southern material culture included paper fans, produced by funeral homes and pervasively used in hot summers, and these fans portrayed the southern version of heaven – typically with pastoral scenes of gentle lambs or angels or peaceful mountain streams. Heaven was a place of calm and relief from the traumas of this vale of tears. Baptismal art on walls above the places of a watery initiation into faith showed scenes of the River Jordan or other images of the biblical Holy Land, colorful scenes in often plain, even stark church edifices. Mainstream churches bought stained glass windows, but the hand-painted windows of vernacular churches suggested authentic indigenous visions of Christian life. Much southern iconography existed outside the confines of church as well. Hill suggests that roadside signs of "Jesus Saves," "Get Right with God," or "Prepare to Meet Thy God" are the southern Protestant equivalents of Roman Catholic saints on the dashboards of cars. They represent in good Protestant fashion the Word made visual. "Jesus Saves" is an evangelical verbal message delivered not orally but through the eye. Material representations of Catholic saints are like good luck charms, talismans, which promote inner devotion. The southern roadside signs seek, on the other hand, to spread the word outwardly, a fitting purpose for a proselytizing religion.[5]

A friendly warning to passers-by from a concerned evangelical Protestant.
Highway 51, Winona, Mississippi. (Photo by Susan B. Lee)

Roadside signs also convey true visual images. While driving down the road in North Carolina years ago, I spotted a homemade sign, on rough wooden planks. It contained the drawing of a hand, with a nail through it and drops of blood, painted in vivid red, spurting out of it. Beneath it were the words HE LOVED YOU SO MUCH IT HURT. That is a raw religious sentiment, an image that fits the sometimes obsessive religiosity of the Bible Belt. The visual detail summons for the believer – and for the nonbeliever as well traveling down the road – the image of Jesus on the cross and all that suggests about death, resurrection, and salvation at the heart of southern evangelical theology.

The combination of words and visual images is often seen in religious folk art in the South. Howard Finster's *Crossing Jordan,* for example, portrays the River Jordan, with Jesus standing in the middle of it and angels standing and flying around him. Words are written on the river: "The Lord Will Deliver His People Across Jordan," "I Want Hafto Cross Jordan Alone," "Things Must Be Better Just Over Jordan." In fact, writing takes up half the canvas, with words describing the evils of bullies, gamblers, adulterers, fornicators, and the "rich who will press the poor out of measure." On the other side of Jordan in the painting are the words *Joy, Kindness, Love, Peace,* and *Eternal Life,* each one leading to a path toward salvation. Scriptural quotes and holy words are not just incorporated onto canvas by southern visionaries. White Alabama preacher Benjamin Perkins painted such messages as PLUNGE IN TO DAY AND BE MADE COMPLETE GLORY TO HIS NAME on a brick pyramid behind a cross with JESUS SAVES emblazoned upon it. Kentuckian Harrison Mayes carved JESUS IS COMING SOON into the numerous concrete crosses he erected across the South, the tangible artifacts of his proselytizing mission.

The words in southern visionary art are often from the Bible, reaffirming the not-surprising fact that is elsewhere apparent of the centrality of the Bible in southern religious culture. It is the ultimate source for the specifics of faith and morals to an unusual degree in the region. Even among the mainstream establishment churches it continues to be the source of faith, often unrestrained by other influences. These visionary artists portray scenes from Christ's life, especially the Crucifixion, and their works visualize the prophecies from the Old Testament and from the Book of Revelation, which contains the vision of a new Jerusalem. The words of these visionaries are often harsh, teaching of the rigor needed for sanctification, to lead a holy life. Southern evangelical churches stress the struggle to subdue the self, to fight the Devil and consecrate the self to the holy. The dangers of failure are visualized in horrific images of sinners burning in hell. The rewards of strict morality likewise appear in words describing good behavior that leads to redemption.[6]

Southern religious history has begun to explore the spiritual experience of religious outsiders, and this theme is a crucial one to bring visionary art more fully into southern religious studies. Today's culturally dominant Baptists and Methodists themselves began as religious dissenters in the 1700s. Once they rose to power in the nineteenth century, a series of protest movements reasserted the primacy of the spirit for the plain folk, frequently representing rural protest against the style of the establishment Baptist, Methodist, and Presbyterian churches. The Landmark Baptists, Primitive Baptists, Churches of Christ, Cumberland Presbyterians, and others began among socially marginal groups that soon found a new identity in their rigorous faiths.[7]

The Holiness movement and later the Pentecostals represent the best examples of such religious outsiders. The 1890s was a watershed in southern religious history because it saw the emergence of a populist religion of the dispossessed rural masses, black and white, comparable to the agrarian political uprising of the decade. Every generation since then in the South has been renewed by the resurgence of an evangelical orientation toward religious experience. In exploring visionary art's cultural significance, scholars need to look more carefully at the time factor, at specifically when these visionaries emerged. Most of the works identified in studies of visionary art in the South date from the 1930s to the 1980s; visionary artists grew up and moved as adults in a world of holiness religion and of small sectarian Baptist churches, which often had pronounced elements of sanctified spirituality in them.

Religious visions have often occurred to religious folk living in secularizing societies, and this was surely a factor in the twentieth-century South. Southern visionaries have combined biblical images with those from modern life. Howard Finster, for example, incorporates Elvis Presley, Henry Ford, and John F. Kennedy into his art as well as the words and images of religious orthodoxy. Finster's visions of the Apocalypse include not only beasts and demons from the Books of Daniel and Revelation but also the submarines and missiles associated with his era's threat of the thermonuclear war.

Scholars of visionary art have placed little stress on the specific church affiliations of their subjects, an attitude that would be incomprehensible to most black and white Southerners who live in a world of contending faiths, each with a specificity understood by those in their communities. In particular, the Pentecostal background to this art is revealing. Pentecostals do believe in those gifts of the spirit often popularly associated with southern Protestantism in general.[8]

God frequently talked directly to these visionary artists. Gertrude Morgan relates that God first spoke to her December 30, 1934, in Columbus, Georgia. Jesus told her to go to Montgomery and Mobile to preach against sin, and later He told her to go to New Orleans. James Hampton, who was born and reared in Elloree, South Carolina, the son of a black Baptist minister, told of his repeated visions. God appeared to him in concrete form, not in an abstract dream but as a physical presence, surrounded by angels. Elijah Pierce, who was born in the Mississippi hill country in 1892, portrays in one of his works God's hand reaching down from heaven to touch him as a child when he put down his Bible and grasped for a Sears Roebuck catalog. Sometimes the words from the Spirit were even spoken in unknown tongues. Minnie Evans's *Prophets in the Air* recounts a dream she had where she heard a beautiful song: "Not that I could understand any of their words, but it was a beautiful song they sang." Alabama's J. B. Murray drew from African tradition but also Pentecostalism in his distinctive aesthetic of "writing in tongues" or, as he called it, "spirit script."

How many of these visionary artists come from the Pentecostal tradition? How many have simply picked up the idea from the South's culture? These questions cannot be answered definitely without an extensive survey of the church backgrounds of these artists, a needed task in the study of visionary art. Many of them were from small rural Baptist church backgrounds, and their individualistic spiritual inspirations may have resulted from dissatisfaction with the definitions of appropriate religious behavior that excluded such explicit visions. On the other hand, those Baptist churches may have been preaching a strong sanctified message themselves. In the rural South, the latter was likely. In any event, the gifts of the Spirit have been active on the southern landscape in the twentieth century. Flannery O'Connor was a good Catholic, and yet she employed southern evangelical imagery from the South's culture to anchor her artistic vision. These self-trained artists were surely different from a well-educated writer like O'Connor, but they may well have picked up these powerful religious symbols from the culture, whether being practicing Pentecostals or not. Pentecostals, in one sense, are an extreme form of Evangelicalism, and that broader shared tradition made possible much borrowing between various Protestant groups in the South.

Exploring the relationship of these visionary artists to southern religious millennialism, a related aspect of evangelical faith, is useful in understanding both the cultural significance of these artists and the importance of millennialism itself in the South. The term *millennialism* has been used in discussions of visionary art, but greater precision in its use would better illuminate this phenomenon. Do visionary artists strike a premillennial theme, evoking images of a fiery Second Coming of Christ before the thousand-year reign of perfection? Or are they postmillennialists, imagining a gradual attainment of a golden age through history, with the establishment of a Kingdom of God on earth after which Christ will return? The exact image is important for correlating millennial themes as they appear in folk art with those in literature and other areas of southern culture. Premillennial views have not been characteristic of mainline Baptist, Methodist, and Presbyterian groups in the South, but they have been pronounced among Pentecostals and holiness people since the 1880s, especially in the subregions of Appalachia, the Carolina Piedmont, and the Ozarks. It has been a major theme in black religion. The slave spirituals promised liberation and a day of judgment on which the last would be first. Nat Turner was inspired by an apocalyptic vision to lead a slave rebellion, and the black exodus from the South to Kansas in 1879 had aspects of a journey to a millennial kingdom of God on earth. The premillennial theme has been prominent among black as well as white visionary artists because it has been a part of the religion of the dispossessed.[9]

Clarifying the relationship between southern religion and visionary art requires, above all, a closer look at the specifically evangelical aspects of visionary art. Although *evangelical* is sometimes used as a near-synonym for fundamentalist, the two are very different impulses and concepts, albeit frequently found together in the South. Evangelical religion stresses the individual's experience of a life-transforming faith, a conversion that leads to the infusion of God's grace. Southern evangelicals downplay liturgies, sacraments, and creeds. Fundamentalists would, of course, passionately disagree with the denial of the importance of doctrinal creeds and enumerated moral agendas. The South has been more evangelical than fundamentalist, and these visionary artists affirm that fact.

The visionary artist embodies and also portrays the evangelical's typical struggle with self, often utilizing striking images of the hellfire and brimstone of millennialism and its judgment. But these artists also display another theme from the tradition, one not often noted by scholars – devotional celebration, the spirit animating those believers seeking "the peace that passeth all understanding." A mellow devotional style picturing Jesus the Comforter and Healer looms large in southern Protestantism. The gap between God and humans is narrowed, and the Lord appears as an intimate presence. Believers speak of peace and joy and sweet hours of prayer. It is a style of the already converted, a form of private worship. It was characteristic of old-fashioned Methodist worship especially, and the mainstream black Baptists and Methodists often have embodied this style, practicing an expressive, joyful, soulful religion. Pentecostal and holiness churches also stress a religious faith that knows the intimate presence of God and celebrates the sheer spiritual power of faith.

Southern visionary artists are in this tradition. Natural images and portrayals of the beauty and wonder of the garden are common. Minnie Evans frequently paints fantastic floral images, suggesting a lush, tropical vision of heaven, and even her images inspired by the Book of Revelation lack an apocalyptic, cataclysmic tone. They are much gentler images, more of peace than of a fiery end. Visionary artists such as Evans are not searching for faith; they have found their religious truth and are celebrating it. They affirm one of the central evangelical concerns – assurance of salvation.

Many contemporary black theologians would deny an evangelical heritage to black religion, but this conclusion seems anomalous given the abiding denominational character of African-American faith. Blacks developed their own unique religious tradition, with its own sacred history and celebrative worship style, but in the South Evangelicalism provided a key language of common discourse between whites and blacks. Understanding its functions for ordinary Southerners, and especially for the rural poor, can provide a way to understand what visionary artists took from evangelical traditions in making their art.[10]

The dynamic imperative of southern Evangelicalism is converting the lost, and visionary artists from the region, black and white, have typically looked upon their art as another way to preach. "Every piece of work I got carved is a message . . . a sermon you might say," according to Elijah Pierce. "A preacher don't hardly get up in the pulpit but he don't preach some picture I got carved." Gertrude Morgan affirms that her paintings are a way to spread the Gospel, and Florida artist Jesse Aaron refers to his inspiration as a calling.

Not all southern visionary artists are religiously driven, but those who are represent visual preachers operating outside the churches but not outside their regional cultures. In one sense, they have been marginal outsiders and their achievements have been "outsider art." Yet they have also been linked to a broad evangelical movement central to understanding the unities and divisions of the South. Mainstream southern Protestants do not speak in tongues, faith heal, or see visions, yet their own biblicism and belief in subjective religious experience, when seized upon by the poor and the suffering, can lead to visions of other worlds of justice achieved through millennial retribution rewarding the spiritually faithful. They are believers who are not so much involved with church organizations as obsessed with portraying religious truth as conveyed to them individually by God. These visionary artists offer a way to understand the pervasiveness of the evangelical religion that influences not only southern public life but private life and creativity as well.[11]

Church Fans

Southerners sitting in church pews sixty years ago likely waved cardboard fans to cool off from the heat in summer or the stifling air inside the sanctuary in winter. Popular religion has its own material artifacts and is especially prone to using the ordinary to apprehend the holy, as seen in these simple artifacts that portray scenes from the faith.

Cardboard fans probably trace back to the 1920s, when printing presses started pouring out the inexpensive items for businesses to use as a cheap way to advertise. Between 1920 and 1930, three major firms produced about 25 million fans each year for banks, insurance companies, tobacco companies promoting snuff or "chaws," political candidates, radio stations, and entertainers. No institution was more associated with the fans than the local funeral home, and this connection transformed the fans into religious icons. Dealing with death in a region whose religion looked to the afterlife, funeral homes used images on fans discreetly to link their work with religion.

The fans pictured scenes from the southern religious imagination.

Above all, Jesus Christ appeared – protecting the lambs, praying in the Garden of Gethsemane, or seated at the Last Supper. One fan, shown here, illustrated the hymn "What a Friend We Have in Jesus." Landscape scenes captured the southern image of heaven: peaceful green meadows, bubbling brooks, lush valleys, and, most common, snow-covered mountains. Sitting in a hot church building, it was easy to believe heaven must be like that.

Cardboard fans were biracial, found among black Protestants as well as white. They shared the image of Jesus (although until recently he tended to be markedly Anglo-Saxon in the South). But African-American advertisers customized their fans for their communities. Black families at worship were typical scenes, as were portrayals of little girls at church. By the 1960s, the Rev. Martin Luther King Jr. was a prominent icon on the fans, sometimes with his mother, or his mother and father, or his wife, or John and Robert Kennedy.

Cardboard fans survive in the modern South, although less often associated with church than with other locales, such as theme parks, political rallies, or festivals celebrating crawfish or watermelons. They serve the same heat-fighting function but have fewer purely sacred images on them. Still, they represent ties to the older South in a world of mass culture. For understanding popular religion they remain significant. Elvis is as likely as Jesus to appear on them, but that reveals connections in itself. The boundaries between the sacred and the secular on these commercialized fans used in churchly settings were always blurred, as with popular religion in general. As theologian Paul Tillich noted, "Religion, like God, is omnipresent."

The most pervasive image on church fans was Jesus Christ, here seen as the gentle shepherd.

A famous painting from high art tradition frequently appears on church fans, as well as on black velvet, porcelain plates, and other forms of popular religion.

WE THANK THEE

The Bible occupies a central position in the southern religion of the Word.

The message is straightforward here: the local evangelical Protestant congregation needs you in the pew.

African-American churches often portrayed Dr. Martin Luther King Jr. in iconography, as here with his parents.

The fan on a stick tradition passed from church to the secular world, as in this fan honoring country comedienne Minnie Pearl, a symbol of the South's plain folk.

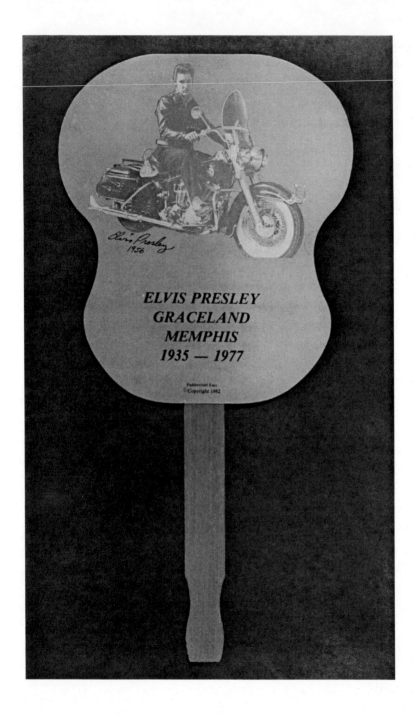

ELVIS PRESLEY
GRACELAND
MEMPHIS
1935 — 1977

Paddlewheel Fans
©Copyright 1982

Elvis Presley was not very churchly in his later life, but some souvenir hawker had the right instinct in putting this exemplar of the southern popular religion on a fan that evoked evangelical Protestantism.

Modernization of the church has surely arrived when lounging Yuppie Southerners replace religious figures on the cardboard fan that began in churches.

Digging Up Bones: Death in Country Music

Since Jessica Mitford published *The American Way of Death* in 1963, interest in death customs and attitudes in the United States has steadily risen. In the late nineteenth and early twentieth centuries, Americans developed a distinctive pattern of coping with death, a way appropriate to a modernizing nation. The American Way of Death has included the embalming of the corpse, the cosmetic beautification of it, the use of elaborate caskets, permanent funeral homes, and professional funeral directors managing the services. Psychologists and sociologists argue that the underlying motive in all this, however, is avoiding the realistic confrontation with the harsh lesson of human limitation. As Philippe Ariès, the foremost student of the history of death, has observed, American funerals "strive to create the illusion of life." Optimistic, youth-oriented, future-oriented Americans have often tried to evade the most profound of human realities, mortality. A society that has known a relatively high degree of success in economic development, political stability, and military engagements has not willingly acknowledged in its death customs and attitudes the ultimate human restriction.[1]

In a 1979 article entitled "The Concept of Death in Popular Music: A Social Psychological Perspective," John C. Thrush and George S. Paulus argued that American popular music reflects and reinforces the dominant death attitudes of this society. They studied forty-eight death-related songs from the Top 40 charts and concluded that death concerns could be divided into five categories: the loss of a loved one, death and old age, suicide, the death of celebrities, and philosophical-religious statements on death and dying.[2]

Have Southerners had a different outlook on mortality than that expressed in the American Way of Death? Although country music has become a national and even international phenomenon, it remains one of the clearest expressions of southern working-class culture, including its attitudes toward life and death. Studies of the historical background of country music, of the geographical origins of country music performers, and of the lyrics in their songs all suggest that the music has been and still is deeply rooted in southern life. An examination of well-known death-related songs in country music, past and present, provides evidence that Southerners learned from their culture an attitude toward death that was distinctly regional.[3]

The modern American Way of Death emerged in the post–Civil War years among the urban middle class in the Northeast, but this new pattern did not spread quickly throughout the South. Funeral innovations were accepted in many southern cities, but few Southerners lived in cities in this period, as the population was scattered across the countryside in rural areas and small towns. Southern poverty, rurality, and the persistence of traditional Christian attitudes limited the initial impact of the American Way of Death in the South. In contrast to the modernizing Northeast, death in the South remained firmly rooted in a concrete regional culture. Death for the typical Southerner was a community and family event. When someone died, the neighbors and family members came with food and assumed responsibility for preparing the body for burial, making a wooden coffin, digging the grave, and participating in the religiously oriented funeral service. The southern funeral itself was a sad, intensely emotional event, with grief openly expressed. Customs such as sitting up all night with the corpse, an open casket funeral service, the singing of sentimental hymns, the preaching of evangelical sermons, and protracted graveside services – all promoted a southern way of death different from the emerging funeral industry ceremonies in the North. Moreover, a person could not hide from death. The death rate for the southern states was traditionally higher than the national average, and the infant mortality rate has been especially high. Southerners have died of particular diseases and illnesses, not necessarily as common elsewhere.[4]

Rather than establishing institutions of death avoidance, as scholars now believe that the Northeast did, Southerners from the late nineteenth century to the mid-twentieth had what can best be characterized as a culture of death. An examination of country music shows six categories of death: the pervasiveness of death, violent and tragic death, songs of love and death, death and the family, celebrity death, and religious influences on death. Together these themes help to chart the landscape of death in the South.

Country music songs typically express an awareness of death and an acceptance of it. Death is everywhere. Children die with disturbing frequency, a reflection of the high southern mortality rate for the young. But songs also tell about mothers dying and going to heaven ("Sweeter Than the Flowers"), sweethearts passing on ("Footprints in the Snow"), and an entire family dying ("Nobody's Darling But Mine"). Even dogs are mourned, as in "Old Shep." "Will the Circle Be Unbroken?" is one of the most famous country songs, and it describes a concrete death experience in precise imagery. One sees a hearse coming to carry away the narrator's mother. He talks to the undertaker, follows close behind the hearse, but confesses, "I could not hide my sorrow / When they laid her in the grave." Although not originally a southern song, it was recorded by the Carter Family in 1935 and became as traditional a song in the South as could be found. It remains a standard piece for country music performers, who thus remind listeners of earlier death attitudes.[5]

Death images in country music are typically not circumscribed but direct and sometimes even grotesque. The American Way of Death has preferred to speak in euphemisms of morticians instead of undertakers, of cemeteries and now lawn gardens instead of graveyards. Country songs call a spade of burial dirt a spade of burial dirt. Older songs like "Oh Death" reflect the starkness of the southern rural past. The song was not written by a Southerner, but southern musicians adapted it often because it spoke of rural realities. It portrays a dying person seeing the figure of death. "What is this that I can see, / Taking hold of me with icy hands? / I am death and none can excell / I'll open the doors to heaven or hell." And a later verse is even more graphic: "Death I come to take the soul / Leave the body and leave it cold / To drop the flesh off of the frame / The earth and worms both have a claim."[6] Such words suggest an almost medieval awareness of death, a memento mori tradition. Think on death, for you cannot escape its cruel realities.

If a culture of death existed in the South, then one would expect that it would be seen in a public, communal context, and indeed it was. Dozens of songs, for example, tell about public executions of murderers, including the "Death of Kirby Cole," about an Athens, Alabama, murder and the "Ballad of Finley Preston," in which the grisly details of a murder are related. Executions in the late nineteenth century and the early twentieth were, in fact, public events in the South, for which people gathered, sometimes even bringing lunches for a day's entertainment. Songs about executions portray the condemned man speaking before his death, confessing his sins and testifying that his tragic life should be a lesson to prevent others from making the same mistakes. It was all moralistic and religious. Even murderers looked toward the afterlife. As Finley Preston says in the song, "I have a hope in heaven / And death I do not fear."[7] Such communal ritualized deaths, and the musical preservation of them, made it difficult for Southerners to hide from their culture of death.

The matter-of-factness with which death is portrayed in country music reflects its deep roots in regional culture. In the contemporary era one sees it in Tom T. Hall's song "Ballad of Forty Dollars." The song is about a gravedigger. That does not seem a likely subject for popular music, with its American attitude of death avoidance, but it is a perfectly acceptable country ballad. The narrator relates the story of seven hours of digging a grave and of drinking "a case of beer" in the process. While waiting in a truck he observes the mourners at the funeral, envies the dead man's "big ol' shiny limousine," and comments on the widow's attire, noting that "some women do look good in black." In the end the narrator confesses his mixed feelings about the situation, with the final line being, "I hope he rests in peace, but trouble is the fella owes me forty bucks." [8] This is a modern song. No longer is death portrayed in grisly detail, but it is still very much a part of life. Death is not fearsome but regarded sardonically, in a concrete way by the narrator, in terms of how it is affecting him personally. Irony and a wry humor about death are perhaps only possible in a culture that has a long history of familiarity with death and acceptance of it.

The central social class orientation of country music, which reflects southern rural folk culture, is significant in terms of its death attitudes. Like most country music protagonists, Hall's character is a working man, from the social class most familiar with the ugly aftereffects of death in any society. If the American middle class dreaded death and constructed ways to avoid it, the southern plain folk culture that nurtured and still supports country music was a realistic one of people compelled by circumstances to confront, sometimes even casually because of their jobs, human mortality.

The lives and careers of country music performers are relevant here. Jimmie Rodgers, the first major star in country music, had to face the reality of an early, slow death from tuberculosis. As Nolan Porterfield notes in his biography, Rodgers displayed "a stoic's tragic sense of life" as he faced death. He accepted the certainty of his own death, "but he was equally certain that he would not meet it cringing or crawling." He made music out of his impending death, singing "My Time Ain't Long," "T.B. Blues," and "Whippin' That Old T.B." Tuberculosis was a common southern way of dying, and the music of the southern people reflected this. But Rodgers also sang "Hobo Bill's Last Ride" and other dying hobo laments. Many of his sentimental songs are about death, such as "Mother, Queen of My Heart," which tells of a gambler who reforms his evil ways after seeing his dead mother's face on a poker card. [9]

Hank Williams was another death-obsessed Southerner. His favorite song was said to be "Death Is Only a Dream," and he wrote such songs as "Six More Miles to the Graveyard" and, as Luke the Drifter, recorded a song called "The Funeral," which has the narrator observing a black funeral in a rundown church. Williams seemed to court death with a fast life, and he died young at age twenty-nine. His hit song on the charts at the time of his death was "I'll Never Get Out of This World Alive." [10]

Hank Williams's tombstone in Montgomery, Alabama, embodies the hope of salvation through "The Light" that might even save someone like Williams on the "lost highway." (Photo by Susan B. Lee)

Rock music, of course, has had its share of death-obsessed performers, but these country musicians reflected the nature of death in the South that produced most of them. W. J. Cash, in *The Mind of the South* (1941), wrote that Southerners were among the most sentimental people in history.[11] This was a little exaggerated, perhaps – hyperbole is also a southern tradition – but Rodgers and Williams did approach life and death with a peculiar combination of sentiment and stoicism, all heavily suffused with religious language and imagery. Rock musicians who seem to court death do not typically write gospel music, but Hank Williams did, and that combination is important to understanding the regional distinctiveness of death attitudes in the past.

In addition to the general pervasiveness of death in country music, a second theme is the violent death. Thrush and Paulus found that suicide was one of the five major death themes in American popular music, but suicide rarely occurs in country music (the South has traditionally had a low suicide rate). Death is, though, often violent and tragic in country music, rooted in many occupations, locales, and experiences. Coal miners sang "Dreadful Memories," a song that, modeled after the sad gospel song "Precious Memories," told of the death of coal mining children. "Shut Up in the Mines of Coal Creek" portrays the death of miners, while "Silicosis Is Killin' Me" (written by black folksinger Josh White) is about the painful fatalities of industrial work. Train songs such as the "Wreck on the Old 97" told of death from railroad disasters. Those songs were later replaced by songs of automobile death. "Wreck on the Highway," written by Dorsey Dixon and one of Roy Acuff's most famous songs, describes an accident scene in graphic imagery. The narrator tells of hearing the "sounds of destruction" and the "groans of the dying" and of seeing "whiskey and blood run together." The song reminds the listener, in Bill C. Malone's words, "that despite the accelerating changes of modern life, some things never change. The Grim Reaper still exacts his deadly toll, and even when life seems its gayest, the very vehicle that has contributed most to one's pleasure may also be the means through which this pleasure turns into tragedy."[12]

Many songs of violent death were related to human relationships. Country music portrays an obsessive and at times violent and fatal relationship between lovers. This is partly a legacy of the British ballad tradition, which portrayed, as historian Thomas L. Connelly has written, "brokenhearted lovers, deaths of sweethearts or children, murder-suicide pacts, and other tragic events." Nineteenth-century folk tunes of the American frontier reinforced this outlook. Songs such as the "Banks of the Ohio" and "Knoxville Girl" graphically depicted the murders of young women. The theme of lover killing lover continues to be a prominent one in commercial country music. In Willie Nelson's chilling "I Just Can't Stand to Say Good-bye," an obsessive lover cannot stand to lose his lover and chokes her to death in the course of the song. The country music parable seems to be, greater love hath no man than that he would kill his beloved before letting her get away. In some southern states the law used to be that a betrayed husband could justifiably kill his unfaithful wife, and country music seems to affirm this in such songs as Porter Wagoner's "Cold Hard Facts of Life," about a husband who kills a straying wife and her lover, and in Tanya Tucker's "Blood Red and Going Down," in which a sexy-sounding child narrator recalls the time when her father murdered her mother and her mother's lover, leaving them in a pool of blood. Given the situation, one doubts, somehow, that these cases ever came to trial.[13]

This is a basic theme of country music and is constantly updated. Johnny Darrel's "Ruby, Don't Take Your Love to Town," later popularized by Kenny Rogers, is a poignant but frightening psychological portrait of a maimed Vietnam veteran. Anticipating his approaching death, he begs Ruby to stay home instead of going to town. She does leave, and he nurtures the hope of vengeance, wishing he could "get my gun and put you in the ground." He is helpless, though, and can only plead with her to come back.[14]

A third theme of death in country music, somewhat separate from the second, is unrequited love and death. Not all songs having to do with love and death, in other words, end in violence. The song of unrequited love has long been a staple of country music, and many a suffering narrator seemed to believe that only death could quiet a brokenhearted lover. One might mention older songs like "The Little Rosewood Casket" and "Little Darling', Pal of Mine." Perhaps the best example of this genre is a recent hit recording by George Jones, "He Stopped Loving Her Today," which tells of a man so devoted to an unrequited love that he has no peace of soul until he dies. The narrator of the ballad relates seeing the dead man in his coffin. He was "all dressed up to go away," and the narrator notes that this was the "first time I'd seen him smile in years." A wreath was on his door and they would soon take him away, his striving for love finally ended.[15]

Many such songs use gothic imagery. "Would You Lay with Me (In a Field of Stone)" is the country music equivalent of William Faulkner's short story "A Rose for Emily," with its overtones of necrophilia. In this song, written by David Allen Coe and popularized by Tanya Tucker, a woman is so unsure of her lover that she demands he pledge his love to the extent of willingness to lie with her, even if she were dead, in a field of stone. "Should my lips grow dry, would you wet them, dear?" she asks, and wants him to "wipe away the blood" from her hand.[16]

Simple songs of a departed lover express a profound grief. Roy Acuff has recorded classics in this area. In "Lonely Mound of Clay" the narrator is mourning "beside a new made grave, heartbroken." He wants to know why the Lord took his love and also why he himself remained alive. He pledges to remain always near her grave and someday to sleep with her beneath the lonely mound of clay. Acuff's "The Precious Jewel" similarly tells of a dead girl, "a jewel for heaven / More precious than diamonds, more precious than gold." He recalls courting her and buying her a ring, but then losing her to heaven. The mood of the song is a lament, with the sad drone of the music a key reinforcement of the mournful lyrics.[17]

A more modern song, "Before Jessie Died," by Tom T. Hall, shows the effects on daily living of the removal of a lover. The narrator recites the story in a monotone, suggesting the dreariness of a life measured in terms of time before and time after the death of the lover. Like many modern country songs of death, not much sentiment is expressed, but rather emptiness. This surely represents evidence for a changing musical tradition and perhaps a changing South, but the overall point remains that the subject of death is still openly discussed and not avoided.[18]

Death and the family is another major category of death-related country songs. Songs about dying and dead children were a part of the older British ballad tradition but became especially popular in the United States during the Victorian era. These older songs survived in the South and became a part of the culture, but new songs in this genre have continued to appear as well. The South's infant mortality rate and its death rate in general were much higher than in other parts of the nation until recently, and these songs again express the feelings of a people who could not ignore death. With close-knit families of extended kin, many Southerners were sooner or later touched by death.[19]

The dead child is usually seen as part of a loving family. Ernest Tubb's song "Our Baby's Book" is about his own son, Rodger Dale, who died in an automobile accident when only seven weeks old. The song proved so popular that, according to Tubb, parents named over three hundred children for his little boy. Tubb's lyrics tell of the happiness the baby gave, and portray him in heaven while the parents are left with only their baby's book, pink and bordered in gold. Feelings of guilt were often brought out in these songs. "Put My Little Shoes Away," a Victorian ballad written in 1873, survived in the land of southern sentiment long after the Victorian era. It shows a dying child urging his mother to save his shoes and give them to the little baby in the family as soon as the "shoes will fit his little feet." Hugh Cross's 1943 song "Don't Make Me Go to Bed and I'll Be Good" tells of a "laughing baby boy" who was sent to bed by his father for making too much noise. In the night the little boy's body is "racked with pain," and he soon dies, leaving his father with nothing but guilt.[20]

At least he did have guilt. Not all dying children in country music were so favored with loving families. Songs of abandoned children and neglected children, for example, play upon parental fears. The child's death is used to urge changed parental behavior. The little girl narrator of "A Drunkard's Child," written in 1929 by the Reverend Andrew Jenkins, recalls that she once had "a happy home" until "daddy went out drinking rum and then he gambled some." Her mother died of a broken heart, and by the end of this sad tale, the little girl says, "I can see your teardrops start." Another example of this genre, "Mommy, Please Stay Home with Me," tells of a mother going out with "the merrymakers," and she "soon was lost in trifling joy," forgetting her baby boy. One can guess that the child was not long for this world, and the mother would willingly give up her life "to hear her baby's voice again." Other such songs are "Little Paper Boy" and the "Death of Little Kathy Fiscus," the latter popular in the 1940s.[21]

These songs are sentimental and maudlin, playing upon fears of children dying and nurturing guilt in survivors of such tragedies. But they also reinforce the culture of death in the South. Death is not hidden. It is not out of the way but openly discussed.

The same is true with parental death, the other major category of family-related death songs. Some of these songs are about the deaths of fathers or of mothers and fathers, but the overwhelming number of songs here are of dying and dead mothers. This is tied up with nostalgia for home. Mothers are identified in such songs with the domestic world of the homeplace and with childhood. The Stanley Brothers sang, for example, Esko Hankins's "Mother Left Me Her Bible." The singer's mother had no treasures to leave when she died, so she left her Bible as a guide to heaven: "I know she'll be waiting for me at the portals. / For she left me the Bible to show me the way." Such songs document southern familialism as poignantly as anything could. A desperate grief is sometimes expressed. In "The Village Churchyard" a man visits a graveyard where his mother lies "in the cold and silent ground." He remembers the night she died, and he prays they will meet again in heaven. In the darkness he puts flowers on her grave and cries, dreaming of a reunion in death. Hank Williams sang many songs like this. "Dear Brother" is in the form of a letter to his brother telling him their mother had died. Standing by her bedside, he says, "I lived my childhood again," thinking of his brother and "of the old homestead." The death of the mother makes him think not only of childhood but of a whole way of life. Grief is openly expressed; there is no effort to hide the tears. Sad as the mood is, though, the song ends by noting that "we'll meet again some day."[22]

Sometimes the death of an older family member causes a philosophical reflection upon life. A modern variation of this is Merle Haggard's recording of "Grandma Harp." The song is a loving, even upbeat, obituary, honoring a ninety-year-old woman, whose maiden name was Ona Lyon, from Newton County, Alabama. It is a simple, but not sentimental, song, in which her death is cause for consideration of changes in the world. She raised "a decent family out of poverty" and lived with the same grandpa for seventy years. The singer concludes that her death marked "a closin' chapter" in "a way of life that I loved within my heart."[23] This is an appropriate sentiment from a region that has indeed lived through enormous changes in the last thirty, much less ninety, years. The song reminds one of the obituaries you can still hear on small-town radio stations in the South, summing up in a few words what a typical person's life has been. Do not expect to hear many songs of mothers, or parents, or grandmothers in popular music, because they are rare indeed. But family and home are what country music is about.

A fifth theme of death in country music is celebrity deaths. A people's heroes can reveal a society's cultural values, and a good way to see who are heroes is to look at who is celebrated and revered when they die. Thrush and Paulus found songs about Marilyn Monroe, about Jimi Hendrix, Janis Joplin, and Jim Croce, and about Abraham Lincoln, Martin Luther King Jr., and John F. Kennedy. "Pop-rock deals with entertainment figures," they note, and with dead political figures who help focus attention on "the unfairness of death." "It seems," they conclude, "that pop-rock is adopting a repressive view toward death by fostering an illusion of impermanence."[24]

Country music has a major tradition of songs about the death of celebrities. Among these are national tributes, such as "Amelia Earhart's Last Flight." They include songs about politicians, such as Tommy Cash's recorded version of "Six White Horses," about the assassinations of the Kennedys and Martin Luther King Jr. A sign of the changing South surely is a recent song heard on the radio, with Johnny Cash singing about the death of "another holy man who dared to make a stand." This song was about King, Jesus Christ, and Mahatma Gandhi. The New South must have finally arrived.[25]

Generally, though, these celebrity death songs are not about national figures. Instead, they fall into two categories, both rooted in regional life. One category contains songs about the deaths of country music performers. When Jimmie Rodgers died in 1933, songwriters mourned through tunes such as "When Jimmie Rodgers Said Good-bye," which described "an old guitar that's lonely" and concluded that Rodgers was now "singing to the angels" in heaven. Hank Williams's death resulted in a spate of tribute songs, including Ernest Tubb's "Hank, It Will Never Be the Same without You," Jimmy Swan's "The Last Letter," and the Virginia Rounders's version of "There's a New Star in Hillbilly Heaven." "The Death of Hank Williams" was written by Jack Cardwell to the same tune as "When Jimmie Rodgers Said Good-bye" (thus striking another victory for southern cultural continuity). The song told of Williams dying in the backseat of his "big blue car" in the hills of West Virginia. The narrator noted that Williams was the "greatest folk song star this world has ever known, but he has now gone to a better land." Celebrities in tribute songs always seem to go to a better land. More recently, David Allen Coe has been haunted by the "Ghost of Hank Williams," and Hank Williams Jr. can hardly do an album without a song, or at least a reference, about "daddy."[26]

Celebrity death songs have continued through the years. Rusty Adams released two songs in March 1963, after the deaths of Patsy Cline, Hawkshaw Hawkins, and Cowboy Copas ("Angels from the Opry" and "Dateline Disaster"). When Elvis Presley died, Merle Haggard sang "From Graceland to the Promiseland," only the most prominent of many tributes to the King. The ultimate country music tribute song, of course, is "I Dreamed of a Hillbilly Heaven," which mentions by name many country stars, both living and dead, suggesting that heaven someday will be the greatest Opry performance ever. The list has been constantly updated in light of the expansion through mortality of hillbilly heaven.[27]

The second category of country songs about dead celebrities covers local southern heroes who capture the imagination. "The Death of Floyd Collins," for example, was about an amateur spelunker in southern Kentucky, who, in February 1925, was trapped in a cave. By the time rescuers reached him he was dead, but media coverage made the story a major event in the region's life. Robert Penn Warren used the Collins story as the central event of a novel, and several folk songs chronicled the tragedy, the most famous written for twenty-five dollars by blind evangelist Andrew Jenkins with Irene Spain. The song tells of young Floyd, whose "face was fair and handsome" and whose heart was "true and brave," but who nonetheless faced an early death. The moral was clear: young people should take warning from this ordinary Kentuckian and "get right with your maker." Another verse raised the specter of ultimate accountability. Not everyone will die in a cave, but "at the bar of judgment / We too must meet our doom."[28]

A more modern version of this theme is Tom T. Hall's "The Year That Clayton Delaney Died." Clayton was "the best guitar picker in our town," says the narrator, who "used to follow Clayton around." Clayton was a hero to the narrator when he was a young boy, although he cannot understand why Clayton was attached to his community and why Clayton "never took his guitar and made it down in Tennessee." Clayton "suffered and cried" in his last days, and he "got religion at the end," which pleased the narrator. The boy went out in the woods and cried when his hero passed on, although he eventually decided "that the Good Lord likes a little pickin' too." As with earlier tribute songs, a religious note appears at the end, as does the attachment to the local community. In *The Enduring South: Subcultural Persistence in Mass Society* (1974), a study of contemporary southern attitudes as reflected in survey data and other sociological evidence, John Shelton Reed argues that localism, a sense of place, is one of the clearest surviving southern characteristics, and this is surely reflected in the treatment of death in country music. More than in other parts of the country, southern heroes, according to Reed, still tend often to be related to members of the community. This makes a particularly striking contrast with popular music. Although celebrity death is one of the categories used by Thrush and Paulus, it is not at all tied in with localism or familialism.[29]

The final major category of death in country music is religious influences. This will come as no surprise because religion has been noted in virtually every other category as well. The South's evangelical Protestantism has aimed to convert lost sinners to Christianity through an emotional conversion experience, a direct encounter with God, and thus to extend salvation and the hope of everlasting life. Reflecting the strong impress of Calvinism, southern religion portrays this life as a vale of tears, wherein suffering is the common lot. This is a terrible commentary on the debilitating poverty and other social and spiritual problems in southern history. Death in this society was a comfort, a release from endless toil and suffering of one sort or another, and not altogether to be feared.[30]

Country music reflects this orientation in general, and these religious precepts have implications for death and dying. Early country performers sang religious songs, a practice still common. Death is an occasion in the country religious song to remind the listener that he or she is a sinner who must get right with God. Country songs portray the peace and hope of heaven as an escape from the troubles and trials of this world. The titles tell the story: "Over in the Glory Land," "This World Is Not My Home," "Beyond the Sunset," "I'll Fly Away," and "Going Up Home" are just a few examples. These songs talk of the spiritual treasures laid up in heaven, angels calling, blissful mornings of judgment day, reunions with loved ones who have gone on before, bright mansions, clouds passing, shadows lifted, burdens lightened, trials over, journeys ended. These songs are a comfort for grieving families, but they are also designed to discomfort the sinning listener – and that means everyone. When the hour of judgment arrived, would mourners hearing the songs be ready to meet their Lord?[31]

In addition to evangelical and Calvinist influences, country music also reflects popular folk religion as well. The traditional South believed in a supernaturalism almost as pronounced as in medieval Europe, and one indeed sees the supernatural at work in country music. Ghosts haunt the music. "The Legend of the Wooley Swamp" tells of the ghost of Lucius Clay, as mean-spirited a character as one is likely to find in country music. His spirit roams while his murderers laugh at him from their swampy graves. Such a superstitious tale, told with many atmospheric touches to create an appropriate mood, is rooted in the deep layer of folk tales and sayings in the rural South. Never officially a part of church doctrines, and indeed opposed by organized religion as irreligious, such folk beliefs nonetheless were combined in a syncretism with church teachings by many average Southerners. One of the best examples of this, and particularly interesting because it is a modern song, is "The Devil Went Down to Georgia." Satan rarely appears in country music, but he does materialize in this song, coming to bargain for the spirit of Johnny, a fiddler in the band. He turns out to be the same Devil whom Daniel Webster bargained with long ago. In these folk tales and superstitions, Southerners could joke about death, and about their fears of evil influences, in a way they never could in their official, formal religion.[32]

Thrush and Paulus listed "Philosophical-Religious Concepts" as one of their categories of death in popular music, but the difference from country music is in terms of the nature of religion in the songs. In popular music, the religion is a generalized religion, one that talks of the "Spirit in the Sky," to cite the Norman Greenbaum song of that title. "Be," by Neil Diamond, is described as a song "giving the means for reaching one's ultimate potential." These songs seems bland and religiously abstract in contrast to country songs, which portray the traditional imagery and tenets of an old-fashioned, God of thunder evangelical faith. One encounters guilt, fatalism, sinning, suffering, and divine retribution. The God of southern country music is a loving figure but a judgmental one as well.[33]

Viewed in a long historical perspective, country music's portrayal of death shows both continuity and change in southern culture. The South has undergone enormous social and cultural changes in the past thirty years, and these are reflected in the music. The region's death customs and attitudes are now like those elsewhere in the country. Southerners, too, in good American fashion, have commercialized death through the funeral industry and the cemetery industry. Country songs no longer display the emotionally wrenching, sentimental attitudes of earlier rural Southerners. Sometimes the songs express the alienation and emptiness of the modern world facing death. But the country songs retain the regional context as well. They continue to focus on such traditional concerns as the family, community, localism, the tragedy of frustrated lovers, the importance of religion. They continue to embody the idea that death should not be segregated from the rest of life but should be dealt with openly as a natural and profound human concern. White Southerners, both individually and collectively, have known much suffering in their long history, especially since the Civil War. The evidence from country music is that this reality has sensitized them to the tragedy of human mortality in a distinctively regional way.

The South's Torturous Search for the Good Books

A teenage boy walks into a pharmacy in the small town of Greenbrier, Tennessee. It is a hot July afternoon in 1961. The nervous teenager leisurely strolls through the store, stopping in front of a rack. He furtively looks around, anxious yet eager. An old woman walks in, shuffling up to the counter, taking endless time for a small purchase. When she finally leaves, he picks something up, holds it in his shaking hands, looks at it carefully, and then glances up again to see whether anyone is watching him. Quickly now, his heart racing, he goes to the counter and hands his purchase to the white-clad pharmacist, who looks at the boy disapprovingly. With his purchase in hand, the teenager leaves the store and races down the street to a quiet place. This is one of my earliest memories of buying a book. The book was Erskine Caldwell's *Tobacco Road,* a novel famed in the South of the mid-twentieth century for its shocking subject matter, dealing openly with sharecropping and, more important, sex.

This scene could have been repeated endlessly in the experience of Southerners in small towns across the region. If a similar southern teen-age boy had been in the Gathright-Reed Drugstore on the Square in Oxford, Mississippi, he might have looked up to see a man clothed in a rather shabby tweed coat staring at him. That would have been William Faulkner. Gathright-Reed was the only place for a good while in Oxford where one could have bought one of Faulkner's books. That books were simply one item among others in the drugstore, to be approached fur-tively and with possible guilt, tells much about the role of books in south-ern culture. Books could be dangerous, they had power, perhaps they were drugs. Efforts were made to prevent their impact in a region ob-sessed through much of its history with defining orthodoxies that should not be questioned by new ideas contained within the bindings of books.

The story of the book in southern history is the story of the percep-tion of dangers associated with reading, of the problems in establishing the communications system essential for making books available, of the differing meanings of books to different groups in southern culture. It is the story, in short, of obstacles overcome before books became com-monplace. Books and other printed material could convey the dogmas and symbols of the sacralized South to a wide regional audience, but they could also undermine that sacralization by questioning it.

The limitations of the book culture in the South can be traced back to the colonial era. Printers in that era served at the pleasure of royal governors, but in the South the governors were suspicious of printing presses, believing they encouraged the questioning of authority. Gover-nors always believe that, don't they? These southern colonial governors prevented the establishment of printing presses much more effectively than in New England, where printing presses existed for a century be-fore they did in Virginia. In 1671, Governor William Berkeley of Virginia insisted, "I thank God *that there are no free schools* nor *printing* and I hope we shall not have these for a hundred years; for *learning* has brought dis-obedience, and heresy, and sects into the world and *printing* has divulged them, and libels against the best government. God keep us from both."[1]

The South failed to develop concentrated urban population centers needed to encourage large publishing houses, it failed to develop distribution routes connecting towns to interior markets, and overall, until well into the nineteenth century, the South remained a cultural colony of England and New England. After the 1830s, Southerners did become interested in publishing books, mostly for nationalistic reasons, as sectional tensions mounted between the South and the North. But by the 1850s, New York and Philadelphia were already well established, dominant American publishing centers. Book publishing in such places had originally been the responsibility of either booksellers who published volumes for their stores to sell or printers who sold their work not only to those who commissioned it but sometimes to others as well. In the new northern publishing centers of the 1850s, publishers became a separate species, choosing books to be marketed based on profits through popular sales.

Charleston's John Russell did become a famed southern bookseller before the Civil War, but few others in the region followed his lead. By the 1850s, to be sure, the South had come to resent northern cultural dominance. Attitudes on books were now tied in with the sectional conflict over slavery. "The pure stream of literature has been corrupted by the turbid waters of Abolition," wrote an author in *DeBow's Review* from New Orleans in 1847, "and it has, at last, become a *necessity* to the South to have a literature of her own." Publishing houses in Richmond and Mobile began issuing volumes for a southern market and regionally oriented periodicals appeared, expressing an explicitly southern ideology. This continued during the war, when the Confederate government actively promoted the book publishing industry as a way to transmit Confederate nationalism. But this effort was of only limited success, because of the nature of southern culture and the realities of culturally and often physically isolated southern life. "The South don't care a d – n for literature or art," wrote William Gilmore Simms in discouragement in 1847. "Your best neighbor & kindred never think to buy books. They will borrow from you and beg, but the same man who will always have his wine, has no idea of a library. You will write for and defend their institutions in vain. . . . At the North the usual gift to a young lady is a book – in the South, a ring, a chain, or a bottle of Eau de Cologne."[2]

Simms had reason to be concerned: he was the first Southerner to be a professional writer rather than to compose simply as a gentleman of leisure. Simms held prestigious editing positions and saw his works published, but to few sales. Northerners often did not buy southern books and, most discouraging, few Southerners did either. Southerners in the antebellum era continued to subscribe to northern magazines and newspapers and to buy books by northern writers while ignoring their own publishers and writers in the region. The war's devastation struck a blow at publishing, and even the few presses working during the postwar era presented mostly only angry denunciations of the North and rote defenses of the South. When the University of North Carolina Press became the first state university press in the early 1920s, it was the only full-time, professionally maintained publisher in the eleven states of the former Confederacy.

Beyond this discouraging historical description, one should note also that the southern cultural worldview was not conducive to appreciation of books. From the early nineteenth century, when southern whites became aware of their minority status within the Union and of threats to the maintenance of their society, many Southerners have been preoccupied with maintaining racial, religious, and regional consensus, through orthodoxies that should not be questioned. When Hinton Rowan Helper published *The Impending Crisis of the Union* in 1857, a book aimed at non-slaveholding whites in the South, he was unable to find a publisher in the region and even found his claim to being a Southerner questioned. Southerners, with the surreptitious acquiescence of federal authorities, searched the mails in the pre–Civil War era, looking for abolitionist books regarded as incendiary in a slave society. This struggle for freedom of thought and expression continued to characterize southern culture until the monumental crisis of the civil rights era, when University of Mississippi historian James Silver could write of the dangers of the "closed society."

After the Civil War, the effort to define a southern way of life, an ideology that all "good" Southerners should affirm and which books should never question, did not vanish but escalated. The Lost Cause movement to honor the Confederacy included efforts to define what the "good books" were in the context of southern culture. The United Daughters of the Confederacy, for example, organized and campaigned tirelessly before school textbook committees to ensure that only pro-southern versions of American history were used in southern schools. The president of the Florida Daughters of the Confederacy told the group that, as a girl, "hot blood came to my cheeks" when reading American histories written by Northerners. The Texas chapter of the United Daughters of the Confederacy, early in this century, reassured parents that public schools had only "good books . . . safe for our pupils . . . truthful in history, literature and tradition."[3]

The idea that unquestioned inherited tradition might be a block to the search for truth in history and literature was hardly considered, suggesting a central problem limiting the growth of a reflective book culture in that era. Even scholars could become caught up in these regional pressures for orthodoxy. University of Mississippi historian Franklin Riley believed in objective, scientific history, but when a textbook he wrote competed with another in Arkansas, he advised his agent to attack the other one for giving more attention to Abraham Lincoln than to Jefferson Davis and for slighting Confederate generals. "No one can say that this is doing justice to the South," he wrote. "What will the little children think about the South after studying this book?" The concern for regional orthodoxy could even affect a topic as seemingly alien from it as mathematics. Daniel Hill, a mathematics professor in North Carolina before becoming a Confederate general, had included this problem in his book *Elements of Algebra:* "A Yankee mixes a certain number of wooden nutmegs, worth 4 cents apiece, and sells the whole assortment for $44; and gains $43.75 by the fraud. How many wooden nutmegs were there?" The number of nutmegs was only one point of knowledge conveyed through the problem, of course, which nicely illustrated what one Southerner referred to as the "dollar proclivities of Yankeedom."[4]

Lost Cause advocates became the first Southerners to work actively to restrict the ideas in textbooks, a tendency surely with dangerous implications. But they were not the only ones. Religious fundamentalism became a second great obstacle to the development of a book culture in the South because of its preoccupation with enforcing orthodoxy of thought. A Georgia legislator, Hal Kimberly, in the 1920s noted: "Read the Bible. It teaches you how to act. Read the hymn book. It contains the finest poetry ever written. Read the almanac. It shows you how to figure out what the weather will be. There isn't another book that is necessary for anyone to read, and therefore I am opposed to all libraries."[5]

The predominant southern religion has been experiential, valuing spiritual experience over written, systematic theology. It stresses the need for individual salvation from sin, and the Bible is the voice of revelation on how to do this. With a pronounced Calvinism teaching that human nature is depraved, religion offered assurance, but assurance often based on not questioning fundamentals. This attitude easily bred intolerance and suspicion of other ideas and ways of thinking.

Let me be clear here. It is not that one should be unconcerned with what children are taught. We live in an age where textbooks are minutely examined for their portrayals of women, African Americans, and others to make sure they are fairly treated, and complaints are properly heard if they are not. Fundamentalists and southern nationalists had and have the same right to concerns. The problem is that when orthodoxies are defined rigidly, the diversity of books and their ideas valued by a free society become unwelcome, and the South through much of its history was a society held in the grip of orthodoxies to be questioned only at profound risk.

The Scopes trial, in the summer of 1925, in Dayton, Tennessee, dramatized the problems of the book culture in the South better than perhaps anything else. It was a conflict over books, the Bible versus a textbook, Hunter's *Civic Biology*. During the trial, a local Dayton man walked up to Clarence Darrow, waved his fist at him, and shouted: "Damn you, don't you reflect on my mother's Bible. If you do, I will tear you to pieces."[6] To this man, the Bible was a talisman, sanctified by his mother.

The Bible was *the book* in the South, the good book, connected in the memories of Southerners with home, family, mothers, idealistic values, occupying a place of extraordinary authority in the regional culture. A central fundamentalist belief was that you must accept the Bible, all or nothing, what defenders now call inerrancy – the belief that nothing in the Scriptures is factually wrong. One true believer in the 1920s, John Roach Stratton, suggested doing away with all schools rather than allowing the teaching of evolution. During debate in the Kentucky Legislature over an antievolutionary law similar to the one Tennessee passed, a Baptist minister delivered an impassioned oration, during which he took a zoology textbook, threw it to the floor, and stomped on it to show his contempt.

Such a scene is, of course, terrifying to book lovers. But religious people were not alone in holding such views. I remind you again that the issue was the power of orthodoxy. *Publishers' Weekly* reported in August 1941 that Governor Eugene Talmadge of Georgia was asking the upcoming legislative meeting "to order the burning of library books which advocate interracial cooperation."[7] The book in question, *We Sing America,* by Marion Cuthbert, told of white and black children attending school together, becoming friends, and sharing a sandwich. "We are going to get rid of that book and all books of that kind," Talmadge reportedly insisted.

To begin to gain perspective on this earlier South and its attitudes, which were so alien to the culture of books and yet could still produce a Southern Literary Renaissance, we must realize that the South in Eugene Talmadge's day was still, in many ways, a traditional society, one in which the written word was regarded as less essential than the spoken word. Well before the South achieved prominence for its book culture in the twentieth century, Southern culture was producing great talkers – lawyers, politicians, preachers, storytellers. Conversation was the creative skill most appreciated. Ellen Glasgow, in *A Woman Within,* noted that in the South "conversation, not literature, is the pursuit of all classes." Southern culture was bound together, beyond social class divisions, by appreciation of the art of speaking. Allen Tate contrasted northern conversation with that of the South. Northerners talk about ideas, he said, whereas "the typical southern conversation is not going anywhere; it is not about anything. It is about the people who are talking." It is not quite fair, though, to say that southern talk was not about anything. It was functional. If you met a typical farmer or merchant, the talk was, as Thomas Nelson Page once observed, of "the crops, the roads, politics, mutual friends, including the entire field of neighborhood matters, related not as gossip, but as affairs of common interest which everyone knew or was expected and entitled to know."[8]

If a cultural predisposition toward the spoken word perhaps values less the written word, an enduring physicality in southern culture also worked against taking the book seriously. Men hunted and fished, and later they carried the football and swung the baseball bat and hopped into their stock cars. One father, trying to develop an appreciation for reading in his son who loved to hunt, placed a book in the boy's trap out in the woods; the young man did not even comment on catching a book and continued hunting, not reading. At least he did not try to skin the book.[9] Southerners loved riding and appreciated horse flesh. They honored physical beauty: Mississippi has produced more Miss Americas than any other state. We are among the leaders in expenditures devoted to beauty pageants; amid the costs for lipstick, diet pills, and hair spray, few can be found for books.

The matter is not just one of gender, though. Consider the case of William Alexander Percy of Greenville, Mississippi. Percy was a poet whose memoir, *Lanterns on the Levee* (1941), told of growing up in the early twentieth-century Mississippi Delta, in a society not oriented toward literary concerns, especially for a boy. But those concerns were decidedly Percy's. "I was a sickly youngster who . . . hated sports partly because they didn't seem important and mostly because I was poor at them, who knew better what I didn't want than what I did." His family was old money, one of Mississippi's most prominent families, and his father was a cigar-smoking, highly social man who, despite a legend of gentility, had long been active in the state's rough-and-tumble politics. "It must have been difficult for Father too," Percy writes. "Enjoying good liquor, loving to gamble, his hardy vices merely under control, he sympathized quizzically and said nothing." His mother, on the other hand, "never understood or forgave me a certain lack of enthusiasm for things social. People, whole throngs of them, delighted her, and her delight was infectious." Percy clung to his books with seemingly little encouragement at home.[10]

For many Southerners, sad to say, reading never became a habit. One traveler from the North to the early nineteenth-century South asked a southern farmer he met whether he liked to read. The man replied, "No, it's damned tiresome."[11] Literary editors faced with stacks of manuscripts might agree on some days, but the man's observation points out how, perhaps, the old saying arose and lasted that more Southerners wrote books than read them.

With little widespread cultural significance given to reading and writing in the traditional South, illiteracy became an enduring obstacle for a widespread book culture. The United States Census of 1870 showed that 4.5 million Americans were unable to read or write; 73 percent of them were in the South. Eighty percent of African Americans, most of whom were in the South, could neither read nor write. The postbellum South lived with a fateful decision of the Old South: it had been illegal to teach slaves to read. Few images from the historical South can be more chilling to consideration of the obstacles to the development of a book culture than that of forbidding someone to read. Some slaveowners, at least, ignored the laws and permitted or even encouraged their slaves to read. Frederick Douglass, for example, learned to read from sympathetic whites, and the role of slaveowning women and children in this encouragement should especially be noted. Sutton Griggs, an African-American Baptist preacher and founder of the Orion Publishing Company in Nashville in the early twentieth century, once noted that reading books sometimes required more courage than fighting. For black Southerners, as for many others in the region, establishment of a book culture would have to overcome the obstacles one does indeed meet in a battle.

I do not mean to suggest that no one read or that few books could be found in the traditional South. The South was not an intellectual culture, but surely we should not be too smug about this. Despite our Emersons and Thoreaus, American culture would never rival European nations in intellectual orientation. Think of the streams of writers who left American Main Streets and exiled themselves temporarily or permanently overseas to escape the bourgeois-dominated middle-class culture of the country.

The South, moreover, like other places, has always had its learned and artistic people, people who will always be a creative minority. The early South was home to extensive private libraries; Thomas Jefferson inherited a library in process for a century, a library that helped make him a Renaissance man, as he himself added to his library's depth and breadth. When earlier generations of Southerners responded to northern attacks on southern culture, they usually cited such libraries as a sign that the region was not the wasteland that northern rhetoric suggested.

No one disputes that the South produced great intellectuals like Jefferson, but the regional culture was less successful at nurturing societal interest in books. You see this in the gap in the development of public libraries, North and South. The library at the College of William and Mary was one of the best in the young nation, and the Charleston Library Society, formed in 1748, was a most successful public club library. But by 1850 the South had the worst library facilities overall of any American region. Despite periodic improvement in libraries, sometimes dramatic, the gap with the North, and particularly New England, always remained. In 1850, New England could assign roughly two people per library book; in the Middle Atlantic states, almost three people per book; but in the South, the ratio was twelve people per book, six times as many as in New England.[12] Public libraries suffered from the destruction of the Civil

War, and Union troops torched the notable private collections of William Gilmore Simms in South Carolina, Joseph Davis in Mississippi, and Edmund Ruffin in Virginia. Afterwards libraries languished, even after other aspects of the region's institutional life recovered from the war.

When an enthusiastic movement to build and support libraries swept the United States in the late 1800s, the South hardly participated. As late as 1926, 72 percent of all Southerners were without access to any public library. Other indicators of book awareness were equally dismal. In surveys of book purchases, the South traditionally has ranked at the bottom of the list. When, after World War II, the southern economy improved so that sales of radios and televisions in the South were on a par with the rest of the nation, the region still was near the bottom in book purchases.[13]

One can overdraw this grim picture. Hardworking librarians assisted those in need to the best of their abilities, and southern states did respond by the 1930s to the need for more extensive library systems. But attitudes deep in southern culture held back such library development, a revealing indicator of book culture. Donald Davidson, one of the Agrarian defenders of southern traditionalism at the end of the 1920s, complained that public libraries tended "ever to become more immense and numerous," perverting "public taste as much as they encourage it." He disapproved of public libraries because they discouraged citizens "from getting their own books and keeping them at home." In defending traditional southern ways, Davidson ridiculed the efforts of the modern age to make books available. He noted that modern society built immense libraries and put "little libraries on wheels"; "the flying library may be looked for eventually." Davidson championed an individualistic ethic long at the heart of the southern way of life, fearing that the modern world's mass culture would appeal to the lowest common denominator, making it harder for high culture to survive.[14]

But the fallacy of this position was to think that one could dissociate the high culture of literary achievements represented by books from society's overall cultural health. The history of the book in the South is the story of the obstacles in regional culture to the widespread valuation of books, a story not just, in other words, of those few who surely did read. The southern gentry was steeped in the classics. They studied their Bibles, read British novels, and even made some books – such as those of Sir Walter Scott – the basis for a deeply felt romantic cult. For them, books had certain clear meanings. They were emblems of a regional elite, holding onto an image of high culture in a rural, provincial world that seemed often uncaring of their ideals. Books were also to the southern aristocracy expressions of a distinctively southern way of life aspiring to romantic visions of greatness and, more down to earth, to political self-control and cultural prestige.

With the gradual rise of a middle-class, town-dwelling merchant class came a greater appreciation of the role of print, of reading, of books, as a way to economic and social success. Many of the distinguished writers of the Southern Literary Renaissance came from middle-class families of businessmen and professionals, who nurtured a love of reading for the knowledge that could be gained, knowledge to be used in the emerging capitalist society of the modern South.

What about the masses of Southerners, those rural small farmers who lived precariously in the nineteenth century and even more insecurely up to World War II in the twentieth century? What did books mean to them? It is easy for those of us who value books to ridicule those in the past who did not read, but we must avoid this temptation and understand their world. In the first place, they probably had access to more books than the discouraging statistics I have cited would suggest. Other studies show that books were available in country stores to be purchased inexpensively, private libraries served family and even neighbors who borrowed and read books, and many southern states did better than others in making public library books accessible.

We also need to remember again that plain folk did not place a higher premium on books because their society was traditional. Most Southerners of the nineteenth and even the early twentieth centuries expected to continue the ways of their parents in farming and looked forward to seeing their own offspring do the same. Schooling beyond minimal literacy was not functional to their economic success, was not as essential as it is in a modern capitalist world. The tragedy was that those leading southern society fought inevitable change so stubbornly and refused to prepare society for it.

By the dawn of the twentieth century and increasingly thereafter, though, the written word was growing more significant in the lives of all Southerners, but the plain folk did not have the societal resources to nurture the understanding of print and the love of books increasingly needed in the newly emerging world. In dealing with landlords, commercial employers, dispensers and collectors of credit, federal government bureaucrats, social welfare reformers, or others representing change, the plain folk were increasingly dependent on understanding print. Even to vote in the South after the turn of the century meant having to read and perhaps interpret the written word, so that one's democratic rights as well as economic status became dependent on the written word, but this was happening at a time before southern society had prepared to assist its citizens to face that reality.

Consider the sharecroppers or tenant farmers, people who suffered grievously from the regional economy, its lack of development, and maldistribution of wealth. If we had mentioned "books" to a sharecropper, he would have thought we were referring to the account books kept by the landowner under the crop lien system. These books bound them to the land legally because of the debts recorded in books. At the end of the year these were read and interpreted by the landowner, often without challenge because the tenant could not read them himself.

In considering the rural poor and books, we are in realms of irony and poignancy. How was the world of print represented to them? We know newspapers were a part of their world because they sometimes had to paper their walls with them. Social scientists in the 1930s reported that farm and home magazines were found in their homes, as were romance and mystery novels. The magazine *True Story* apparently would have won popularity awards in southern rural areas. The Sears Roebuck catalog, or the Sears Roebuck Bible as a Zora Neale Hurston character called it, represented the book to many rural Southerners. It was popularly known as the Wish Book, a name that makes clear that it represented the appeal of print as few things did in that rural culture. Writer Harry Crews insists that the federal government should issue a medal to the Sears Roebuck Company "for bringing all that color and all that mystery and all that beauty into the lives of country people."[15]

Through such simple and unsophisticated examples, southern rural folk gained increasing access to the world of print. School textbooks should especially be noted. They were a part of the rural household, even of the poor, by the 1930s. This was thanks to politicians such as Huey Long, James Vardaman, and others, men who were less than admirable in many of their actions, leaders we characterize as demagogues, but who appealed for votes on a platform of cheap textbooks and delivered on the promise. This was a hard-won victory and as much as anything represented an extension of the idea of book culture throughout southern society.

One group of Southerners had a special fascination with books because of experiencing their forbidden nature most dramatically. Black Southerners pursued education as soon as it was available, idealized teachers, and sought books after freedom wherever they could find them. The complicated meaning of books in this specifically southern black context was seen in the story of a fugitive slave observed hauling a big Bible with her as she roamed the woods and swamps. She was unable to read, but her old mistress had turned down the pages at the passages she knew by heart, and she would often sit in the woods, opening the Bible at these verses, repeating them aloud to bring consolation and peace of mind. For her, the book was an icon as powerful as any in her life.

Black Southerners, moreover, understood better than anyone the connection in the region between the spoken word and the written word, a relationship central to the flowering of literature in the twentieth century. On the one hand, black southern writers drew from oral culture for their narratives, characters, and even language. "An average southern child, white or black," wrote Zora Neale Hurston, "is raised on simile and invective. They know how to call names. It is an everyday affair to hear somebody called a mullet-headed, mule-eared, wall-eyed, hog-nosed, 'gator-faced, shad-mouthed, screw-necked, goat-bellied, puzzle-gutted, camel-backed, butt-sprung, battle-hammed, knock-kneed, razor-legged, box-ankled, shovel-footed, unmated so-and-so!" Southerners, she continued, "can furnish a picture gallery of your ancestors, and a notion of what your children will be like," all of it full of "images and flavor." She added that rural southern folk were "not given to book-reading," and so "they take their comparisons right out of the barnyard and the woods."[16]

One can see modern southern literature in general drawing from such oral lore, growing naturally out of this cultural resource that emerged unconnected to any thoughts of a book culture, but helping a book culture emerge well rooted in regional culture. Modern southern literature, in a sense, has taken the stories of generations of Southerners, converted them into high art, and deepened their meaning.

On the other hand, and perhaps less recognized, the written word influenced oral culture. The premiere example here must be the Bible, and that book is one we must consider further to recognize its extraordinary significance in nurturing a book culture in the South. For no one was this more true than African Southerners. The great black historian Carter Woodson once noted that blacks adored the Bible, and their desire to read it promoted their learning. Countless sermons, the spirituals before the Civil War, and the gospel songs afterward converted the descriptions of the Bible into oral lore. Noah and the flood, Jonah and the whale, Job and his tribulations, Samson and his strength, Father Abraham wrestling Jacob, Daniel in the lion's den, John the Baptist in the New Testament, Peter the rock on whom the church is built, weeping Mary, grieving Martha – all these became like current events in oral lore, teaching lessons on human nature.

Flannery O'Connor once observed that "what has given the South her identity are those beliefs and qualities which she has absorbed from the Scriptures and from her own history of defeat and violation: a distrust of the abstract, a sense of human dependence on the grace of God, and acknowledgment that evil is not simply a problem to be solved, but a mystery to be endured."[17] The Good Book in the South reinforced and interpreted the suffering growing out of southern historical experience.

Any examination of the relationship between books and traditional southern culture should dispel, finally, the idea that books were un- important in the South. Despite the suspicion of books, exactly the opposite was the case. Books had the power of a dangerous force, with almost magical properties to disturb everyday life. Because of the power attributed to books, the discovery of books by individuals in this cul- ture could be a life-transforming experience. The transforming power of books could be seen in the experiences of countless writers. Southern lit- erary history is replete with authors who grew up as insatiable, obsessive readers. Thomas Wolfe pledged to read every book in a public library and came close to doing so. Carson McCullers devoured books, from Greek drama to French literature, British and American novels, and nineteenth-century realists. She described reading Dostoevsky as giving her "a shock that I shall never forget."[18]

The transforming power of books in the South is best seen through the challenges they raised to the orthodoxies of race relations. Think of young Richard Wright, having fled Mississippi, working in Memphis, picking

The South's Search for the Good Books **123**

It is stunning to consider the effect of these letters on a page, conveying meaning, thought, emotion, culture, civilization etc.

up the Memphis *Commercial-Appeal,* and reading that H. L. Mencken was a fool – that and many other editorial denunciations of him. Wright goes to the riverfront library, equipped with a library card borrowed from a sympathetic white man (an Irish Catholic), and he reads Mencken. "I pictured the man as a raging demon," Wright notes, "slashing with his pen, consumed with hate." Learning that Mencken was fighting with words, he too gains this dream. "I hungered for books, new ways of looking and seeing. It was not a matter of believing or disbelieving what I read, but a feeling something new, of being affected by something that made the look of the world different." Through books, he now defined his dream, a dream that the institutions and folkways of the Jim Crow South had tried to thoroughly inhibit. For Wright, the power of the written word became the way to challenge orthodoxy.[19]

Consider also Will Campbell, the Mississippi white Baptist minister active in the civil rights movement. He grew up with the typical southern white attitude of the time, an assumed white supremacy, but in his memoir *Brother to a Dragonfly* (1977) he relates reading a book that changed his life while he was in the jungles of the South Pacific during World War II. *Freedom Road,* a popularized historical novel by Howard Fast, told of an illiterate freed slave, Gideon Jenkins, who organized poor whites and freed slaves to gain increased political power during Reconstruction. Campbell read the book all night and into a hot Sunday morning. "They were the most powerful and compelling words I had read in my nineteen years." He recognized that the poor whites in the novel "were my people" and "the black men and women were those we grew up thinking we had to oppose." From his reading, he came to believe that he had been taught racial antagonism because it promoted the power of the entrenched southern ruling class that must have feared an alliance between poor blacks and poor whites. "I knew that my life would never be the same. I knew that the tragedy of the South would occupy the remainder of my days. It was a conversion experience comparable to none I had ever had, and I knew it would have to find expression."[20] The language is that of religious experience, the psychology of conversion. The South took words seriously, at times with a religious intensity rooted in the region's predominant style of spiritual experience. Other activists, black and white, in the civil rights movement, the preeminent challenge to older southern orthodoxies, drew also from the Bible, the South's Good Book.

The books of the renowned writers of the Southern Literary Renaissance and those of today who continue the tradition have made their good books, their great books, by appreciating the word and the mind and the free pursuit of truth, questioning orthodoxies to advance truth. In doing this, they have drawn from the regional culture's appreciation of oral lore and the good book.

In *One Writer's Beginnings* (1984), Eudora Welty gives a charming memoir about the importance that books played in her development as a writer, and from her we see how books could assume tangible physical meaning to Southerners who appreciated them. "It had been startling and disappointing to me," she writes of her childhood, "to find out that story books had been written by *people,* that books were not natural wonders, coming up of themselves like grass. Yet regardless of where they came from, I cannot remember a time when I was not in love with them – with the books themselves, cover and binding and the paper they were printed on, with their smell and their weight and with their possession in my arms, captured and carried off to myself."[21] These words suggesting the pleasures of books to a twentieth-century master should not mislead us; they represent a triumph over deeply embedded obstacles in southern culture to appreciation of reading. Welty's parents instilled in her a love of books, and she in turn used the materials of her life in the South to give readers the gifts of her own books, which illuminate human existence. This is now a legacy the South can be proud of and on which it can continue to build.

Icons
and
Spaces

The Iconography of Elvis

Elvis Presley was music, sound, the voice, words. He came out of the South's oral culture that produced political orators, preachers, conversationalists, and storytellers. But Elvis was also a look and an image. He was likely the most photographed person in history, and his image has made him one of the most pervasive icons of mass culture.

Iconography is the study of the content of visual images, and the Elvis Icon suggests meanings related to the enduring public fascination with the King of Rock 'n' Roll. Human icons were originally promoted and maintained by religious institutions. In the modern world of popular

Medieval saints had their relics, and a saint of the southern popular religion has his vial of sweat. (Photo by Tom Rankin)

culture, business commercializes iconography and makes icons of public figures accessible to a wide audience. An Elvis Icon in the form of a keychain surely does not evoke the same feelings as that of a saint on a church altar, but pop icons still embody heroic models for human behavior and represent a striving for transcendence from the everyday world. The Elvis Icon reflects his Time, Place, and People.

The Elvis Icon burst into public consciousness in the 1950s, and the initial image from that decade still has power. It was a decade of anti-heroes – Marlon Brando in a leather jacket, James Dean as a misunderstood teenage rebel, and Elvis as a punk singer. His look is insolent, sullen, and sneering. He is dressed often in black – or as a black. He is the rebel against middle-class white convention. There are the swept-back, slicked-down dark hair and the baggy pants, oversized jackets, and "zoot suity" fashions, purchased on Memphis's Beale Street, a symbolic center of Deep South black culture. This was the revolutionary Elvis, shaking American culture to its foundations and liberating it from a middle-class outlook. This image represented the dark side of Elvis's persona – the mysterious, somewhat menacing young man awakening sexuality in young girls. Parents of the 1950s would likely never broaden their understanding of the Elvis Icon beyond this image.

Visual images and sounds were not altogether separate with Elvis. The icon emerged from the raw rhythms and lyrics of his early rockabilly songs as well as from visual images from his performances, album covers, marketed artifacts, and photographs. The Elvis Icon of the 1950s was softened somewhat by song-lyric images that were associated with him for the rest of his career: blue suede shoes, teddy bears, and hound dogs.

Icons are not stationary, trapped in time. If they survive, they adapt, lose meanings, and take on new significance. The 1960s Elvis Icon evolved from the youthful rebel to the fun-loving American young man. The titles told all: "Live a Little, Love a Little," "Fun in Acapulco," "Harum Scarum," and "Girls, Girls, Girls!" Elvis was now in Technicolor, and he became an energetic prop in colorful settings. Elvis was frolicsome, wholesome, living a life of mostly leisure to which he seemed well suited. The Elvis Icon symbolized escape into a fantasyland. If the Elvis of the 1950s was a symbol of a changing culture, the Elvis of the following decade represented an escape from the radical turmoil related to race relations, social reform, and overseas war. Elvis had been remade into a bland icon, but the popularity of the movies suggested that this was not an unwelcome development for believers in the icon.

The 1970s began for Elvis in 1969 – when he wore his first jumpsuit in a public performance. The jumpsuit was 1970s fashion, but Elvis made it the central artifact of a new image of royalty. He was now the King. He wore brightly colored, bejewelled, sequined clothes; wide, glittering belt buckles like those of championship wrestlers; and necklaces with crosses and other religious symbols. The Icon was now on stage, posing for cameras, stalking the crowd, and striking martial arts stances. Elvis was part of a royal pageant for the faithful.

Elvis Presley died in August 1977, but the icon lived on. The 1980s witnessed the continued marketing of Presley's music, with new releases of old recordings and bootlegged albums. But the icon survives in an amazing variety of material artifacts that lie at the center of a cult based on a legend. The Elvis Icon can still be found on posters, banners, postcards, magazine covers, comic books, bubblegum cards, dolls, caps, jackets, T-shirts, scarfs, sunglasses, shoes, socks, shoestrings, slippers, ties, mittens, bracelets, earrings, watches, rings, keychains, necklaces, pins, magnets, and many more objects.

The Elvis Icon was a secular object, but it had meaning in terms of societal values. Presley's Graceland was surely his place, and since his death it has taken on increased significance as the context for the Elvis Icon. Graceland is a major tourist attraction, drawing hundreds of thousands of visitors annually. The Elvis Icon lived on at Graceland, but, more broadly, its "place" was the geographic South. Elvis Presley was born in Mississippi, grew up in Tennessee, burst into iconic significance at the Sun Record Studio in Memphis, and, after years away in California, Hawaii, and Las Vegas, he came home in the 1970s to live in the South.

Elvis, of course, had national and international appeal. His "poor boy made good" story had wide appeal to the working class. But his "people" were above all working-class southern whites, and the Icon reflects this. He touched generational, musical, and national feelings, but the Elvis Icon has had special meaning for the people stereotyped as poor white trash, rednecks, and crackers. He symbolized Southerners in general with his polite manners and belief in mama and Jesus (despite his late-in-life lifestyle), combined with the threat of violence inherent in his image as 1950s rebel or 1970s martial arts fighter.

Curiously, the Elvis Icon has little hint of the southern obsession with history. Historian C. Vann Woodward writes of the "burden of southern history," and novelist William Faulkner sees the past surviving in the present for Southerners, but the Elvis Icon is notable for its attempt to transcend the past. This attempt is a clue to an enduring meaning of the Elvis Icon for his people. "He hated antiques," write Jane and Michael Stern in *Elvis World* (1987). "They reminded him of being poor."[1] The Elvis Icon emerged from the 1950s South – no longer a world of sharecroppers but of poor people moved to the cities. Given access to plentiful American goods in an age of increasing southern prosperity, the Elvis Icon teaches that they should be enjoyed.

Elvis's people valued also, though, such spiritual-moral qualities as religion and manners. From the beginning of Elvis's career, the Icon reflected a sentimental, almost Victorian religiosity. The sweet Elvis had a soft, effeminate look, including dreamy eyes and long eyelashes. Photographers portrayed him visiting with polio victims, drinking milkshakes, hugging his mother, and engaging in other wholesome activities. Fans repeatedly said they admired Elvis because he loved his mother, Gladys, was a good boy who lived with his family all his life, was mannerly (saying "yes, sir" and "no, ma'am"), was gentlemanly in behavior with women, and was generous in giving gifts – "happies," as he called them. He embodied a genteel, moral-religious version of the southern identity and did so convincingly.[2]

Elvis Presley was a product, however, of an earthy, seemingly ungenteel variety of southern religion, which shaped his personality, achievements, and image. He was a Pentecostal raised in the Assembly of God church. This tradition stresses the wonder-working power of the spirit, and it produced many of the legendary early rock performers, black and white. "Since I was two years old," Elvis remembered, "all I knew was gospel music. That was music to me." He exhibited the evangelical's touchstone – religious experience. The child Elvis disappeared one day and when he returned, crying, he told his family that "he had been talking to Jesus." When he was nine, he received the baptism of the Holy Spirit. After the Presleys moved to Memphis in the late 1940s, Elvis

...Take My Hand Precious Lord...

Elvis floats in the heavens in this poster image that includes words from a popular southern gospel song. (Photo by Tim Rankin)

began attending the all-night gospel singings, hearing groups that would influence his performing style. While talking with Jesus and hearing gospel music were not atypical experiences for Southerners, Presley's story possessed an intensity and focus that made him exceptional.[3]

Many Southerners saw his people, Pentecostals, as socially marginal, insulting them with the term "Holy Rollers," and his own religious background suggests another meaning to the Elvis Icon. *Liminality* is not an indigenous southern word – one would not find it in those "How to Speak Southern" books sold at Stuckey's. The word could have been created, though, to describe Elvis Presley and the generations of Southerners who lived through the dramatic social, economic, and political changes of the mid-twentieth century. Liminal is transitional, a stage of life or of ritual, a point between the separation from the old and incorporation into the new. Sometimes, according to its leading theorist, Victor W. Turner, the liminal can become a permanent category for those people who appear to be in a state "betwixt and between."[4]

liminal

Such people may include tricksters, actors, poets, monks, and other individuals – surely rock stars – who live on the margins of conventional social behavior and generate intense emotional responses from the broader society. They may appear innocent, paradoxical, anomalous, or disorderly to the middle class. They can be dangerous yet are also sources of renewal. They are people on the threshold of new experiences, new ways of life, that others may later follow, after the dangers of liminality are overcome.

The Elvis Icon was indeed liminal and especially so as a symbol from and of the American South. His career exhibited movement, a progression from youthful rebellion against middle-class conventionalities, symbolized by the creative musical energy of the 1950s, into a transcendent royal presence as the King in the 1970s. Elvis's career itself can be seen going through separation, transition, and incorporation, but the deeper reality that popular religion embraces is that his whole life represented an enduring liminality for the South. He was permanently "betwixt and between."

Presley was never conventional. His many seemingly conventional characteristics were taken to excessive extremes and often combined with iconoclastic ones in a complex mix. He may have gone to church as a young man, but that fact was subsumed by his perceived dark and threatening rebel image in the wider culture. Presley's 1960s movie character type may have seemed easygoing and nonthreatening, but the character was, in fact, always a working-class fellow who had earned quick success and lived out a dream of sexual liberation that was far from middle class.[5] His 1970s Vegas persona was a southern version of a royal performance that placed Presley far outside, and above, the experiences of ordinary mortals.

Liminal figures are significant because they are symbolically on the edge not just of society but for society. In this sense, the Elvis Icon was a lightning rod that absorbed the dangerous rays of social change. Such a role is controversial and fearful. The early Presley was often seen as taboo. He wore long, greasy-looking hair, pink shirts, and black pants with a pink stripe – not exactly reassuring to a southern middle class that was often socially insecure itself. "That boy needs to wash his neck," commented the wife of a Louisiana country entertainer after meeting Presley early in his career, and she summed up this fear of the "dirt" he represented. Soon after, in 1957, a Jacksonville, Florida, Baptist minister sparked a national furor by accusing Presley of giving a "dirty" show. "I don't do no dirty body movements," Elvis responded, but the minister was soon in *Life* magazine, railing against the young performer, Bible in one hand, an Elvis poster in the other. Presley and his mother were deeply hurt by the implication of his irreligion, the worst possible charge for this believing Pentecostal family.[6]

For all his uniqueness, Elvis symbolized a quality often linked with liminality, namely, the search for community among those in transition. This community of those on the southern margins was based on qualities outside the mainstream. The Elvis Icon evoked radical egalitarianism, especially a biracial musical culture and the dreams of success by the rural and working-class Southerner. It also touched feelings of deep humility, as seen in the legend of his polite, deferential *southern* manners. Elvis's persona was androgynous, blurring gender lines. He even wore eyeliner in his early performing days, and young toughs beat him up once – was it for his championing of black music or his androgyny? Each was deeply troubling to the conventional regional wisdom of the day. The Elvis legend of beneficence, openhearted charity, and humanitarianism illustrated a final trait that is often identified with the liminal community – an undifferentiated concern for humanity.[7]

Toward the end of Elvis Presley's life, he seemed to move closer some-

Elvis is a central modern figure of the southern civil religion earlier associated with Confederate heroes, as symbolized by this flag. (Photo by Tom Rankin)

how to his southern origins. He had never moved far beyond them, but symbolically he self-consciously claimed that heritage – even a sense of its history – with his 1970s concert performances of the "American Trilogy," which combines fragments from the peaceful slave spiritual "All My Trials," the rousing crusader's hymn "Battle Hymn of the Republic," and the southern anthem "Dixie." Presley reassembled these pieces and made them his own, delivered in a slow, reflective, melancholy performance that suggested an awareness of the complex past of regional conflict and southern trauma. At the end, he added the overt religious language to the other elements, shouting "Glory, Glory, Hallelujah!"[8]

The Icon now mediated between Northerners and Southerners, blacks and whites, expressing the new ideology of the post–Jim Crow South of the 1970s – a biracial ideal at the heart of a southern civil religion. Southerners responded to his death in 1977 with a tumultuous outpouring of emotion, in one of the largest funerals in southern history. Elvis's cult was grassroots, a populist upswelling of civil religious sentiment that used supernatural legends, marketed souvenirs, and other cultural forms to tie Elvis to a regional (as well as national) patriotism. His image soon appeared in tandem with the Confederate battle flag, linked usually with other southern heroes, and on religious relics such as "Elvis sweat."[9]

Elvis's historical era was liminal for the South, a transitional time, when heritage weakened but the future was unclear. He was a symbolic mediator who moved through history but seemed outside of history. The Elvis Icon came from a certain specific time period, place, and people to teach that human beings, even in the complex modern world, can still reach awesome levels of achievement. Elvis's immanence in his tangible, earthly, this-world life story is paralleled for popular religion by the theme of his transcendence through special qualities. Elvis was a southern country boy in legend, but magic spiritual qualities seemed to cluster about him.

Sunday at the First Baptist Church

Dallas's First Baptist Church might be regarded as a Baptist Vatican, if Baptists had such a thing. Spiritual home to 27,000 members, the church owns five blocks of prime acreage, worth $50 million, on the north end of downtown Dallas. W. A. Criswell has pastored this congregation for half a century and now serves as senior pastor. He was a key player in the fundamentalist takeover of the Southern Baptist Convention in the 1980s, making this congregation a source of doctrinal authority. Criswell himself is something of a saint to hard-nosed biblical inerrantists who see every word of the Scriptures as inspired, but he is a dark figure to moderates nursing their wounded souls.

The Reverend Criswell's influence is palpable here. As one walks to the church, you pass the Criswell Center for Biblical Studies and the Criswell Bookstore. The Bible on the back of the church pew is the *Believer's Study Bible,* edited by – guess who.

They tell a story in Dallas. The Reverend Criswell dies and knocks on the pearly gates. St. Peter asks him who he is, and Criswell gives him his name. "I'm sorry, but you're not in the book," says St. Peter. "I can't understand it. How can *I* not go to heaven?" St. Peter thinks for a minute, goes into the backroom, and when he returns says, "Okay, you can go in. It was under real estate."

H. L. Mencken, in his understated, good-natured way, complained that the South was "a cesspool of Baptists," and sometimes it has seemed like they have been more common than mosquitoes in Louisiana. The South has changed enormously over the last two decades, but the Baptists and other evangelical Protestants continue to recruit and nurture members in greater numbers than other churches. Perhaps no church can be a symbol of how evangelical Protestantism is faring in the contemporary South, but a visit to First Baptist on a Sunday morning shows why Evangelicalism continues to dominate the modern South. Those folks baptized in the past in countless local River Jordans in the southern countryside or who worshipped once in austere, hard-pewed settings would hardly recognize the new version of the old-time religion, though.

First Baptist is huge. Its main sanctuary seats eighteen hundred bodies, but the church supports twenty-seven chapels in all, including those for Chinese, Hispanics (several here), and a deaf congregation of 250 "signing" Baptists. Young marrieds worship in one of the chapels. First Baptist had a Laotian chapel, but the pastor left to do missionary work. Everyone understood. One begins to wonder whether one First Baptist can be found; is "the church" now a series of them, each reflecting separate group identities, each serving different Baptist constituencies?

The church is typical of modern urban churches in the South, trying to provide a "total life" environment. The church sponsors a K–12 academy and daytime activities for young children. At last year's summer camp, five hundred young ones spent a week in the wilds, in a camp geared single-mindedly to evangelism, with the resulting 146 decisions for Christ. Dallas's urban life is not that of the east Texas Piney Woods that nurtured Evangelicalism in earlier times, but proselytizing is still the message and method of this faith.

This is a busy church, reflecting the traditional Baptist view that you do the Lord's work in overdrive. Historians call the old New England Puritans moral athletes, but First Baptist Baptists are evangelical sprinters, energetically racing toward the goal line and thinking of it not in some long-distance future but now.

A third of the congregation comprises single adults, and a new singles class ministers to them. Efforts are directed at such categories as "separate again," "single parent," "pregnancy crisis," "divorced recovery," and the "career group." A new group is for those between college and career, targeted perhaps to those souls going through the Dustin Hoffman as Graduate Syndrome.

As an institution of a self-respecting modern middle class, First Baptist especially seems to target business people. The Nautilus machines provide weight training, and a racquetball court helps keep the body as fine-tuned as these Baptist souls aspire to be. Business luncheons provide an occasion for men and women to meet away from work, in a setting apart from worship. Church workers then follow up with contacts to attract them to Sunday services.

Church as business

First Baptist is an urban institution and does not seem to ignore certain responsibilities that come with its favored position. The Dallas Life Foundation is a secular wing of First Baptist, coordinating the church's social services activities, which are extensive. It operates a huge warehouse, providing housing for the homeless, three meals a day, basement appliances, and a devotional chapel on the first floor. The church regards this as its secular mission, but it is surely a part of evangelical proselytizing – its abiding mission.

On a Sunday morning, the congregation appears prosperous, earnest, busy, and successful. When you enter the sanctuary, it is like going to the beach on a sunny day; the blazing lights are needed for the seven television cameras that broadcast weekly services. Microphones dangle from the ceiling by long wires, looking like stalactites in a cave.

The choir, clothed in bright blue robes, collectively sprawls across the altar, behind the pulpit, and in front of the raised baptismal font. The singing is spirited. "Standing on the promises of Christ my King, /

Through eternal ages let His praises ring" – these classic lines sung that morning attach these modern Baptists to countless evangelical Protestants across time, space, and denomination. The singing is powered by a booming thousand-pipe organ, producing a sound that puts the fear of God in you in the unlikely event that the sermon does not.

On this particular Sunday, the Reverend Criswell is away, leading a tour of eighty of the faithful in the Holy Land. Guest preacher is Coach Grant Teaff, head football coach of the Baylor Bears for twenty-one years. "I think Paul would have made a fantastic football coach," Teaff said at an adult service meeting – the Impact Class – between Sunday morning worship services. It was a fitting comparison for that church's effort to extend the old-time southern gospel into the modern, middle-class, urban and suburban South, where sports is a new kind of religion but one closely allied with traditional Evangelicalism.

Baylor University, Teaff's school, has been caught in the crossfire of the bitter Southern Baptist Convention divisions. But Coach Teaff, who is now head of the board governing the Fellowship of Christian Athletes, is here not to dispute theology but to preach the story of the Crucifixion. The television lights might be glaring, but the message is the same one heard as long as Baptists have been seeking assurance of salvation.

Teaff began by linking his story to the news – the pervasive popular culture story of the 1990s, the O. J. Simpson murder case. "We've heard about what has been called the murder of the century. I want to talk about the murder of all time, the death of Jesus Christ." The sermon was awash in the blood of the Lamb, wanting to make you feel the pain of the cross. "It was a horrible, terrible, bloody murder," Teaff preached, "an excruciating, painful, humiliating event."

The Reverend Coach described the torture of Jesus. The wreath of two-and-a-half-inch-long thorns on His head brought "drops of blood" that would "drip down the face." A "master flogger" then used an eighteen-inch-long cat-o'-nine-tails to "literally shred the flesh." Jesus would then "have been standing in a pool of his own blood, awaiting his sentence." Roman soldiers later would nail the spikes in the wrists, and Teaff's evocative sermon made you feel each hammer blow as it landed. "When the soldiers lifted the cross into place, you could have seen the outline of Jesus' body on the ground, through the outline of blood where he had laid."

This is a classic conservative Protestant sermon theme, but Teaff buttressed his story by citing forensics authorities, including "a pathologist at the Mayo Clinic," who had written about the Crucifixion. Citing scientific authorities, Teaff explained, for example, that the membrane of the sweat band can burst as a result of stress, and blood will break into the sweat glands. "Jesus literally sweated blood," said Teaff, corroborating the Bible with science. Coach Teaff is a vigorous man, who looks like he could take on Satan's legions if need be. He delivered an athlete's sermon, roaming across the platform punctuating his words with firm gestures and animation. His presence in the pulpit gave poignancy to a sermon describing the physical debilitation of Jesus Christ.

The service closed with the invitation, as the coach noted, "There may be some here who've been playing at it, talkin' the talk. It's easy to do." The congregation sang the ultimate song of invitation, "Just as I Am," and eight new members joined the church that Sunday morning.

The sermon was a powerful one, people sang the old songs, and new members committed to the flock. The setting of this modern Southern Baptist icon seemed sanitized – the place and people well scrubbed, brightly lit, and well appointed. But the message was traditional, bred in the hardscrabble, rural South and still realistically, graphically aware of human limitations. Its answers seem too simple to critics and its believers sometimes too intolerant of other messages, but the energy, confidence, and single-mindedness of this congregation help explain why Evangelicalism continues to dominate southern religious life.

The Cult of Beauty

The beauty queen seems an unlikely type to consider for religious significance, and especially so in a South dominated by the strict moral code of evangelical Protestantism. The parade of flesh that is the beauty pageant, the image of the swimsuit competition that dominates perceptions of it, appears to be far from the moralistic teachings of the evangelical churches.

The worldview seen in twentieth-century southern popular religion, however, has accepted the images and rituals of the beauty culture along with strictures for modest behavior for women. Any tensions between the two have somehow been bridged, and to understand this accommodation one must see the beauty queen in the South as an embodiment of the southern civil religion. She represents values long associated with a South that saw special symbolic meanings in its women, meanings with moral-religious overtones. Popular religion can find significance in the events of everyday life, much less the pageantry of the beauty cult.

To understand the relationship between beauty and popular religion in the South one needs to understand the history of the beauty culture. Beauty has been tied in with central themes of southern traditional life.

"The modern Southern belle has, of course, long been the Pageant ideal," writes Frank Deford of the Miss America contest, "so that – even in those years when a Southerner does not win – the likely winner is still probably patterned after that type." The "fundamental Southern-belle personality" that has become the nation's beauty ideal is "vivacious, sparkle-eyed, full of fun, capable of laughing at herself, and incapable of speaking either (a) briefly, or (b) without using the hands to illustrate all points." She has poise and personality beneath the outward physical at-tractiveness.[1]

Beauty pageants such as the Miss America competition suggest the in-fluence of southern ideas in shaping national ideals of beauty. Within the specifically southern context, beauty pageants are part of a cult of beauty, with certain definite ideas on what beauty is and why it is significant to be beautiful. The South's cult of beauty reflects southern attitudes on race, social class, and especially gender and sexuality, and these attitudes have changed significantly over time.

Beauty has long been related in the South to color. English colonists in North America brought European concepts of beauty, which became a factor justifying the enslavement of black Africans. Historian Win-throp D. Jordan has noted that "the English discovery of black Africa came at a time when the accepted standard of ideal beauty was a fair com-plexion of rose and white. Negroes not only failed to fit this ideal but seemed the very picture of perverse negation." Judged on this standard, blacks were seen as "pronouncedly less beautiful than whites." In his age, Thomas Jefferson asked whether skin color is not "the foundation of a greater or less share of beauty in the two races?" He insisted that "the fine mixtures of red and white" were "preferable to that eternal monotony" of black skin. Jefferson's concept of beauty included "flowing hair" and an "elegant symmetry of form," both of which he attributed to whites more

The Cult of Beauty **145**

than to other races. "The circumstance of superior beauty," he wrote, "is thought worthy of attention in the propagation of our horses, dogs, and other domestic animals; why not in that of man?"[2] The idea of beauty was tied in for southern whites with ideas of sexuality and morality. Southern whites used the dark skin color of slaves as an outward indicator of the immorality of blacks, attributing to them impurities, lasciviousness, and evil.

The myth of the Old South included a prominent role for the beautiful white lady. Indeed, as W. J. Cash noted in *The Mind of the South* (1941), she became identified "with the very notion of the South itself." Physical beauty was a part of the definition of southern womanhood. The nineteenth-century conception of woman's appearance emphasized her fragility, purity, and spirituality rather than her physical nature. The southern lady, according to Anne Firor Scott, was to be "timid and modest, beautiful and graceful." Anne Goodwyn Jones has pointed out that white women in the Old South "became not only the perfect embodiments of beauty" but also "the appropriate vehicles for the expression of beauty in language." Beauty itself, like the lovely woman who best represented that quality, "was fragile and ethereal, or sensuous and pleasurable, but it was finally irrelevant to the serious business of life."[3] Beauty was a culturally admired trait, but it was also a limiting one for women.

The identification of whiteness and women with beauty has survived in the twentieth century. Cash wrote that the southern woman was "the South's Palladium," "the shield-bearing Athena gleaming whitely in the clouds," "the lily-pure maid of Astolat." Carl Carmer wrote in *Stars Fell on Alabama* (1934) of the University of Alabama fraternity dance that included a toast: "To Woman lovely woman of the Southland, as pure and chaste as this sparkling water, as cold as this gleaming ice, we lift this cup, and we pledge our hearts and our lives to the protection of her virtue and chastity."[4]

The southern ideal of the beautiful woman has evolved, though, in this century. The Scarlett O'Hara type, who is associated with the Old South, is beautiful but somewhat artificial. Sexuality is much more openly associated with beautiful women in the modern South. Victoria O'Donnell's typology of images of southern women in film points out that one dominant type is the "Sexual Woman": "She is beautiful, voluptuous, only partially clothed, and openly erotic. She is able to give sexual fulfillment,

This grave monument might suggest that Southerners want to preserve a beautiful visage in stone even after death. Baker County, Georgia. (Photo by Tom Rankin)

but she does so in order to impart strength to her man." Sometimes the beautiful southern woman becomes the "Rich, Spoiled Woman," who has "beauty, money, men, and friends" but is "spoiled and wild." Another film image of the modern southern woman portrays her as "earthier, gaudier" than women of the past, embodying open "carnal qualities, for she has lost her purity and chastity and is glad of it." The "Unfulfilled Sexual Woman" wants to be sexually appealing, but she is frustrated because "she has little to offer in terms of physical beauty." For all of these social types in the southern imagination, beauty remains an important ingredient of culturally determined happiness, which now includes sexual satisfaction.[5]

Changing attitudes toward the sun have affected the southern ideal of beauty. In Western Civilization white, pallid skin was traditionally a sign of upper-class status, and such makeup as face powder and rouge highlighted whiteness. With industrialization, upper-class Europeans and white Americans, including eventually Southerners, developed an interest in outdoor life. The laboring class now worked indoors, so the upper class sought suntans and outdoor recreation as an indicator of social-class status. "The lithe, sun-tanned, tennis-playing, outdoor woman," writes Marvin Harris, "became a respectable alternative to the cloistered, snow-and-alabaster ideal of the old regimes."[6] Soon the middle class adopted this ideal of a physically healthy, athletic, sun-tanned woman.

This cultural change had special significance in the South, where the sun is intensely felt and "whiteness" has its most deeply rooted racial-cultural meaning. The sun has long helped determine southern social status – rednecks were laborers, and their women were said to be less beautiful because they were less pallidly white than the plantation wife. By the 1920s the South, according to historians Francis Butler Simkins and Charles Pierce Roland, had "learned to regard its very hot and very bright sun as a beneficent friend instead of as a cruel tyrant." Sunbonnets and long, tight-fitting clothes were abandoned for lighter garments, and the sun was soon regarded as a source of health. Sun bathing gradually became common, and "the acme of Southern comeliness became blue eyes, blond hair, and brown skin."[7]

Black attitudes toward beauty have gone through their own changes. Illustrations of African Americans up to the 1880s show a predominance of natural hair and little cosmetic beautification of the face. By the turn of the twentieth century, though, black males were beginning to use hot combs to straighten hair, while black women were using oils and pomades. Evidence suggests that many blacks internalized white ideals of beauty. They used cosmetics to lighten skin color and hair straighteners to "conk" the hair. This probably reached a peak during the 1940s. Beauty parlors became important institutions of the black community, and cosmetic manufacturers were among the wealthiest of black Americans.

Skin color has been a symbol of social class status within the black community. John Dollard noted in *Caste and Class in a Southern Town,* his 1937 study of Indianola, Mississippi, that "consciousness of color and accurate discrimination between shades is a well-developed caste mark in Southerntown; whites, of course, are not nearly so skilful (*sic*) in distinguishing and naming various shades." Toni Morrison's novel *The Bluest Eye* (1970) portrays the tragic results of a black family's self-hatred because of a "white skin" ideal of beauty. Lawrence Levine cautions, however, against overemphasizing the effect of a cultural ideal of white beauty on blacks. For many blacks a light skin did not suggest social status within the black community, but rather a corruption of the race. If some black people have admired white skin, others have viewed black skin as natural, and many cosmetics have existed not to cloak that color but to highlight it. Moreover, when color preference has been seen in such black cultural expressions as blues lyrics, it has most often been brown, rather than either black or white-yellow. Paul Oliver's study of blues lyrics, *Blues Fell This Morning* (1960), found that rural folk expressed an ideal of beauty somewhat different from the urban black and white ideal of "the streamlined woman." Bluesmen admired the "big, fat woman with the meat shaking on her bone." They also celebrated certain physical features, such as teeth that "shine like pearls" as a natural and attractive contrast with dark skin.[8]

The civil rights movement of the 1950s and 1960s surely strengthened pride in a black ideal of beauty. "Black Is Beautiful" reflected a new appreciation of dark skin specifically as well as a more general pride in black culture. Magazines such as *Beauty Trade* and *Essence* are now published by blacks outside of the South, but their ideas influence the southern beauty industry and black ideals of beauty. Beauty pageants have become a fixture on black campuses and in black communities across the South.[9]

The beauty pageant is the ritual event that best displays modern national and regional attitudes about beauty. Predecessors of American beauty pageants were European festivals that crowned queens. European May Day activities have included selection of beautiful women as symbols of fertility. In the colonial era this custom took root more in the South than among the Puritans. Schools for young southern white women throughout the nineteenth century included contests for selection of attractive, popular queens. Southern romanticism expressed itself in antebellum tournaments, re-creating medieval pageants, and these festive occasions included queens selected for their beauty. Postbellum festivals also included selection of beauties. Mardi Gras chose its first queen in 1871, despite the protest of some moralists who objected to any public display of women. These May Day, tournament, and festival queens were upper-class figures, and as historian Lois Banner has written, these contests reinforced "the centrality of physical beauty in women's lives and made of beauty a matter of competition and elitism and not of democratic cooperation among women."[10]

Commercial beauty pageants appeared first in the late nineteenth century. P. T. Barnum sponsored a female beauty pageant in 1854, but it involved only the display of daguerreotypes of women, with observers voting on winners. Carnivals in the South, often attached to agricultural fairs, helped pave the way for beauty contests displaying beautiful women in native costumes from around the world. The Atlanta International Cotton Exposition of 1895 had a beauty show on its midway, and this part of the exposition was described as "the Mecca of the show." By 1900 chambers of commerce and fraternal groups in the South sponsored carnival beauty shows at fairs, but it was still not considered appropriate for middle-class women to be on display in competitive contests. The first true competition was the Miss United States contest at Rehobeth Beach, Delaware, in 1880, but the South's beach resorts did not follow suit generally until after the turn of the century.[11]

The Miss America pageant began in 1921, but the judges did not select a Southerner until Texan Jo-Carrol Dennison was chosen in 1942. With the Americanization of the South – and the southernization of the United States – in recent decades, Southerners have become identified with love of beauty pageants. *Newsweek* estimated that 750,000 beauty contests are held each year in the United States, ranging from pageants for school homecoming queens, county and state fair queens, and festival representatives to the Miss America contest. "The phenomenon is strongly regional," according to *Newsweek*. "The 'Pageant belt' stretches from Texas (where there are men who will date only titleholders) throughout the South, overlapping the Bible belt with odd precision." The article cites the conclusion of Tom Ryan, a corporate executive who worked with beauty contests: "Pageantry *is* like an evangelical movement."[12]

Beauty pageants in the South are part of a regional cult of beauty. Young southern white ladies have long been encouraged in the feminine arts, and aspects of beauty have been taught in female academies, charm schools, and modern modeling salons. Cosmetologists, beauticians, and hairdressers are well-known figures in small and large southern towns, where concern for "looks" is endemic. Eudora Welty reproduced the ambience and conversational sound of the southern beauty parlor in her short story "Petrified Man."

Cosmetics were slow to take root in the poor rural South of the early twentieth century. Even today, some Pentecostal-Holiness groups stress an ascetic ideal of outward plainness and inner beauty. Nevertheless, most women in small southern towns and cities have long accepted national views on cosmetics. Mary Kay Ash, founder of the successful Mary Kay Cosmetics, is from Texas; a key figure in the black cosmetic industry in this century, Madame C. J. Walker, came from Louisiana. Changes in contemporary southern religion's attitude toward beauty are evinced by Tammy Faye Bakker, the television celebrity formerly on the Pentecostal-oriented show, the *PTL Club*. Bakker flaunted her makeup by using a great deal of it. She even launched her own line of cosmetics.

Small-town, middle-class life in the South and the nation supports the ceremonies of beauty. In 1970, for example, only eight of fifty contestants in the Miss America pageant were from the nation's twenty-five largest cities. Few large urban areas sponsor contests, and even statewide beauty pageants tend to take place in smaller cities and towns. James Rucker, a former executive director of the Miss Mississippi contest, notes that whereas big-city northern girls enter the contest for the scholarship money or a chance at show-business success, "in Mississippi, it's tradition for the best girls to come out for the Pageant. In Mississippi, the best girls just want to be Miss America."[13]

Beauty contests are community events in towns and small cities. Beauty-contest winners are contemporary regional celebrities – the female equivalents of football stars. Beauty queens, whether Miss America or

In Mississippi, beauty is not simply the concern of the teenage belle, as seen in this image of a recent Mrs. Mississippi, Donna Russell, and her children. (Photo by Tom Rankin)

Southerners start early in the beauty culture. (Photo by Tom Rankin)

Miss Gum Spirits (representing the southern timber industry), make personal appearances, travel extensively, earn scholarship money, and have their photos on calendars. Meridian, Mississippi, rewarded Susan Akin, Miss America in 1985, with an enthusiastic hometown parade. She rode through town before a cheering crowd that included young girls who had won their own honors as Deep South Beauty Queen, Cameo Girl, Mini Queen, and Miss Cinderella Queen. This ritual event showed an intense American middle-class patriotism. The band played "This Is My Country" and "God Bless America." United States Congressman Sonny Montgomery was there to praise her, and Meridian's mayor named the day in her honor. Religion was a central feature. The pastor of the First Baptist Church gave an invocation, thanking God for "letting us live in a country where a neighborhood girl could be selected Miss America." The Baptist kindergarten students had penned portraits of the queen. A friend from childhood told the crowd that Susan Akin was "the one of us who earned immortality."[14]

Participants in the Miss America pageant and those who have studied it believe that Southerners who compete have an advantage. After Tennessee's Kellye Cash won in 1986, another contestant claimed that Cash had won because judges desired a "sweet kind of nonaggressive Southern belle." Cash revealed her regional consciousness when she said she was "basically a conservative Southern gal." The contestant representing Mississippi that year insisted Southerners had no special advantage, except that "they just work harder." Eight of the ten finalists, in any event, were from former Confederate states. Miss Montana, Kamala Compton, gave no evidence of knowing about John C. Calhoun's concept of the concurrent majority, which proposed presidents from the North and the South, but she suggested a variation of it. Southerners were "just a lot more prepared than us Western girls who try once for a title," she told a reporter. "I mean, they should have a Southern Miss America and a Western Miss America."[15]

Southerners clearly devote considerable time and resources to doing well in the Miss America pageant. University of Southern Mississippi sociologists Don Smith, Jim Tent, and Gary Hansen have theorized that southern contestants likely do better in the national contest because of three factors: (1) pageant officials, judges, and contestants assume, based on past experience, that Southerners will do well; (2) the southern states encourage beauty contestants; (3) and southern states have strong pageant systems. Twenty-five states have never won the contest, whereas Texas, Alabama, and Arkansas have won twice, and Mississippi has won four times. For contestants' clothes Texas spends more than twice as much as Vermont spends for its entire pageant. Vermont has never placed a contestant in the top 10 at Miss America, but Texas obviously values its success. From 1945 to 1970 California led the nation in scholarship prize money ($47,300) awarded to contestants. Mississippi was second ($43,000), but Mississippi's commitment was much greater, given that the state had a tenth of California's population. Four of the top seven states in awarding scholarship money up to 1970 were Arkansas, Alabama, South Carolina, and Mississippi.[16]

The Miss America contest and beauty pageants in general earn the condemnation of many men and women. "The whole gimmick is one commercial shell game to sell the sponsors' products," said critic Robin Morgan in 1968. She saw beauty pageants as embodying an ugly Americanism. "Where else could one find such a perfect combination of American values? Racism, militarism, and capitalism – all packaged in one 'ideal' symbol: a *woman*." Spokesmen for the Miss America pageant defend it, noting it is the largest provider of scholarships for women in the United States. Women themselves are, of course, actively involved as participants and, behind the scenes, as trainers and managers, but men run the Miss America contest and other beauty contests. In September 1986, for example, no women served on the twelve-member commission that represented the state pageants. The Jaycees sponsor most local Miss America contests, and men's service clubs are involved in other beauty contests. Pageants are hobbies for many men, a time for having fun and for theatrical displays. The head of the Miss Arkansas contest wears a hog suit and cheers for his choice each year; the state chairman in Mississippi dresses in a tuxedo made from Confederate flags. Regional symbols are thus displayed and linked to woman. Miss America pageant director Albert Marks Jr. notes that "watching pretty girls" is "the greatest spectator sport in America." Southerners have been unusually involved in this sport as both participants and spectators.[17]

Beauty, then, had distinctive regional meanings and connotations for Southerners, which reflected woman's role as symbol of southern culture. As seen, that symbolic role began far back, its origins a part of the idealization of the regional identity in the plantation myth of the Old South. The culture of beauty in the twentieth-century South, as in other parts of the United States, has been, however, a middle-class and working-class phenomenon, and one must look at the evangelical religious attitudes coming out of those classes for the final aspects of beauty's role in embodying the southern civil religion.

The evangelical ideal of woman centered on her special moral and spiritual nature. Woman was not so much an idealized symbol of region as a specific symbol of home and family. She represented the restraint, zealous morality, refinement, and self-discipline valued by evangelical culture. Samuel S. Hill sees the extreme version of the southern religious woman as represented by the ideal of sainthood in the region. "In the imagination of southern Christians," Hill writes, "a saint is typically female, past middle age, white, southern in manner, and gregarious." The southern saint does have a personality that could be that of the beauty queen. "She" is gentle, kindly, supportive. "She" is concerned with others and sacrifices herself for individuals and groups in need. "She" is not to be glamorous, sophisticated, or public-minded, though. "She" is certainly not to be notable in appearance nor erotically appealing. "In other words," Hill concludes, " 'she' is not likely to be perceived in corporeal terms."[18] The contrast with the other southern ideal of conspicuous display of beauty seems stark here.

Hill's image of the saintly southern woman is of a female older than a beauty queen, of course, and its images do not necessarily embody the same expectations for younger women. On the other hand, Southerners do extend the category of beauty queen beyond belles, as seen in the category of "Mrs." queens as well as "Miss." In any event, modern southern evangelicals have redefined their culture so that the beauty queen seems a quite acceptable role for a moral southern woman. One can see the process through the example of Cheryl Prewitt, Miss America of 1980. Prewitt grew up in Choctaw County, Mississippi, the daughter of pious evangelicals. Her father's name alone, Hosea Amos Prewitt, could put the fear of God in you. When her father saw her for the first time after her birth, he "prayed over me, committed me to the Lord, and dressed me in my first diaper."[19] She attended church every time the church doors opened and sang gospel music with her performing family, the Prewitts.

Prewitt was severely injured at age eleven in an automobile accident, which left one leg two inches shorter than the other. Overcoming the physical injury became the focus of Prewitt's testimony to God's power. Her recovery was slow, including much wheelchair time, but, as she revealed in her testament, *A Bright-Shining Place,* she grew in faith. At a revival she realized the need to be born again and to "discover for what reason God had put me into the world." She realized she would never be alone because she "would always have Jesus as my very real friend and guide." She saw herself at this point "on the threshold of a very big adventure." She also reflected on the automobile accident, in which a neighbor was killed, and wondered, "*Why should I have been spared?*" (66–68).

Prewitt's book notes the importance of a biblical passage to her. Matthew 5:48 says, "You, therefore, must be perfect, as your heavenly Father is perfect." These words inspire her, and she even comes in her self-examination to see her physical appearance in perspective. "As far as my looks were concerned – at this, I had to laugh. With a mouth crowded with crooked teeth, a face tracked with scars, and two legs of unequal length, I was hardly an All-American beauty!" (70).

Prewitt read her Bible and soon prayed for a healing, like those Jesus performed. A Pentecostal preacher, Kenneth Hagin, placed his hands on Prewitt's head during a prayer meeting and invoked, "In the name of Jesus." A warm feeling washed over Prewitt, "as though I'd been immersed in a hot tub," and she lost all track of time. She was transported "to some faraway bright-shining place – a private place inhabited only by myself and Jesus." Afterward, her crippled left leg extended by two inches, until her heels met, "like two perfectly matched bookends." She now testified that the miracle was "to serve as a sign to others . . . of God's existence and love." (114–18).

This account is a classic of southern popular religion, centered on a small-town Mississippi girl, member of a gospel-singing family, touched by a miracle of God, through the refuge of Jesus and the more direct hands of a Pentecostal faith healer. The image of her healing is a physical one, with waves washing over her body, but the physicality is linked to spirituality. The body is made whole through the spirit.

The healing miracle set the stage for the transformation of the evangelical woman into a beauty queen, which represents the final stage of the miracle. Prewitt enrolled, against her father's stern wishes, in the Miss Choctaw County beauty contest in hopes of winning scholarship money to college. The economic meaning of beauty pageants to modern southern plain folk families is of paramount importance, even overcoming stern fathers' anxieties. Prewitt lost that first contest, but she won the Miss Mississippi State contest, singing the sacrificial pop hymn "He Ain't Heavy . . . He's My Brother."

Prewitt later won the Miss America Pageant. Her father finally relented his opposition and attended the pageant, telling her afterwards, "I believe it's God's will that you won tonight. . . . Now you just be sure you live up to the big job He's given you, hear?" (223).

In Prewitt's persona, the beauty queen has become an icon of religious edification. The flesh, once broken, has been healed and it can now testify to God's power. Prewitt's example is, of course, an extreme case of southern religiosity validating the beauty culture. But the general expectations for beauty queen behavior seem easily reconcilable now with evangelical morality. The beauty queen represents a conspicuous display of corporeality, in one sense, but in another sense the display is within carefully regimented and restricted codes. The beauty queen represents purity. She is also a triumphant contestant, who wins by embodying – in the evangelical view – not just outward beauty but inner beauty. She represents values and retains her virtue. She has a quality, physical beauty, that is widely admired in the South, and she can use it and her success to testify to her faith.

The cult of beauty exemplifies an important tenet of popular religion: all aspects of life can provide religious illumination when believers see them in a sacred perspective.

Unifying the Symbols of Southern Culture

When the film *Mississippi Burning* came out in 1989, it brought back bitter memories for southern blacks and whites. Public controversy over the movie focused on its historical inaccuracies. Less noticed was the film's role as part of a larger process fraught with regional significance: the memorialization of the civil rights movement.

Indeed, while the fight for equal rights and improved race relations continues today, the civil rights movement of the 1950s and 1960s is becoming remembered history through attempts to honor its early leaders and to portray the era on film and in books. These efforts, in turn, have become part of a broader cultural conflict between blacks and whites over southern symbolism and identity. We are at a historic moment in which Southerners are struggling to define their public culture in a biracial, postsegregation society.

The South has once before gone through the experience of memorializing a central event in its history. Two decades after the end of the Civil War, Southerners intensified their memorialization of the Confederate effort. They erected hundreds of the ubiquitous Confederate monuments in small towns throughout the region, as well as larger, more elaborate statues of Robert E. Lee, Jefferson Davis, Stonewall Jackson, and other leaders. The United Daughters of the Confederacy undertook a campaign to place paintings of the heroes of the Lost Cause in schoolrooms across the South.

Through most of the twentieth century, then, symbols of the South were tied to the Confederacy, the supreme moment of southern collective consciousness or, more precisely, southern white consciousness.

Black Southerners have recently begun a serious challenge to the use of Confederate symbols to represent the southern experience. In the early 1980s, for example, the first black cheerleader at the University of Mississippi declined to carry the Confederate battle flag, which students and alumni identified at the time as the school's unofficial school emblem – the rebel flag of the Ole Miss Rebels. Black legislators and civil rights groups in several Deep South states have demanded an end to the practice of flying that flag over state capitols. Douglas Wilder, the first black elected to a state executive office in the South since Reconstruction and later governor of Virginia, led an unsuccessful movement to change his state's official song, "Carry Me Back to Old Virginny," because of its demeaning racial imagery.

Underlying these challenges is the argument that the Confederacy and the Civil War had different meanings for blacks and whites and that images associated with the white past should not be used as publicly sanctioned symbols for the South as a whole.

Yet the objections have met with much resistance and resentment from white Southerners. For many southern families, the Confederacy represents not an ideology defending slavery but rather inherited stories of family danger, adherence to principle, sacrifice, and love of history. Calls to abandon these past symbols represent, to these Southerners, a genealogical and cultural lobotomy.

The recent attempts to memorialize the civil rights movement are part of this challenge to traditional southern symbolism. The meaning of this central event in modern southern history is undergoing definition, through a process shaped by forces both outside and inside the South. We are now witnessing a development comparable to the southern creation of the Lost Cause a century ago – the conversion of history into a cultural memory that will survive a generation and live on to provide meaning.

During the two decades since Dr. Martin Luther King Jr.'s death, civil rights groups and individual communities have honored local martyrs with plaques, grave markers, and, most notably, the impressive crypt for Dr. King at the Martin Luther King Jr. Center for Nonviolent Social Change in Atlanta. The first memorial to the civil rights movement as a whole was at the Southern Poverty Law Center in Montgomery, Alabama. It was tangible evidence that the South's fascination with the past increasingly focused in the last decade on the struggle of the 1950s and '60s for racial equality.

The celebration of the civil rights movement has often collided with the earlier public symbols of southern culture. White students at one Mississippi high school, for example, unveiled the Confederate battle flag during ceremonies honoring Dr. King as part of Black History Month in 1989, triggering racial tensions that forced authorities to cancel classes and declare an early spring holiday. White hate groups, such as the Ku Klux Klan and the white supremacy movement, continue to exploit this division.

Can this conflict over southern cultural symbols be resolved? The fundamental issue in the conflict is the nature of community in the South, which obviously includes both blacks and whites with deep ancestral roots. The public cultural symbols of the region must now reflect that common past.

Older emblems associated with the Confederacy and with racial segregation no longer are appropriate as public symbols. The Confederate battle flag, for example, is associated as much with the Ku Klux Klan as with the Confederacy, and its supercharged racial meaning can never unify the region's people. Public symbols will never last long unless they bring people together.

Yet to banish all symbols suggesting a racially divided history to museums and private homes would violate the shared experience of southern blacks and whites. Writer Robert Penn Warren notes that the Confederate leaders offer the student of history "a gallery of great human images for our contemplation," and the same can be said for those leading the early civil rights protests.

The Civil War left the South defeated and divided. In a sense, the civil rights movement finally ended the Civil War, offering Southerners the chance for racial reconciliation. The challenge now is to combine past symbols that suggest the region's struggles and best ideals into a new symbolic structure.

In fact, this process is already under way. In Virginia, Mississippi, and a few other southern states, the Martin Luther King Jr. holiday is celebrated on the same third Monday in January as Confederate heroes day. It may be that images of Robert E. Lee and Martin Luther King Jr. should hang side by side in our grammar schools – regional heroes embodying positive human virtues. Whites may at first honor white heroes, and blacks their leaders, but combining the symbols will represent public recognition of a joint history.

Ideologues will never be satisfied with this solution, but Southerners will likely have to go beyond ideology in order to live together. A shared appreciation of the region's troubled history must provide a common bond.

The contemporary South understands the moral complexities involved in looking back to the nineteenth century. The simultaneous display of images from the Confederacy and the civil rights movement should not blur the distinction between them but rather preserve the historical significance of each as landmarks on the road to achieving a society of black-white mutual respect. Southern cultural symbols can no longer be rallying cries for protest. They must teach of the tragic costs of past racial divisions and the need for reconciliation.

Memorializing heroes should not lead to a mindless mythology. A romantic view of the Confederate heroes eventually made them into marble men, their human struggles forgotten by the modern world, and Dr. King is in danger of becoming a sanctified saint, destined in retrospect to easy success. Incorporating civil rights heroes into southern public symbolism should remind Southerners and other Americans of the slow, painful efforts required to overcome injustice.

The South is searching, moreover, for new symbols. Musicians, writers, athletes, and other contemporary heroes are becoming fresh new representatives of a culture that managed to overcome legally imposed racial segregation.

Southern culture reflects a merging of three hundred years of Western European and West African cultural continuity. The question now is whether Southerners will acknowledge this reality through their public symbols.

In Atlanta, the portrait of Dr. King at the State Capitol is displayed on a wall next to a revolving glass case of tattered Confederate battle flags used by troops in the Civil War. Such a juxtaposition suggests a complex new burden of southern history – not to forget the Civil War but to remember that the civil rights movement was the other great event in regional life, not only freeing blacks from legal oppression but liberating whites from obsession with the racial status quo.

12 Sacred Southern Space

The concept of sacred space suggests places designated for the encounters between humans and the Divine. These places may be buildings dedicated to worship. They may be natural sites, as in boulder-marked sacrificial spots, mountain tops where inspirational events occurred, or rivers for ritual baptisms. They become locales for popular religion when they involve mass behavior and give evidence of the supernatural at work.

Photography can document sacred space and provide a visual image of popular religious behavior. Tom Rankin's photographs chart the spiritual geography of African Americans in the Mississippi Delta. For the ancient

Greeks, the unseen presences in a place determined its nature as sacred or profane. Rankin's images are haunted by palpable if hidden signs of the spirituality of a people in a distinct time and place.

The black Delta Christians captured in these photographs are linked to other African-American worshippers through a long tradition. Before the Civil War, blacks in the South generally worshipped in biracial churches, mostly Baptist and Methodist. They took part in the First and Second Great Awakenings in the eighteenth and early nineteenth centuries and later in summer revivals, drawing from European church traditions in the process but also influencing the shape and content of the Evangelicalism that would come to dominate the South. The "invisible institution" was the religion of the slave quarters, a secret religion practiced in the woods or away from the masters' attention. Here God did not sanction slavery but condemned it. The new children of bondage waited, trusting in the Divine for their liberation. The praise house was the setting and shouting was the ritual that marked this religion as distinctive, the worshippers drawing on an African heritage of danced religion.

Emancipation enabled freed slaves to withdraw from white-dominated biracial churches and to form their own separate congregations and denominations. The National Baptist Convention came to be the umbrella group representing many local, mostly independent churches. The African Methodist Episcopal church, the African Methodist Episcopal Zion church, the Colored (later Christian) Methodist Episcopal church, spin-offs from the National Baptists, and later holiness and Pentecostal groups all organized African-American religious impulses into enduring institutions represented in the Mississippi Delta.

Under slavery and later under Jim Crow segregation, the church became central to black group identity. It was a social center, a locus for protest against racial discrimination, and a training ground for leaders in the black community. It also carried forward African-American cultural traditions, including storytelling, dance, and drama, and its influence on music is recognized around the world. The local church, in short, gathered together widely scattered rural blacks to form a community that could implement common objectives and maintain the culture's traditions.

The religion illustrated here is a part of that tradition. Many of the churches and graveyards in the Delta go back a century; some are older.

The inside of a Mississippi Delta African-American church presents words, images, and artifacts of the faith. (Photo by Tom Rankin)

The land was a great swampy forest then. Not until the railroad came into the Delta, along with timber workers to clear the land and federal government money to help with flood control along the Mississippi River, did large numbers of settlers appear. Among them were the freedmen, seeking opportunity on a new frontier in the South.

In the twentieth century, many African Americans whose toil had made the Delta a wealthy place for others left because they did not share in the land's bounty. But these home churches have a powerful hold on their people, those who have gone to live elsewhere as well as those who stayed. Between 20 and 25 percent of all African-American churches are rural (a figure double the size of the black rural population), and churches in the nonmetropolitan South have the highest rates of membership among all African Americans. Many of the Delta congregations were founded in the late 1800s and early 1900s, originally housed in wooden frame buildings; these photographs show some that are still around. In other cases, groups have decided to build with brick because of its greater prestige and durability.

Many of the congregants of these churches are poor in worldly goods. It is often said that the church has been a survival mechanism for people with hard lives. Tom Rankin's photographs enable us to look more deeply into black religious life, beyond easy categorizations. Perhaps some of us have not been able to see what has always been there, because we think of black religion so much in terms of voices rather than images: the chanting preacher, the "amens" of the congregation, the sweet choirs, the distinctive piano sounds. Rankin helps to open our eyes.

These photographs of sacred spaces provide a visual metaphor for African-American religious experience. One notices first the settings. The buildings are on flat land that often stretches toward the horizon. The environment is lush, with shrubs, bushes, vines, and weeds all around. The church grounds are often adjacent to a cottonfield: in the distance is the daily work area of the people who worship here. One picture shows cotton growing almost to the church door. Churches and graveyards cling to a small territory, indicating their vulnerability to the profane world. This is God's acre, but it is not always at ease.

These spaces assert the division of the sacred from the profane. Sacred phenomena are separate from daily life, from the commonplace. Religion is intentional: people make clear by naming and by practice what is sacred, and maintaining these boundaries is a function of all religion. The spaces illuminated in these photographs are set aside for a purpose beyond work, beyond the daily harshness and injustice known by generations of black people in the Delta.

Natural features of the landscape often take on religious meaning, as an entryway to the divine. Trees – cypresses, great oaks, and others – are especially important religious symbols here. Vertical objects, like the branches of these Delta trees reaching heavenward, represent the intersection of the spiritual and human worlds. Other natural forms as well as trees create shadows that haunt these landscapes. Rankin's photographs are filled with the interplay of light and dark.

Inside the churches, the small spaces and low ceilings create an especially intimate setting for contact with the Divine. The interiors suggest a fundamental appeal of the holy: orderliness. They are places of purity, with none of the messiness of the profane world. The enclosed space is clearly divided into levels: the congregation is separated from the pulpit and choir and piano. Yet the space is so small that the congregation and those involved in conducting the worship service can interact freely, so that it is easy to imagine the lines between them dissolving.

The iconography is striking: Leonardo da Vinci's *Last Supper* hangs from a wall; nearby is a Church Covenant (indicating that these people are resolutely Protestant). A ceiling fan hangs from on high, and an awareness of time is indicated by a clock inside a bell and by a calendar. Jesus is the key figure. Crosses suggest his sacrifice and, surprisingly, even a crucifix hangs starkly on a paneled wall. He is especially prominent on painted windows, which suggest stained glass. My favorite is the church where Jesus is painted on four windows; the fourth window also holds an air conditioner, creating a bifurcated Jesus. These interiors, true sanctuaries, are miniature celestial cities offering vivid images of hope.

If churches are often situated so that light plays off them, suggesting illumination, graveyards are places of darkness. Sometimes overtaken with scrub brush and weeds, mostly they are scraped clean, all contaminants gone. Thrusting up out of these burial places are imaginative grave markers: homemade angels with wings, carved in the solidity of concrete. The cemeteries are usually located under prominent trees, resulting in a dark and sometimes forbidding atmosphere that suggests the fear and dread humans often bring to encounters with the sacred.

A church in the Mississippi Delta portrays Jesus Christ on each window, although one window also makes rooms for air-conditioning. (Photo by Tom Rankin)

The holy in most religious traditions evokes dread and awe. Ghosts could indeed be about, reminders of the history of this land, of the suffering borne by its black inhabitants. But these burial sites are also cool and refreshing in the Mississippi climate, places of refuge, offering welcome relief from the scalding summer sun.

The cemeteries show the boundaries between the sacred and the profane. Clumps of bushes along the edges roughly but clearly demarcate these sacred spaces. Medieval European walls were military fortifications, but they began as magical protection lines against the forces of chaos embodied in demons beyond the enclosure. Past the lines of bushes here lie the cottonfields. Sometimes that land is literally dead, a wasteland created by poisonous chemical sprayings. It is close geographically but spiritually well removed.

Rituals sanctify a sacred space. Salvation is a central part of the predominant religion of the Delta, and conversion and initiation are fraught with meaning. The baptism ritual embodies the essence of the faith, and the people in these photographs of river baptisms are pilgrims, black-clad holy men and white-clad holy women standing in water, seeking sanctification. It is a timeless scene, these holiness people marching off as to glory, to a ceremony recharging a people's faith.

As we look at these places and people, they seem quiet and peaceful and calm. That is one dimension of the holy. Another is the power of exaltation. Contact with the Divine results in urgent, compelling, and spontaneous energy. Religion infuses its black followers with energy, this emotional power.

In studying the cultural significance of African-American religion, we often do not look closely enough at the sources of its power. Rankin helps us to understand those sources. The sacred can be disturbingly paradoxical: gentle, nurturing, and serene for believers, yet also violent and unpredictable. These sacred spaces in the Mississippi Delta have indeed nurtured tranquility for suffering souls; they have also been the source of a divine energizing. Power carries with it the possibility of renewal and freedom, ideas that have long driven African-American spirituality. Now we can see what it has meant to people who have lived through hard times to maintain sacred spaces such as these.

The ceremonies of African-American spirituality depicted here do not provide merely cathartic release; they represent the opportunity for tran-

A graveyard behind a Mississippi Delta church suggests the power of light and dark in a sacred landscape. (Photo by Tom Rankin)

The central ritual of southern Protestant Evangelicalism is baptism, portrayed here in the 1980s in the Mississippi Delta. (Photo by Tom Rankin)

scendence. Each new initiate renews the group and its fellowship with God. Access to the Divine leads to the hope of perfection in earthly lives.

African-American churches in the Mississippi Delta are much more than social and service centers for the community, important as those functions are. Profound mysteries are at work here; lives can be transformed, hope given for the future.

These sacred places represent the transition between the world of the invisible institution of slave times and the modern black church, between folk religion and popular religion. They are holy relics of the traditional world of an older South. Many of the churches seen here no longer exist; at least one of the preachers has passed away. Tom Rankin's photographs are sensitive renderings of a world of primordial attachments, full of fears and joys and expectations. They are tangible artifacts from a South where people of faith sense the continuing manifestation of the Spirit even in the modern world.

Afterword:
Popular Religion
and the Southern
Cultural Passage

This volume has revealed glimpses of the southern worldview at a time of social transformation. Flannery O'Connor noted that the South was Christ-haunted, and I have tried to show that popular religion can be a useful way to illuminate her observation. Popular religion, as used here, has been the religion of the masses, of the people, as distinct from that of the theologians, preachers, and institutions (although they appear occasionally as well). The popular religion I have sought is also mostly nonecclesiastical, an expression of spirituality outside the church doors. Examples of southern popular religion are touched by open supernaturalism, evoking the mysteries of religion in seemingly secular activities.

This volume makes no claim, certainly, to systematic exploration of popular religion in the South. Such obvious topics as televangelists and gospel music, for examples, are unexamined. Some of these essays have not been focused exclusively on religion but have been more about southern culture in general. Yet these case studies have shown how evangelical Protestantism so permeated southern culture as to enter profoundly into many of its features. Evangelical Protestantism provides the bridge be-

The cross combines with an urgent word message in this familiar southern icon. Highway 72, North Alabama. (Photo by Susan B. Lee)

tween popular religion and such other forms as folk and denominational. Some of these pieces have been set in sacred spaces, but even here the boundaries of religious categories are not clear and thus overlap. Coaches preach rousing sermons, television cameras broadcast what might otherwise be a folk sermon, and African-American churches in the Delta are sources of a supernaturalism that blurs sacred-secular distinctions usually important to ecclesiastical religion.

The civil religion of regional patriotism has been a key focus because it provides access to distinctively and characteristically "southern" dimensions of popular religion. Civil religion has provided the archetypes and rituals at the heart of the symbolic mediation that popular religion represents. Civil religion comes partially from above in culture – an example of invented tradition – but it is also rooted in the people, cropping up at certain times and events. Beauty queens, musicians, writers, artists, and football coaches have become modern celebrants of a southern civil religion that celebrates regional cultural customs, rituals, and values that have survived the many changes in the cultural passage of the last half century.

The symbols of twentieth-century popular religion in the South show the seeming contradictions in regional social psychology. How does one reconcile black people and white people, rich and poor, agrarian and industrial, rural and urban, glamour belles and saintly women, lost causes and civil rights, folk religion and ecclesiastical worship? Liminal symbols, as seen in the essay on Elvis Presley, are those that are on the threshold of new ways but are rooted still in the old, a separate category "betwixt and between." They offer a view of cultural transition that may be useful in thinking of the modern South. Symbiosis is a particular form of liminality, which represents a way to structure religious symbols. Seemingly contradictory beliefs must be seen as logically related, held in balance, not by a third trait but by the awareness that the existence of each depends on the other. They are all part of one system; to properly understand one requires knowledge of its opposite.[1]

David Potter has written of the "enigma of the South," and others have written of its paradoxes. The concepts of liminal transition and symbiotic meanings from popular religion emphasize that the southern belief system holds the seeming southern contradictions together as simply parts of one symbolic universe, as lived in everyday life. To understand fully the southern belle, you must understand the female saint of virtue. To understand white culture, one must examine black culture as well. In each case, neither category would have the same meaning without the presence of the other.

Poor Southerners experienced the regional cultural passage of the twentieth century with special fury – uprooting rural lives, pushing them off the land, but bringing new opportunities with new ways. Religion helped mediate that transition. Regional cultural icons from the modern South blended with intentionally Christian ones to form new expressions of "God's project." After traveling through the South in search of Elvis in 1989, newspaper reporter David Treadwell quoted one unnamed Southerner he met who concluded that the homes of poor whites and poor blacks in the South differed in a revealing detail – "black houses got two pictures on the wall – Jesus and Martin Luther King; white houses got Jesus and Elvis."[2] Jesus mediates between King and Elvis, tying them and the cultures they represent closer together. James McBride Dabbs saw the South, finally, as under God's judgment and grace. The judgment stemmed from the fragmentation and divisions in the region, in a sense from its people failing to realize the symbiosis at the heart of their culture. "God's grace," said Dabbs, came from those magical moments of reconciliation, when the region's people came together, sometimes simply in shared everyday customs and rituals. God's project was the biracial South, a project unfinished in Dabb's day and still in the making. God's judgment or God's grace.

Notes

Introduction

1 James McBride Dabbs, *Haunted by God: The Cultural and Religious Experience of the South* (Richmond: John Knox Press, 1972), 134.

2 The following discussion of popular religion is indebted to Peter W. Williams, *Popular Religion in America: Symbolic Change and the Modernization Process in Historical Perspective* (1980; rpt. Urbana: University of Illinois Press, 1989). See also Charles H. Long, "Popular Religion" and Segundo Galilea, "Popular Christian Religiosity," in *The Encyclopedia of Religion,* ed. Mircea Eliade (New York: Macmillan, 1987), vol. 11; David D. Hall, *Worlds of Wonder, Days of Judgment: Popular Religious Belief in Early New England* (Cambridge, Mass.: Harvard University Press, 1990); and Robert Anthony Orsi, *The Madonna of 115th Street: Faith and Community in Italian Harlem, 1880–1950* (New Haven: Yale University Press, 1985).

3 Williams, *Popular Religion in America,* 12. For a useful discussion of the relationship between evangelical Protestantism and modernity, see James Davison Hunter, *American Evangelicalism: Conservative Religion and the Quandary of Modernity* (New Brunswick: Rutgers University Press, 1983).

4 Samuel S. Hill Jr., *Southern Churches in Crisis* (New York: Holt, Rinehart and Winston, 1967).

5 See, for example, the articles in Russell E. Richey and Donald G. Jones, eds., *American Civil Religion* (New York: Harper and Row, 1974).

6 Don Yoder, "Toward a Definition of Folk Religion," *Western Folklore* 33 (January 1974): 2–15. Jeff Todd Titon, *Powerhouse for God: Speech, Chant, and Song in an Appalachian Baptist Church* (Austin: University of Texas Press, 1988), 149.

7 William M. Clements, "The American Folk Church: A Characterization of American Folk Religion Based on Field Research among White Protestants in a Community in the South Central United States," Ph.D. diss., Indiana University, Bloomington, 1974; Titon, *Powerhouse for God,* 141–62.

8 Richard M. Weaver, "The Older Religiousness in the South," *Sewanee Review* 51 (spring 1943): 238–48.

1. The Southern Religious Culture

1 Lee Seifert Greene, *Lead Me On: Frank Goad Clement and Tennessee Politics* (Knoxville: University of Tennessee Press, 1982), 232–34.

2 Ibid., 235–36.

3 John Lee Eighmy, *Churches in Cultural Captivity: A History of the Social Attitudes*

of Southern Baptists (Knoxville: University of Tennessee Press, 1972); Samuel S. Hill Jr., "The South's Two Cultures," in *Religion and the Solid South,* ed. Samuel S. Hill Jr., Edgar T. Thompson, Anne Firor Scott, Charles Hudson, and Edwin S. Gaustad (Nashville: Abingdon Press, 1972), 24–56.

4 Rhys Isaac, *The Transformation of Virginia: Community, Religion, and Authority, 1740–1790* (Chapel Hill: Published for the Institute of Early American History and Culture, Williamsburg, Va., by the University of North Carolina Press, 1982).

5 John B. Boles, *The Great Revival, 1787–1805: The Origins of the Southern Evangelical Mind* (Lexington: University Press of Kentucky, 1972); David T. Bailey, *Shadow on the Church: Southwestern Evangelical Religion and the Issue of Slavery, 1783–1860* (Ithaca: Cornell University Press, 1985). Boles develops the idea of a regional religious culture in *Religion in Antebellum Kentucky* (Lexington: University Press of Kentucky, 1977).

6 C. C. Goen, *Broken Churches, Broken Nation: Denominational Schisms and the Coming of the American Civil War* (Macon, Ga.: Mercer University Press, 1985); Mitchell Snay, *Gospel of Disunion: Religion and Separatism in the Antebellum South* (New York: Cambridge University Press, 1993).

7 Charles Reagan Wilson, *Baptized in Blood: The Religion of the Lost Cause, 1865–1920* (Athens: University of Georgia Press, 1980).

8 John B. Boles, ed., *Masters and Slaves in the House of the Lord: Race and Religion in the American South, 1740–1870* (Lexington: University Press of Kentucky, 1988); C. Eric Lincoln and Lawrence H. Mamiya, *The Black Church in the African-American Experience* (Durham, N.C.: Duke University Press, 1990).

9 Hunter D. Farish, *The Circuit Rider Dismounts: A Social History of Southern Methodism, 1865–1900* (Richmond: Dietz Press, 1938); Rufus B. Spain, *At Ease in Zion: A Social History of Southern Baptists, 1865–1900* (Nashville: Vanderbilt University Press, 1967).

10 David E. Harrell Jr., "Religious Pluralism: Catholics, Jews, and Sectarians," in *Religion in the South,* ed. Charles Reagan Wilson (Jackson: University Press of Mississippi, 1985), 59–82; Wilson, *Baptized in Blood,* chap. 4.

11 Kenneth K. Bailey, *Southern White Protestantism in the Twentieth Century* (New York: Harper and Row, 1964); James J. Thompson Jr., *"Tried as by Fire": Southern Baptists and the Religious Controversies of the 1920s* (Macon, Ga.: Mercer University Press, 1982); George M. Marsden, *Fundamentalism and American Culture: The Shaping of Twentieth-Century Evangelicalism, 1870–1925* (Oxford: Oxford University Press, 1980).

12 Hill, *Southern Churches in Crisis;* Randall M. Miller and Jon L. Wakelyn, eds., *Catholics in the Old South: Essays on Church and Culture* (Macon, Ga.: Mercer University Press, 1983); Eli Evans, *The Provincials: A Personal History of Jews in the South* (New York: Atheneum, 1973).

13 David E. Harrell Jr., *Varieties of Southern Evangelicalism* (Macon, Ga.: Mercer University Press, 1981).

14 The best discussion of Evangelicalism as the dominant Southern religious tradition is in Hill, *Southern Churches in Crisis.* For a discussion of these issues at the folk level, see also James L. Peacock and Ruel W. Tyson Jr., *Pilgrims of Paradox:*

Calvinism and Experience among the Primitive Baptists of the Blue Ridge (Washington: Smithsonian Institution Press, 1989).

15 Joel A. Carpenter, "Evangelical Protestantism," Donald G. Mathews, "Evangelicalism," and Joel A. Carpenter, "Fundamentalism," in *Encyclopedia of Religion in the South,* ed. Samuel S. Hill (Macon, Ga.: Mercer University Press, 1984), 239–43, 243–44, 275–78.

16 David E. Harrell Jr., "Fundamentalism," in *Encyclopedia of Southern Culture,* ed. Charles Reagan Wilson and William Ferris (Chapel Hill: University of North Carolina Press, 1989), 1288–89.

17 Hill, *Southern Churches in Crisis,* chap. 7. See also John Patrick McDowell, *The Social Gospel in the South: The Woman's Home Mission Movement in the Methodist Episcopal Church, South, 1886–1939* (Baton Rouge: Louisiana State University Press, 1982); and Robert Moats Miller, "Social Gospel," in *Encyclopedia of Religion in the South,* Hill, 699–700.

18 Hill, *Southern Churches in Crisis,* 27–28; Clements, "The American Folk Church."

19 Lincoln and Mamiya, *Black Church;* Albert J. Raboteau, *Slave Religion: The "Invisible Institution" in the Antebellum South* (New York: Oxford University Press, 1978). See also Samuel S. Hill, "Religion," *Encyclopedia of Southern Culture,* 1265–1331.

20 Mechal Sobel, *The World They Made Together: Black and White Values in Eighteenth-Century Virginia* (Princeton: Princeton University Press, 1987); Boles, *Masters and Slaves.*

21 Robert C. McMath Jr., *Populist Vanguard: The History of the Southern Farmers' Alliance* (Chapel Hill: University of North Carolina Press, 1975), 133.

22 Ibid., 134.

23 Ibid., 136; James R. Green, *Grass-Roots Socialism: Radical Movements in the Southwest, 1895–1943* (Baton Rouge: Louisiana State University Press, 1987), 138–39, 162–75.

24 Wilmer C. Fields, "On Jordan's Stormy Banks: Religion in a Changing South," in *Dixie Dateline: A Journalistic Portrait of the Contemporary South,* ed. John B. Boles (Houston: Rice University Studies, 1983), 65–80.

25 John Shelton Reed, *The Enduring South: Subcultural Persistence in Mass Society* (Chapel Hill: University of North Carolina Press, 1974), chap. 6.

26 "Southern Family Bulwark Loses Some of Its Stakes," *Memphis Commercial Appeal,* 5 July 1993.

27 See Carol Flake, *Redemptorama: Culture, Politics, and the New Evangelicalism* (Garden City, N.Y.: Doubleday, 1984).

28 Ibid., 52. For a fuller discussion of Dallas's First Baptist Church, see chapter 9.

29 Flake, *Redemptorama,* chap. 6.

30 Nancy Tatom Ammerman, *Baptist Battles: Social Change and Religious Conflict in the Southern Baptist Convention* (New Brunswick: Rutgers University Press, 1990).

31 Flannery O'Connor, *Mystery and Manners,* ed. Sally and Robert Fitzgerald (New York: Farrar, Straus, and Giroux, 1969), 59; V. S. Naipaul, *A Turn in the South* (New York: Alfred A. Knopf, 1989), 164.

2. "God's Project"

1 Robert N. Bellah, *The Broken Covenant: American Civil Religion in Time of Trial* (New York: Seabury Press, 1975), 145; John F. Wilson, *Public Religion in American Culture* (Philadelphia: Temple University Press, 1979), 20, 21.

2 George Tindall, *The Ethnic Southerners* (Baton Rouge: Louisiana State University Press, 1976), 23.

3 Wilson, *Baptized in Blood;* C. Vann Woodward, *The Burden of Southern History* (Baton Rouge: Louisiana State University Press, 1960).

4 The religion of the Lost Cause was the most important manifestation of regional religious patriotism in the South, but the full history of the southern civil religion would include such topics as the founding of Jamestown, the myth of a colonial Eden, the sectional-national antebellum dichotomy, the southern role in national wars, and southern ideas on regional destiny.

5 Wilson, *Baptized in Blood,* chap. 8; John Shelton Reed, *Southerners: The Social Psychology of Sectionalism* (Chapel Hill: University of North Carolina Press, 1983), 85–91.

6 W. J. Cash, *The Mind of the South* (New York: Alfred A. Knopf, 1941), 392; Allen Tate, *Essays of Four Decades* (Chicago: Swallow Press, 1968), 592; Thomas L. Connelly and Barbara L. Bellows, *God and General Longstreet: The Lost Cause and the Southern Mind* (Baton Rouge: Louisiana State University Press, 1982), 107–13, 121–27; C. Hugh Holman, *The Immoderate Past: The Southern Writer and History* (Athens: University of Georgia Press, 1977), 39; Daniel Aaron, *The Unwritten War: American Writers and the Civil War* (New York: Oxford University Press, 1973), 327–42.

7 Holman, *Immoderate Past,* 96.

8 Tindall, *Ethnic Southerners,* 43–58.

9 Allen Tate, "Ode to the Confederate Dead," in *Poems: 1928–1931* (New York: Charles Scribner's, 1932), 50.

10 Allen Tate, "Remarks on the Southern Religion," in Twelve Southerners, *I'll Take My Stand: The South and the Agrarian Tradition* (1930; rpt. Baton Rouge: Louisiana State University Press, 1977), 174.

11 Daniel Joseph Singal, *The War Within: From Victorian to Modernist Thought in the South, 1919–1945* (Chapel Hill: University of North Carolina Press, 1982), 232–60; Fred Hobson, *Tell about the South: The Southern Rage to Explain* (Baton Rouge: Louisiana State University Press, 1983), 204–5; Louis D. Rubin Jr., *The Writer in the South: Studies in a Literary Community* (Athens: University of Georgia Press, 1972), 91–93. Connelly and Bellows, *God and General Longstreet,* 137.

12 Lewis P. Simpson, "Southern Spiritual Nationalism: Notes on the Background of Modern Southern Fiction," in *The Cry of Home: Cultural Nationalism and the Modern Writer,* ed. H. Ernest Lewald (Knoxville: University of Tennessee Press, 1972), 190, 206.

13 Walker Percy, "Red, White and Blue-Gray," *Commonweal,* 22 December 1961, 338; Walter Lord, *The Past That Would Not Die* (New York: Pocket Books, 1967), 31, 63,

134, 137, 178; James W. Silver, *Mississippi: The Closed Society* (New York: Harcourt Brace and World, 1964), 5; Connelly and Bellows, *God and General Longstreet*, 117–19; Numan V. Bartley, *The Rise and Fall of Massive Resistance: Race and Politics in the South during the 1950s* (Baton Rouge: Louisiana State University Press, 1969), third illustration.

14 The University of Mississippi never officially adopted the Confederate battle flag as the school symbol, but its use was encouraged from 1948 on, especially after the home economics department there made the largest battle flag in the world in 1949.

15 William Faulkner, *Requiem for a Nun* (1951; rpt. New York: Vintage Books, 1975), 212; Connelly and Bellows, *God and General Longstreet*, 113–19.

16 Robert Penn Warren, *The Legacy of the Civil War: Meditations on the Centennial* (New York: Random House, 1961), 54, 57.

17 Percy, "Red, White and Blue-Gray," 338.

18 Walker Percy, *The Last Gentleman* (New York: Farrar, Straus, and Giroux, 1966), 236–37; J. O. Tate, "Civility, Civil Rights, and Civil Wars: Walker Percy's Centennial Novel," in *Perspectives on the American South*, ed. James C. Cobb and Charles R. Wilson, vol. 4 (New York: Gordon and Breach, 1985).

19 See Reed, *Southerners*, 86–87; Connelly and Bellows, *God and General Longstreet*, 137–48; Thomas L. Connelly, *Will Campbell and the Soul of the South* (New York: Continuum, 1982).

20 Reed, *Southerners*, 87–91.

21 Hill et al., *Religion in the Solid South*, 29; Lord, *Past That Would Not Die*, 77–78; Silver, *Mississippi*, 26–27.

22 Richard M. Weaver, "The South and the American Union," in *The Lasting South: Fourteen Southerners Look at Their Home*, ed. Louis D. Rubin Jr., and James J. Kilpatrick (Chicago: Henry Regnery, 1957), 64; Rubin, *Writer in the South*, 91–92.

23 Frank Lawrence Owsley, "The Irrepressible Conflict," in *I'll Take My Stand*, 66; John Shelton Reed, "For Dixieland: The Sectionalism of *I'll Take My Stand*," in *A Band of Prophets: The Vanderbilt Agrarians after Fifty Years*, ed. William C. Havard and Walter Sullivan (Baton Rouge: Louisiana State University Press, 1982), 46, 48, 54.

24 Reed, "For Dixieland," 57; Hobson, *Tell about the South*, 329, 333; Richard M. Weaver, *The Southern Tradition at Bay: A History of Postbellum Thought* (New Rochelle, N.Y.: Arlington House, 1968), 391.

25 Leslie W. Dunbar, "The Annealing of the South," *Virginia Quarterly Review* 37 (autumn 1961): 507; Morton Sosna, *In Search of the Silent South: Southern Liberals and the Race Issue* (New York: Columbia University Press, 1977), 201, 207; Charles L. Black Jr., "Paths to Desegregation," *New Republic*, 21 October 1957, 15.

26 Sosna, *In Search of the Silent South*, 173–74, 201, 197, 208–9. These liberals frequently had conversion experiences, born again into the belief in brotherhood. See Will D. Campbell, *Brother to a Dragonfly* (New York: Continuum, 1980), 98–99.

27 Richard H. King, "Stoking the Fires and Polishing the Pinnacles," in *Perspectives*

on the American South, ed. John Shelton Reed and Merle Black, (New York: Gordon and Breach, 1984), 2:61–72; Woodward, *Burden of Southern History,* 3–26, 187–212.

28 Martin Luther King Jr., *The Wisdom of Martin Luther King In His Own Words* (New York: Lancer Books, 1968), 41, 23, 64, 75; Martin Luther King Jr., *Why We Can't Wait* (New York: Harper and Row, 1963), 80.

29 King, *Why We Can't Wait,* 116; King, *Wisdom,* 77; *New York Times,* 28 August 1983, 16.

30 See John Shelton Reed, "Up from Segregation," *Virginia Quarterly Review* 60 (summer 1984): 378, 391–93; "The South Today: Carter Country and Beyond," *Time,* 27 September 1976.

31 James McBride Dabbs, *Who Speaks for the South?* (New York: Funk and Wagnalls, 1964), 343–44; Robert M. Randolph, "James McBride Dabbs: Spokesman for Racial Liberalism," in *From the Old South to the New: Essays on the Transitional South,* ed. Walter J. Fraser Jr. and Winfred B. Moore Jr. (Westport, Conn.: Greenwood Press, 1981), 254–56; Hobson, *Tell about the South,* 335–52; Charles P. Roland, *The Improbable Era: The South since World War II* (Lexington: University Press of Kentucky, 1976), 191.

32 Dabbs, *Who Speaks for the South?* 369, 371; Dabbs, *Haunted by God,* 40; Dabbs, "The Religion of a Countryman," *Forum* 91 (May 1934): 305–9; Dabbs, "The Land," in Rubin and Kilpatrick, eds. *Lasting South,* 79–80, 83.

33 Dabbs, *Who Speaks for the South?* 368; Dabbs, "The Land," 78; Dabbs, *The Southern Heritage* (New York: Alfred A. Knopf, 1958), 267–68.

34 Dabbs, *Who Speaks for the South?,* 371–73, 377.

35 F. Garvin Davenport Jr., *The Myth of Southern History: Historical Consciousness in Twentieth-Century Southern Literature* (Nashville: Vanderbilt University Press, 1967), 188; Dabbs, *Who Speaks for the South?,* 370; Warren, *Legacy of the Civil War,* 54–58.

36 Robert Penn Warren, *Democracy and Poetry* (Cambridge: Harvard University Press, 1975), 56; Howard Zinn, *The Southern Mystique* (New York: Alfred A. Knopf, 1964).

3. The Death of Bear Bryant

1 Ed Hinton, "Fifty-three Miles of Mourners Watch Bear Pass By," *Atlanta Journal-Constitution,* 29 January 1983, 4G.

2 Harold Kennedy, "Solemn, Silent, Sad: Campus Says Good-bye to Bryant," in The Birmingham News Staff, *Remembering Bear* (Indianapolis: News and Features Press, 1983), 80–82; "5,000 Attend Memorial for Bryant," *Memphis Commercial Appeal,* 28 January 1983, 2D.

3 Mike Fleming, "Thousands Gather to Pay Respects to Bryant," *Memphis Commercial Appeal,* 29 January 1983, 1D; "Players Will Be Closest to Bryant at Large Funeral," *Jackson Clarion-Ledger,* 28 January 1983, 1C; Rick Cleveland, "Thousands Pay Tribute to the 'Bear,'" *Jackson Clarion-Ledger,* 29 January 1983, 1A; Wen-

dell Rawls Jr., "Bryant Is Given a Hero's Farewell," *New York Times*, 29 January 1983, 16.

4 "Full Text of Sermon for Bryant Funeral," *Birmingham News*, 28 January 1983, 2A; Hinton, "Fifty-three Miles."

5 Rheta Grimsley Johnson, "Simple Tributes Speak Loudest for the Bear," *Memphis Commercial Appeal*, 29 January 1983, 1A; Tom McCollister, "Farmer Came into Town 'To See Bear Off,'" *Atlanta Journal-Constitution*, 29 January 1983, 4G.

6 Will Grimsley, "Millions Mourn Bryant," *Cleveland Plain Dealer*, 29 January 1983, 3C; Frank Sikora, "'This Man Was Loved by Many,'" *Birmingham News*, 29 January 1983, 1A; Mike Fleming, "Sports Figures Pay Homage to Bryant," *Memphis Commercial Appeal*, 29 January 1983, 3D; Allen Barra, "Dixie's Goal-Line Stand," *Village Voice*, 28 September 1982, 19; Frank Deford, "'I Do Love the Football,'" *Sports Illustrated*, 23 November 1981, 102.

7 Johnson, "Simple Tributes"; Hinton, "Fifty-three Miles"; "Hundreds of Thousands Come to Bid the Bear Farewell," *Jackson Clarion-Ledger*, 29 January 1983, 1C; Grimsley, "Millions Mourn Bryant," 3E.

8 Wendell Rawls Jr., "Bryant Doctor Tells of Lengthy Illness," *New York Times*, 28 January 1983, 23; Sikora, "'This Man Was Loved by Many,'" 1; Deford, "'I Do Love the Football,'" 107–8.

9 John McGrath, "Bear Buried amid Tide of Emotion," *Atlanta Journal-Constitution*, 29 January 1983, 1C.

10 A. C. Bancroft, ed., *The Life and Death of Jefferson Davis* (New York: J. S. Ogilvie, [1889]); "200,000 Pay Tribute to King," *Atlanta Journal-Constitution*, 10 April 1968, 1; and Albert Goldman, *Elvis* (New York, McGraw-Hill, 1981).

11 Grimsley, "Millions Mourn Bryant," 3E; "Hundreds of Thousands Come," *Jackson Clarion-Ledger;* "In Farewell to Bear: 'Thanks for His Influence on Young,'" *Birmingham News*, 28 January 1983, 1A, 10A.

12 McGrath, "Bear Buried amid Tide of Emotion," 1C, 5C; Sikora, "'This Man Was Loved by Many,'" 10A; Rheta Grimsley Johnson, "Stadium Crowd Came to Mourn," *Memphis Commercial Appeal*, 29 January 1983, 1D ("tailgate party" quote); "Birmingham's Modern Lawn-Park Cemetery," *Park and Cemetery*, 26 (March 1916): 17.

13 Tindall, *Ethnic Southerners*, 23; Patrick Gerster and Nicholas Cords, eds., *Myth and Southern History*, 2 vols. (Chicago: Rand McNally, 1974).

14 Cash, *Mind of the South*, 130; Clyde Bolton, "Bryant: A Winner's Journey," *Remembering Bear*, 9–10; Rick Cleveland, "Bryant Rose from Poverty to Greatness," *Jackson Clarion-Ledger*, 30 January 1983, 2; Bryant quote is in Richard Hoffer, "Bear Bryant Dies of Heart Attack," *Los Angeles Times*, 27 January 1983; Dave Anderson, "Time Out for the Bear," *New York Times*, 27 January 1983, 21.

15 William Faulkner, *The Hamlet* (1931, rpt. New York: Vintage, 1956), 9.

16 Thomas Rogers, "Bryant Recalled as Helpful Coach," *New York Times*, 27 Janu-

ary 1983, 20 (Paterno quote); "Mississippians Are Stunned, Shocked by Bryant's Death," and "What They Said about the Bear" in *Jackson Clarion-Ledger,* 27 January 1983, 3C; Al Dunning, "We've Lost More Than the Greatest Football Coach," *Memphis Commercial Appeal,* 27 January 1983, 1D; Mike Fleming, "Longtime Friends Shocked by Bryant's Death," *Memphis Commercial Appeal,* 27 January 1983, 1D; "The Talk of the Town," *New Yorker,* 14 February 1983, 36.

17 Johnson, "Simple Tributes" (Aliceville quote); George Vecsey, "The Bear Was 'Worn Out,'" *New York Times,* 28 January 1983, 23; Nina Goolsby, "Bear Buried Today," Oxford, Mississippi *Eagle,* 28 January 1983, 4; Rawls, "Hero's Farewell," 16.

18 David Davidson and Tom McCollister, "Bryant Was 'One Person Blessed by the Lord'" *Atlanta Journal-Constitution,* 29 January 1983, 5C ("greatest leader" quote); "Alabama's Bear Bryant Dies," *Jackson Clarion-Ledger,* 27 January 1983, 7A (Reagan quote); Tom McCollister, "Bear's 'Boys' Gather Together, Pay Bryant Their Last Respects," *Atlanta Journal-Constitution,* 29 January 1983, 4G (Dodo quote); Tom Barley, "Bear's Power Turned Boys into Winners," *Remembering Bear,* 44–47; Deford, "'I Do Love the Football,'" 100.

19 Billy Mitchell, "Man in Wheelchair Poignant Tribute to Bryant," *Tuscaloosa News,* 30 January 1983, 1A; Charles Land, "As the Memories Come Back, They Are of Fond Times," *Tuscaloosa News,* 30 January 1983, 3B; Alf Van Hoose, "Class Was Bryant's Magnificent Possession," *Remembering Bear,* 16; Deford, "'I Do Love the Football,'" 106; "Paul 'Bear' Bryant," *Jackson Clarion-Ledger,* 28 January 1983, 14A. For a discussion of the symbolism of the Confederate heroes, see Wilson, *Baptized in Blood,* chap. 2.

20 Herschel Nissenson, "He Could Have Coached 38 More, and It Wouldn't Have Been Too Much," *Remembering Bear,* 83; Cleveland, "Bryant Rose from Poverty," 2.

21 "Reflections on a Hero" (editorial), *Remembering Bear,* 91–92; "The Bear: His Life, His Legend," *Jackson Clarion-Ledger,* 30 January 1983, special section; "Remembering the Bear" (editorial), *Memphis Commercial Appeal,* 28 January 1983, 5; Grimsley, "Millions Mourn Bryant," 3E. The conclusions in this paragraph are based on a survey of the stories on the Bryant death in the following newspapers: the *Boston Globe,* the *Cleveland Plain Dealer,* the *Los Angeles Times,* the *New York Times,* the *Arkansas Gazette,* the *Memphis Commercial Appeal,* the *Jackson Clarion-Ledger,* and the *Birmingham News.* The "never beat Notre Dame" quote was from John Powers, "Bryant Towered over 'Bama,'" *Boston Globe,* 27 January 1983, 25.

22 Paul Borden, "Bama's Bear Belonged to All of Us," *Jackson Clarion-Ledger,* 30 January 1983, 3; Bill Crowe, "A Genuine Southern Hero," *Remembering Bear,* 28. See also Howell Raines, "Good-bye to the Bear," *New Republic,* 24 January 1983, 10–11.

23 Bill Crowe, "A Genuine Southern Hero" (Pepe quote), 28; Raad Cawthon, "Saying Good-bye to the Legendary Bear Is No Easy Task," *Jackson Clarion-Ledger,* 30 January 1983, 8; Vecsey, "Bear Was 'Worn Out'" 23; Joseph Dorso, "Bear Bryant Dies, Coached Most Victories," *New York Times,* 27 January 1983, 41.

24 Woodward, *Burden of Southern History*, 23.

25 See John Shelton Reed's essay, "Grits and Gravy: The South's New Middle Class," *One South* (Baton Rouge: Louisiana State University Press, 1982), 119–28.

26 For a recent discussion of football in the South, stressing its importance in race relations, see Willie Morris, *The Courting of Marcus Dupree* (Garden City, N.Y.: Doubleday, 1983).

4. William Faulkner and the Southern Religious Culture

1 H. L. Mencken, "The Sahara of the Bozart," in *Prejudices: Second Series* (New York: Alfred A. Knopf, 1920), 136–37; Mencken, editorial, *American Mercury* 7 (January 1926), 32.

2 Malcolm Cowley, introduction to *The Portable Faulkner* (New York: Viking Press, 1940); Irving Howe, *William Faulkner: A Critical Study* (Chicago: University of Chicago Press, 1951); George Marion O'Donnell, "Faulkner's Mythology," in *William Faulkner: Three Decades of Criticism,* ed. Frederick J. Hoffman and Olga W. Vickery (New York: Harcourt, Brace, and World, 1963); J. Robert Barth, ed., *Religious Perspectives in Faulkner's Fiction* (Notre Dame: Notre Dame University Press, 1972); John W. Hunt, *William Faulkner: Art in Theological Tension* (New York: Haskell House, 1973).

3 Mary Dell Fletcher, "William Faulkner and Residual Calvinism," *Southern Studies* 18 (summer 1979): 199–216; Robert L. Johnson, "William Faulkner, Calvinism, and the Presbyterians," *Journal of Presbyterian History* 57 (spring 1979): 66–81; William H. Nolte, "Mencken, Faulkner, and Southern Moralism," *South Carolina Review* 4 (December 1971): 45–61; Alwyn Berland, *"Light in August:* The Calvinism of William Faulkner," *Modern Fiction Studies* 8 (summer 1962): 159–70; Harold J. Douglas and Robert Daniel, "Faulkner and the Puritanism of the South," *Tennessee Studies in Literature* 2 (1957): 1–13; Ilse Dusoir Lind, "The Calvinistic Burden of *Light in August,*" *New England Quarterly* 30 (September 1957): 307–29.

4 Edith Hamilton, "Faulkner – Sorcerer or Slave?" *Saturday Review,* 12 July 1952, 10.

5 See Hill, *Southern Churches in Crisis,* 14; Hill et al., eds., *Religion and the Solid South;* Boles, *Great Revival 1787–1805;* Johnson, "Faulkner, Calvinism, and the Presbyterians." For analysis of church membership figures in Mississippi, see Harold F. Kaufman, "Mississippi Churches: A Half Century of Change," *Mississippi Quarterly* 14 (summer 1961): 138–47.

6 William Faulkner, *The Town,* 306–7, 452; Hill, *Southern Churches in Crisis,* 18.

7 Hill, *Southern Churches in Crisis,* 14.

8 Donald G. Mathews, "Evangelicalism," in *Encyclopedia of Religion in the South,* 243–44; Hill, *Southern Churches in Crisis,* 25.

9 William Faulkner, *Soldiers' Pay* (New York: Boni and Liveright, 1926), 261; Robert L. Johnson, "William Faulkner," in *Encyclopedia of Religion in the South,* 250–52.

10 Frederick L. Gwynn and Joseph L. Blotner, eds. *Faulkner in the University: Class Conferences at the University of Virginia, 1957–58* (Charlottesville: University Press of Virginia, 1959), 41. See also Joseph Blotner, *Faulkner: A Biography* (New York: Random House, 1974), 1:88; Malcolm Cowley, ed., *Writers at Work: The Paris Review Interviews* (New York: Viking Press, 1958), 136. I have profited from a fine study of Samuel Clemens's ambivalent relationship to southern Evangelicalism: Lloyd A. Hunter, "Mark Twain and the Southern Evangelical Mind," *Bulletin of the Missouri Historical Society* 33 (July 1977): 246–64.

11 James J. Thompson Jr., "Erskine Caldwell and Southern Religion," *Southern Humanities Review* 5 (winter 1971): 33–44; Louis D. Rubin Jr., "Flannery O'Connor and the Bible Belt," in *The Curious Death of the Novel: Essays in American Literature* (Baton Rouge: Louisiana State University Press, 1967); Robert H. Brinkmeyer Jr., "A Closer Walk with Thee: Flannery O'Connor and Southern Fundamentalists," *Southern Literary Journal* 18 (spring 1986): 3–13.

12 William Faulkner, *Mosquitoes* (New York: Liveright, 1927), 11; Faulkner, *Absalom, Absalom!* (New York: Vintage Books, 1972), 109; Faulkner, "Golden Land," in *Collected Stories* (New York: Vintage Books, 1977), 704. See also Walter Taylor, *Faulkner's Search for a South* (Urbana: University of Illinois Press, 1983), 52–64; William Van O'Connor, *The Tangled Fire of William Faulkner* (New York: Gordian Press, 1968), 72–87.

13 William Faulkner, *Requiem for a Nun,* 89; Faulkner, *Sartoris* (New York: New American Library, 1964), 25.

14 William Faulkner, *Absalom, Absalom!* 82; Faulkner, *Soldiers' Pay,* 278; Faulkner, *Mosquitoes,* 36.

15 Robert N. Burrows, "Institutional Christianity as Reflected in the Works of William Faulkner," *Mississippi Quarterly* 14 (summer 1961): 139.

16 William Faulkner, *Light in August* (New York: Vintage Books, 1972), 461, 347; Gwynn and Blotner, *Faulkner and the University,* 189.

17 Robert N. Bellah, "Civil Religion in America," *Daedalus* 96 (winter 1967): 1–21; Hill et al., *Religion and the Solid South,* 24–56.

18 Wilson, *Baptized in Blood.*

19 Faulkner, *Light in August,* 42, 300, 452.

20 Ibid., 56, 80, 57, 69.

21 Ibid., 69, 361, 357, 325.

22 See David M. Potter, *The South and the Sectional Conflict* (Baton Rouge: Louisiana State University Press, 1968); John C. Messenger, "Folk Religion," in *Folklore and Folklife: An Introduction,* ed. Richard M. Dorson (Chicago: University of Chicago Press, 1972), 217–32; Don Yoder, "Official Religion versus Folk Religion," *Pennsylvania Folklife* 15 (winter 1965–66): 36–52; Bruce A. Rosenberg, *Can These Bones Live? The Art of the American Folk Preacher* (Urbana: University of Illinois Press, 1988).

23 William Faulkner, "Shingles for the Lord," in *Collected Stories,* 27–43.

24 William Faulkner, *As I Lay Dying* (New York: Vintage Books, 1929), 7; Alan Dundes, "Folk Ideas as Units of World View," *Journal of American Folklore* 84 (January–March, 1971): 93–103.

25 Faulkner, *As I Lay Dying,* 67–68, 8.

26 Ibid., 23, 32, 8.

27 Ibid., 37, 49, 81, 104, 105.

28 See William H. Wiggins Jr., "The Black Folk Church," in Richard M. Dorson, ed., *Handbook of American Folklore* (Bloomington: Indiana University Press, 1983); Newbell N. Puckett, *Folk Beliefs of the Southern Negro* (Chapel Hill: University of North Carolina Press, 1926).

29 William Faulkner, *The Sound and the Fury* (New York: Vintage Books, 1956), 362–64.

30 Ibid., 370–71. See also Cleanth Brooks, *William Faulkner: The Yoknapatawpha County* (New Haven: Yale University Press, 1963), 345.

31 Gwynn and Blotner, *Faulkner in the University,* 190.

32 Roger M. Williams, *Sing a Sad Song: The Life of Hank Williams* (Urbana: University of Illinois Press, 1980), 195.

5. Southern Religion and Visionary Art

1 For discussion of the idea of a southern religious culture, see Boles, *Great Revival, 1787–1805;* Charles Reagan Wilson, "William Faulkner and the Southern Religious Tradition," in *Faulkner and Religion,* ed. Doreen Fowler and Ann Abadie (Jackson: University Press of Mississsippi, 1991). A good brief discussion of evangelical religion is Donald G. Mathews, "Evangelicalism," in *Encyclopedia of Religion in the South,* 243–44; see also Donald W. Dayton and Robert K. Johnston, eds., *The Variety of American Evangelicalism* (Knoxville: University of Tennessee Press, 1991).

2 John B. Boles, "The Discovery of Southern Religious History," in *Interpreting Southern History: Historiographical Essays in Honor of Sanford W. Higginbotham,* ed. John B. Boles and Evelyn Thomas Nolen (Baton Rouge: Louisiana State University Press, 1987).

3 Lisa McGaughey Tuttle, "Revelations: Visionary Content in the Work of Southern Self-Trained Artists," *Art Papers* 110 (November–December 1986): 35–38. For African dimensions of southern visionary art, see Robert Farris Thompson, *Flash of the Spirit: African and Afro-American Art and Philosophy* (New York: Random House, 1983); and Judy McWillie, "Another Face of the Diamond: Black Traditional Art from the Deep South," *Clarion* 12 (fall 1987): 42–53.

4 Hill, *Southern Churches in Crisis,* 97.

5 Hill, *Encyclopedia of Religion,* 645.

6 For the role of the Bible in another expressive form of southern culture, see

Charles Wolfe, "Bible Country: The Good Book in Country Music," in *The Bible and Popular Culture in America,* ed. Allene Stuart Phy (Philadelphia: Fortress Press, 1985).

7 A good beginning place for thinking about religious outsiders in the South is Harrell, *Varieties of Southern Evangelicalism.*

8 For a brief introduction to the Pentecostal faith see Edith L. Blumhofer, "Pentecostalism," in *Encyclopedia of Southern Culture,* 1296–97.

9 See James H. Moorhead, "Millennialism," in *Encyclopedia of Religion,* 277–79.

10 Milton G. Sernett, "Black Religion and the Question of Evangelical Identity," in Dayton and Johnston, *Variety of American Evangelicalism,* 135–47. See also Lincoln and Mamiya, *Black Church.*

11 For a careful study placing visionary artists in a southern context, see Joyce Ann Miller, "In the Handiwork of Their Craft Is Their Prayer: African-American Religious Folk Art in the Twentieth-Century South" (master's thesis, University of Mississippi, southern studies program, 1992).

6. Digging Up Bones

1 Philippe Ariès, *The Hour of Our Death* (New York: Alfred A. Knopf, 1981), 596–601. See also Jessica Mitford, *The American Way of Death* (New York: Fawcett, 1963); James J. Farrell, *Inventing the American Way of Death, 1830–1920* (Philadelphia: Temple University Press, 1980), 3–15, 213–24; and David E. Stannard, ed., *Death in America* (Philadelphia: University of Pennsylvania Press, 1975).

2 John C. Thrush and George S. Paulus, "The Concept of Death in Popular Music: A Social Psychological Perspective," *Popular Music and Society* 6, no. 3 (1979): 219–27.

3 For studies suggesting the southern nature of country music, see James C. Cobb, "From Muskogee to Luckenbach: Country Music and the Southernization of America," *Journal of Popular Culture* 16 (winter 1982): 81–91; Peter V. Marsden, John Shelton Reed, Michael D. Kennedy, and Kandi M. Stenson, "American Regional Culture and Differences in Leisure Time Activities," *Social Forces* 60 (June 1982): 1044; Richard A. Peterson, "The Fertile Crescent of Country Music," *Journal of Country Music* 6 (spring 1975): 19–25; Stephen S. Smith, "Sounds of the South: A Rhetorical Saga of Country Music Lyrics," *Southern Speech Communication Journal* 45 (winter 1980): 164–72; George O. Carney, "Country Music and the South: A Cultural Geography Perspective," *Journal of Cultural Geography* 1 (fall/winter 1980): 16–33; George O. Carney, "T for Texas, T for Tennessee: The Origins of American Country Music Notables," *Journal of Geography* 78 (November 1979): 218–25; George O. Carney, "From Down Home to Uptown: The Diffusion of Country-Music Radio Stations in the United States," *Journal of Geography* 76 (March 1977): 104–10.

4 Charles R. Wilson, "The Southern Funeral Director: Managing Death in the New South," *Georgia Historical Quarterly* 67 (spring 1983): 49–69; Farrell, *Inventing the American Way of Death*, 146–83; Christopher Crocker, "The Southern Way of Death," in J. Kenneth Morland, ed., *The Not So Solid South: Anthropological Studies in a Regional Subculture* (Athens: University of Georgia Press, 1971), 114–29.

5 "Can the Circle Be Unbroken?" was recorded by the Carter Family on May 6, 1935. The lyrics appear in Dorothy Horstman, ed., *Sing Your Heart Out, Country Boy* (New York: Dutton, 1975), 37–38. See also Bill C. Malone, *Country Music, U.S.A.,* (Austin: University of Texas Press, 1985), 67. Robert Cantwell develops the importance of death to modern bluegrass music in "Believing in Bluegrass," *Atlantic Monthly,* March 1972, 58–59.

6 "Oh Death" was recorded by Dock Boggs on *Dock Boggs,* Folkways FA 2351.

7 "The Ballad of Finley Preston" was recorded by Clint Howard, Fred Price, and their sons on *The Ballad of Finley Preston,* Rounder 0009.

8 "The Ballad of Forty Dollars" was written and recorded by Tom T. Hall, copyright 1968, Newkeys Music, Inc. Lyrics are printed in *The Songs of Nashville: The 100 Greatest Country and Western Songs Ever Recorded* (New York: Chappell, [1975]), 8.

9 Nolan Porterfield, *Jimmie Rodgers: The Life and Times of America's Blue Yodeler* (Urbana: University of Illinois Press, 1979), 216, 266–68, 278–80, 315, 332–34.

10 Williams, *Sing a Sad Song,* 42–43, 74–75, 128, 220.

11 Cash, *Mind of the South,* 127.

12 "Wreck on the Highway," copyright 1946, Acuff-Rose Publications. Lyrics are in Horstman, 89. See Malone, *Country Music, U.S.A.,* 132.

13 Connelly, *Will Campbell and the Soul of the South,* 109; "I Just Can't Stand to Say Goodbye," written and recorded by Willie Nelson, on *Willie Nelson Live,* RCA APLI-1487; "Cold Hard Facts of Life," recorded by Porter Wagoner, RCA 9067; "Blood Red and Going Down," recorded by Tanya Tucker, *Tanya Tucker's Greatest Hits,* Columbia, 1972.

14 "Ruby, Don't Take Your Love to Town" was written by Mel Tillis, BMI, and featured on *Kenny Rogers's Twenty Greatest Hits,* Liberty Records, 1983.

15 Malone, *Country Music, U.S.A.,* 18; George Jones, "He Stopped Loving Her Today," Epic ETX 38323 (the song was written by Bobby Braddock and Curly Putnam).

16 Ruth A. Banes, "From Wolverton Mountain to Wooley Swamp: Gothic Elements in Country Music," *Canadian Journal of American Studies.* "Would You Lay with Me (In a Field of Stone)" was featured on *Tanya Tucker's Greatest Hits,* Columbia, 1972.

17 "Lonely Mound of Clay" and "Precious Jewel" appear on Acuff's *Wabash Cannonball,* Pickwick JS-6162.

18 "Before Jessie Died" was written and recorded by Tom T. Hall on the album *Natural Dreams,* Mercury 822-425-1.

19 Malone, *Country Music, U.S.A.,* 67; Martha Hume, *You're So Cold I'm Turning Blue* (New York: Penguin, 1982), 94–96.

20 "Our Baby's Book," copyright 1941, Noma Music, Inc. "Put My Little Shoes Away" was written by Samuel Mitchell and Charles E. Pratt in 1873. "Don't Make Me Go to Bed and I'll Be Good," copyright 1943, Peer International Corporation, was recorded by Roy Acuff. The lyrics of these songs appear in Horstman, *Sing Your Heart Out, Country Boy,* 80–81, 82–83, and 74–75.

21 "A Drunkard's Child," copyright 1930, Peer International Corporation. "Mommy, Please Stay Home with Me" was written by Wally Fowler, Eddy Arnold, and J. Graydon Hall, copyright 1933, M&M Cole/ABC Paramount.

22 "Mother Left Me Her Bible" and "The Village Churchyard" appear on the Stanley Brothers's *16 Greatest Gospel Hits,* Gusto GT-0016; "Dear Brother" was written by Hank Williams and appears on *I Saw the Light,* Polygram SE 3331.

23 "Grandma Harp" was written and recorded by Merle Haggard. Lyrics appear in *The Songs of Nashville,* 68.

24 Thrush and Paulus, "Concept of Death in Popular Music," 223–24.

25 Horstman, *Sing Your Heart Out, Country Boy,* 67–68.

26 "When Jimmie Rodgers Said Good-bye" was written by Dwight Butcher and Lou Herscher, copyright 1933, Jerty Vogel Music. "The Death of Hank Williams," copyright 1953, Fon Knox Music Co. The lyrics of these songs appear in Horstman, *Sing Your Heart Out, Country Boy,* 87, 71–72.

27 Ellis Nassour, *Patsy Cline: An Intimate Biography* (New York: Tower Books, 1981), 378–79; "I Dreamed of a Hillbilly Heaven" was written by Hal Southern and Eddie Dean, copyright 1960, Singletree Music Co.

28 "The Death of Floyd Collins," copyright 1925, P. C. Brockman, Atlanta. The lyrics to this appear in Horstman, *Sing Your Heart Out, Country Boy,* 70–71.

29 "The Year That Clayton Delaney Died" was written and recorded by Tom T. Hall. Lyrics of this song appear in *The Songs of Nashville,* 292–93. Reed, *Enduring South,* 35.

30 Hill, *Southern Churches in Crisis,* 73–88, 123–24.

31 Malone, *Country Music, U.S.A.,* 16–18; Horstman, *Sing Your Heart Out, Country Boy,* 31–35.

32 Fred Edwards, Jim Marshall, Charlie Hayward, Tom Crain, and Taz DiGregorio, "The Legend of the Wooley Swamp" and Jim Marshall, Fred Edwards, Tom Crain, Taz DiGregorio, Charlie Hayward, Charlie Daniels, "The Devil Went Down to Georgia," both featured on *The Charlie Daniels Band: A Decade of Hits,* Epic 50706, 1983.

33 Thrush and Paulus, "Concept of Death in Popular Music," 224–27.

7. The South's Torturous Search for the Good Books

1 Berkeley is quoted in John R. Stilgoe, *Common Landscape of America, 1580 to 1845* (New Haven: Yale University Press, 1982), 242. The following works were espe-

cially useful in preparation of this chapter: David D. Hall and John B. Hench, eds., *Needs and Opportunities in the History of the Book: America, 1639–1876* (Worcester, Mass.: American Antiquarian Society, 1987); the annual James Russell Wiggins Lectures in the History of the Book in American Culture, particularly Robert A. Gross, *Printing, Politics, and the People* (Worcester, Mass.: American Antiquarian Society, 1989); and J. Wayne Flynt, *Ban, Burn, and Ignore: Writing and Publishing Books in the South* (Tuscaloosa: University of Alabama Press, 1989).

2 Clement Eaton, *The Mind of the Old South,* 2d ed. (Baton Rouge: Louisiana State University Press, 1967), 264.

3 Fred Arthur Bailey, "Textbooks of the 'Lost Cause,'" *Georgia Historical Quarterly* 75 (fall 1991), 507–33.

4 Gaines Foster, *Ghosts of the Confederacy: Defeat, the Lost Cause, and the Emergence of the New South, 1865 to 1913* (New York: Oxford University Press, 1987), 185; Avery Craven, *The Growth of Southern Nationalism, 1848–1861* (Baton Rouge: Louisiana State University Press and the Littlefield Fund for Southern History of the University of Texas, 1953), 255–58; J. W. Morgan, "Our School Books," *DeBow's Review* 28 (April 1860): 434–40.

5 Ray Ginger, *Six Days or Forever? Tennessee v. John Thomas Scopes* (Boston: Beacon Press, 1958), 15.

6 Ibid., 17.

7 "Talmadge Threatens Book Burning," *Publishers Weekly,* 16 August 1941, 460.

8 Allen Tate, "A Southern Mode of the Imagination," in *Essays of Four Decades,* 584; Waldo W. Braden, "Conversation," in *Encyclopedia of Southern Culture,* 621; Ellen Glasgow, *The Woman Within* (New York: Harcourt, Brace, 1954), 152.

9 Grady McWhiney, *Cracker Culture: Celtic Ways in the Old South* (Tuscaloosa: University of Alabama Press, 1988), 212.

10 William Alexander Percy, *Lanterns on the Levee: Recollections of a Planter's Son* (1941; rpt. Baton Rouge: Louisiana State University Press, 1973), 126, 130.

11 McWhiney, *Cracker Culture,* 206.

12 Ronald L. Numbers and Janet S. Numbers, "Science in the Old South," in *Science and Medicine in the Old South,* ed. Ronald L. Numbers and Todd L. Savitt (Baton Rouge: Louisiana State University Press, 1989), 26 (Table 9).

13 Robert M. Willingham Jr., "Libraries," and Carol Johnston, "Publishing," in Wilson and Ferris, *Encyclopedia of Southern Culture,* 25–57, 864–67; John Ezell, *The South since 1865,* 2d ed. (Norman: University of Oklahoma Press, 1975), 306.

14 Donald Davidson, "A Mirror for Artists," in Twelve Southerners, *I'll Take My Stand,* 33, 40.

15 Harry Crews, *A Childhood: The Biography of a Place* (New York: Harper and Row, 1978), 53–54.

16 Zora Neale Hurston, *Dust Tracks on a Road: An Autobiography* (Urbana: University of Illinois Press, 1985), 135–36.

17 Flannery O'Connor, *Mystery and Manners,* 209.

18 Virginia Spencer Carr, *The Lonely Hunter: A Biography of Carson McCullers* (Garden City, N.Y.: Doubleday, 1975), 32.

19 Richard Wright, *Black Boy* (New York: Harper, 1937), 271–73.

20 Will D. Campbell, *Brother to a Dragonfly,* 97–98.

21 Eudora Welty, *One Writer's Beginnings* (Cambridge: Harvard University Press, 1984), 5.

8. The Iconography of Elvis

1 Jane and Michael Stern, *Elvis World* (New York: Alfred A. Knopf, 1987), 118.

2 Ibid.; Linda Ray Pratt, "Elvis, or the Ironies of a Southern Identity," in *The Elvis Reader,* ed. Kevin Quain (New York: St. Martin's Press, 1992), 93–103.

3 Peter Guralnick, *Lost Highway* (Boston: David R. Godine, 1979), 120–21; Vester Presley, as told to Deda Bonura, *A Presley Speaks* (Memphis: Wimmer Brothers Books, 1978), 117; Cheryl Thurber, "Elvis and Gospel Music," *Rejoice* 1 (summer 1988): 6. See also Dannal Perry, "From the King of Rock and Roll to the King of Kings: Elvis Presley and Religion," unpublished paper, University of Mississippi, southern studies program.

4 Victor W. Turner, *The Ritual Process: Structure and Anti-Structure* (Chicago: Aldine, 1970), 94–129.

5 Vernon Chadwick, "Camp Elvis: Totem and Taboo, Hawaiian Styles," *Southern Reader* 3 (September–October 1991): 1, 2, 24–25.

6 Peter Guralnick, *Last Train to Memphis: The Rise of Elvis Presley* (Boston: Little, Brown, 1994), 137; *Life,* 27 August 1956, 108–9; Elaine Dundy, *Elvis and Gladys* (New York: Macmillan, 1985), 258–59.

7 Wayne Elzey, "Liminality and Symbiosis in Popular American Protestantism," *Journal of the American Academy of Religion* 43 (December 1975): 741–56.

8 Connelly and Bellows, *God and General Longstreet,* 147–48.

9 Greil Marcus, *Dead Elvis: A Chronicle of a Cultural Obsession* (New York: Doubleday, 1991).

10. The Cult of Beauty

1 Frank Deford, *There She Is: The Life and Times of Miss America* (New York: Viking Press, 1971), 23, 31, 80–82.

2 Winthrop D. Jordan, *White over Black: American Attitudes toward the Negro, 1550–1812* (Chapel Hill: University of North Carolina Press, 1968), 9, 458–59, 464, 490.

3 Cash, *Mind of the South,* 116; Anne Firor Scott, *The Southern Lady* (Chicago: University of Chicago Press, 1970), 4; Anne Goodwyn Jones, *Tomorrow Is Another Day:*

The Woman Writer in the South, 1859–1936 (Baton Rouge: Louisiana State University Press, 1981), 41–42.

4 Cash, *Mind of the South,* 86; Carl Carmer, *Stars Fell on Alabama* (New York: Farrar and Rinehart, 1934), 15.

5 Victoria O'Donnell, "The Southern Woman as Time-Binder on Film," *The South and Film,* ed. Warren French (Jackson: University Press of Mississippi, 1981).

6 Marvin Harris, "The Human Strategies: The Rites of Summer," *Natural History* 82 (August–September 1973): 20–22.

7 Francis Butler Simkins and Charles Pierce Roland, *A History of the South,* 4th ed. (New York: Alfred A. Knopf, 1972), 383.

8 John Dollard, *Caste and Class in a Southern Town* (1937; rpt. New York: Doubleday, Anchor Books, 1949), 69; Paul Oliver, *Blues Fell This Morning: The Meaning of the Blues* (New York: Horizon Press, 1961). See also Lawrence W. Levine, *Black Culture and Black Consciousness: Afro-American Folk Thought from Slavery to Freedom* (New York: Oxford University Press, 1977), 289–93; Toni Morrison, *The Bluest Eye* (New York: Holt, Rinehart and Winston, 1970); "Cosmetology," in *Encyclopedia of Black America,* ed. W. Augustus Low and Virgil A. Clift (New York: McGraw-Hill, 1981), 289–90.

9 "Campus Queens at Black Colleges," *Ebony,* May 1983, 41–42; Deford, *There She Is,* 249–54.

10 Lois W. Banner, *American Beauty* (Chicago: University of Chicago Press, 1984), 255.

11 Ibid., 265; Deford, *There She Is,* 108.

12 "A Controversial Spectator Sport," *Newsweek,* 17 September 1984, 58.

13 Deford, *There She Is,* 80–81.

14 Alan Huffman, "It's Home Sweet Homecoming for Meridian Native Susan Akin," *Jackson Clarion-Ledger,* 20 October 1985, 3B.

15 "Back to Apple Pie," *Memphis Commercial Appeal,* 15 September 1986, 1A, 10A; "Miss America Losers Ponder Question: Who's the Fairest of Them All?" *Jackson Clarion-Ledger,* 17 September 1986, 1A.

16 *Jackson Clarion-Ledger,* 15 October 1986, 1C; Lisa DePaulo, "The 10 Biggest Myths about the Miss American Pageant," *TV Guide,* 6 September 1986, 3–7; Deford, *There She Is;* "A Controversial Spectator Sport," 57.

17 DePaulo, "The 10 Biggest Myths," 7; "A Controversial Spectator Sport," 56.

18 Samuel S. Hill, "Toward a Charter for a Southern Theology," in *Religion and the Solid South,* 205–7.

19 Cheryl Prewitt, *A Bright-Shining Place* (Garden City, N.Y.: Doubleday, 1981), 5–6.

Afterword

1 Elzey, "Liminality and Symbiosis in Popular American Protestantism."

2 David Treadwell, "King Elvis Still Reigns in Southern Lore," *Los Angeles Times,* 10 August 1987, 1, 3.

Index

Civil religion (*continued*)
Bryant as symbol, 39; in William
Faulkner, 65–67; Elvis Presley as symbol,
138; in beauty culture, 145, 156
Civil rights movement, 12, 35, 42, 113, 159;
and James McBride Dabbs, 33; and Will
Campbell, 124; and black pride, 149,
161–63
Civil War, 160, 162–63; and religion, 5;
post–, 6, 95; southern defeat in, 17, 19, 33,
50, 56; as Lost Cause, 20–29 passim, 47,
65, 113; pre–, 58, 112–13, 123, 165;
destruction in, 118–19
Civil War centennial, 26
Clemens, Samuel, 60, 61
Clement, Frank, 3–4
Cleveland, Rick, 47
Cline, Patsy, 106
Coca-Cola, xvi
Coe, David Allen, 102, 105
College of William and Mary, library of, 118
Colonial era, 32, 150; religion in, 4, 57; book
culture in, 111
Compton, Kamala, 154
Confederacy, xv, 35, 42, 45, 47; and religion,
xx; as Lost Cause, 5, 19–28 passim, 113–14,
160–62; in Faulkner, 63, 65, 66, 70; and
African Americans, 70
Confederate battle flag, 26–28, 48, 49, 155;
and Elvis Presley, xvi, 138; and the Lost
Cause, 20; and Allen Tate, 23; and the Ku
Klux Klan, 25; and African Americans,
160–63 passim
Confederate memorial day, 20, 21, 65
Confederate monuments, 20, 22, 160
Confederate nationalism, 112
Confederate veterans, 20, 51, 65
Congregationalists, 8
Connelly, Thomas L., 101
Copas, Cowboy, 106
Country music, xvii, xx, 28, 94–109 passim
Cowley, Malcolm, 56
Crews, Harry, 121
Criswell, W. A., xxi, 139–42
Crockett, Davy, 44
Cross, Hugh, 103
Crowe, Bill, 49
Cuthbert, Marion, 116

Dabbs, James McBride, xv, xvi, 32–35, 178

Dallas First Baptist Church, xxi, 14, 139–43
Dallas Life Foundation, 141
Daniels, Charlie, 28
Darrel, Johnny, 101
Darrow, Clarence, 115
Davenport, F. Garvin, 34
Davidson, Donald, 119
Davis, Jefferson, 114; and the Lost Cause,
19–20, 160; and Allen Tate, 23; funeral of,
42
Davis, Jimmy, 27
Davis, Joseph, 119
Dean, James, 131
Death: Bear Bryant funeral, 37–51 passim;
and country music, 94–109 passim; and
cemeteries, 170
Deford, Frank, 145
Democratic National Convention of 1956,
3–4
Dennison, Jo-Carrol, 150
Diamond, Neil, 108
"Dixie" (song), 20, 25, 26, 28, 138
Dixon, Dorsey, 100
Dodd, Bobby, 46
Dollard, John, 149
Douglass, Frederick, 118
Dukes of Hazzard, 27
Dunbar, Leslie W., 30
Dundes, Alan, 69

Eighmy, John Lee, 4
Electronic church, 16, 175
Elmore, Joe, 40
Episcopalians, 8; in the South, 20; in
Faulkner, 58–60, 63
Evangelicalism: and southern
distinctiveness, 5–6, 8, 29, 58; and biracial
South, 30–31; modern, 39, 75–76, 140; and
southern culture, 59–60, 73–74, 107
Evans, Minnie, 80, 82

Falwell, Jerry, 16
Family, 102–4
Farmers, 44, 120–21
Farmers' Alliance, 12–13
Fast, Howard, 124
Faubus, Orval, 27
Faulkner, William, xvi, xx, 55–72 passim,
102, 111, 133; and the Lost Cause, 26; and
religion, 74. Works: *Requiem for a Nun*, 26;

Patton, George, 54
Paulus, George S., 95, 100, 107, 108
Pentecostalism, xx, 6, 59, 61, 75, 82;
emergence of, 8, 79; and visionary art, 80;
and premillenialism, 81; and Elvis Presley,
133–36 passim; and asceticism, 151; and
Cheryl Prewitt, 157; and African
Americans, 165
Pepe, Phil, 49
Percy, Walker, 25–27
Percy, William Alexander, 117
Periodicals, 121
Perkins, Benjamin, 78
Perkins, Ray, 41
Pierce, Elijah, 80, 83
Pink shirts, 136
Place, sense of, 106–7
Politics and religion, 4
Popular culture, 28
Popular religion: defined, xvi, 175; and civil
religion, xvii; and official religion, xvii;
and folk religion, xviii; and
modernization, 175–78
Populism, 12
Porterfield, Nolan, 98
Potter, David, 67, 177
Preachers, 64
Presbyterian Church in the United States, 5, 7
Presbyterians, 32, 79, 81; predominance in
the South, xvii, 5, 8, 75; and the Lost
Cause, 20; in Faulkner, 58; and Calvinism,
60
Presley, Elvis, xvi–xvii, xxi, 178; death of,
37, 40, 42, 106, 132, 138; religious
influences on, 74; iconography of, 79, 85,
129–38; as liminal figure, 135–38, 177
Presley, Gladys, 133
Preston, Finley, 97
Prewitt, Cheryl, 156–58
Prewitt, Hosea Amos, 156, 157
PTL Club, 151
Public religion. See Civil religion
Publishing, 111–12
Puritanism, 57, 141, 150

Rankin, Tom, xxi, 164–73 passim
Reagan, Ronald, 46
Reconstruction, 6, 20, 66, 124, 160
Reed, John Shelton, 28, 29–30, 50, 107
Rehobeth Beach, Del., 150

Religion, official, xvii, 64–65. See also Civil
religion; Folk religion; Popular religion
Republicans, 3
Riley, Franklin, 114
Ripley, Miss., 61
Roberts, Oral, xvi, 16
Robertson, James, 16
Robertson, Pat, 16
Robinson, Eddie, 40–41
Rock music, xvii, 100, 105; and Elvis Presley,
129
Rodgers, Jimmie, 98, 100, 105
Rogers, Kenny, 101
Roland, Charles Pierce, 148
Roman Catholicism. See Catholicism
Rubin, Louis D., Jr., 29
Rucker, James, 151
Ruffin, Edmund, 119
Russell, John, 112
Ryan, Tom, 151

Sacred Harp singing, 56
Sayers, Roger, 39
Scarlett O'Hara, 146
Scopes trial, 23, 61, 115
Scott, Anne Firor, 146
Scott, Sir Walter, 119
Sears Roebuck catalog, 80, 121
Sectarians, 6, 79
Selma, Ala., 25, 36
Sentimentalism, 46–47, 100, 103
Sexuality, 146–48
Sharecropping, 6, 44, 50, 121, 133
Shealy, Steadman, 39
Silver, James, 113
Simkins, Francis Butler, 148
Simms, William Gilmore, 112, 113, 119
Simpson, Lewis P., 24
Simpson, O. J., 142
Slavery, 160; and churches, 5–6, 165; and
African-American religion, 70; and
books, 117–18, 122
Smith, Don, 154
Social class, 12–13
Socialism, 13
Sons of Confederate Veterans, 20
Southern Baptist Alliance, 16
Southern Baptist Convention, 9, 11, 13, 58;
founding of, 5; and Fundamentalism, 7,
16, 139, 142

Southern identity, 13–14; post–Civil War, 19; crisis of, 23; and Agrarians, 29; and Elvis Presley, 132–33; and civil rights movement, 159–63

Southern Literary Renaissance, 17, 22, 116, 120, 125

Southern Poverty Law Center, 161

Southern Regional Council, 30, 32

Southern religious studies, 74–75

Southwestern humorists, 61

Spain, Irene, 106

Sports, 116–17. *See also* Football

Stanley Brothers, 104

"Star-Spangled Banner" (song), 25

Stern, Jane, 133

Stern, Michael, 133

Stratton, John Roach, 115

Stuckey's, 135

Sun Record Studio, 132

Supernaturalism, xvii–xviii, 108, 175–76

Swaggart, Jimmy Lee, 16

Swan, Jimmy, 105

Talmadge, Governor Eugene, 115–16

Tate, Allen, 22, 23–24, 116

Teaff, Grant, 142–43

Televangelism, 16, 175

Tennessee, 110, 115, 132

Tent, Jim, 154

Texas A&M University, 47

Theology, 7, 20–21

Thoreau, Henry David, 33, 118

Thrush, John C., 95, 100, 107, 108

Tillich, Paul, 85

Tindall, George, 19, 23, 43

Titon, Jeff Todd, xviii

Treadwell, David, 178

Tubb, Ernest, 103, 105

Tucker, Tanya, 101, 102

Turner, Nat, 81

Turner, Victor W., 135

Twain, Mark, 60, 61

United Confederate Veterans, 20

United Daughters of the Confederacy, 20, 113, 160; Texas chapter, 114

University of Alabama, 28, 146; and Bear Bryant, 39–50 passim

University of Mississippi, 113, 114; and Lost Cause symbolism, 25, 26, 160; in Faulkner, 44

University of North Carolina Press, 113

Upper class, 119–20, 148

Vanderbilt University, 23

Vardaman, James, 121

Vecsey, George, 45, 49

Vermont, 155

Vietnam War, 101

Violence, 100–101

Virginia Rounders, 105

Wagoner, Porter, 101

Walker, Madame C. J., 151

Warren, Robert Penn, 22, 26, 35, 106, 162

Wayne, John, 45

Weaver, Richard M., xxi, 29

Webster, Daniel, 108

Welty, Eudora, xvi, 125, 151

We Sing America, 116

Wesley, John, 60

White, Josh, 100

White Citizens' Council, 25

Wilder, Douglas, 160

Will Barrett, 27

Williams, Don, 28

Williams, Hank, Jr., 28, 106

Williams, Hank, Sr., xvi, 72, 98, 104, 105

Williams, Peter W., xvi, xvii

Williams, Tennessee, 20

Wilson, John F., 19

Wolfe, Thomas, 123

Women, 144–58 passim

Woodson, Carter, 123

Woodward, C. Vann, 21, 31, 49, 133

Wordsworth, William, 33

Working class, 40; and books, 97–98, 100; and Elvis Presley, 132; and ideal of beauty, 148

World War I, 21, 32

World War II: post-, 113, 119; pre-, 120; and Will Campbell, 124

Wright, Richard, 123–4

Yoder, Don, xviii

Yoknapatawpha County, 61, 63, 64, 65, 66, 71, 72. *See also* Faulkner, William

Zinn, Howard, 35